DIVIDENDS UNDER
THE INCOME TAX

.

NATIONAL BUREAU OF ECONOMIC RESEARCH

Fiscal Studies

Dividends Under the Income Tax

DANIEL M. HOLLAND

SCHOOL OF INDUSTRIAL MANAGEMENT
MASSACHUSETTS INSTITUTE OF TECHNOLOGY

A STUDY BY THE
NATIONAL BUREAU OF ECONOMIC RESEARCH, NEW YORK

PUBLISHED BY
PRINCETON UNIVERSITY PRESS, PRINCETON
1962

Printed in the United States of America

Dividends Under the Income Tax by Daniel M. Holland

ERRATA

Page 5, line 25: *read* "dividend underreporting is most serious among dividend recipients with income of"

Page 29, line 34: *read* "through 1953 they had to be estimated."

Page 32, source notes, line 3: for "Column 3" *read* "Column 4"; line 4, for "Column 4" *read* "Column 5"

Page 72, Chart 3, title: *read* "Percentage of Dividends and Wages and Salaries Not Accounted for on Tax Returns, 1936-1958"

Page 74, Table 18, date in title: *read* "1936-1961"; last column heading: *read* "1954-1961"

Page 82, Table 20, note a: *read* "Adjusted for comparability with tax return data; see line 14 of Table 26 in note"

Page 83, line 16: *read* "most sizable item for which estimates much different from ours are a real possibility is dividend receipts of nonprofit organizations (see line"; line 18: *read* "estimated entries, feasible alternative values would have only a slight"

Page 91, line 2: for "footnote 44" *read* "footnote 43"

Page 99, lines 30 and 31: *read* "Jr. of the Internal Revenue Service. Their values are such that in every year σ_R^2 dominates the results"

Page 134, note b: *read* "10 to 20 for 1956."; note c: *read* "20 to 50 for 1956."

Page 154, following line 7 of text, first term of formula: *read* " $\dfrac{N_A}{E\text{-}P_1E}$ ";
following line 8 of text, first term of formula: *read* " $\dfrac{N_A}{E\text{-}P_2E}$ "

Page 164, line 11: for "70.8" *read* ">0.8"; for "70.1" *read* ">0.1"

Page 171, footnote 31, line 2: for "footnote 3" *read* "footnote 6"

RELATION OF THE DIRECTORS
TO THE WORK AND PUBLICATIONS
OF THE NATIONAL BUREAU OF ECONOMIC RESEARCH

1. The object of the National Bureau of Economic Research is to ascertain and to present to the public important economic facts and their interpretation in a scientific and impartial manner. The Board of Directors is charged with the responsibility of ensuring that the work of the National Bureau is carried on in strict conformity with this object.

2. To this end the Board of Directors shall appoint one or more Directors of Research.

3. The Director or Directors of Research shall submit to the members of the Board, or to its Executive Committee, for their formal adoption, all specific proposals concerning researches to be instituted.

4. No report shall be published until the Director or Directors of Research shall have submitted to the Board a summary drawing attention to the character of the data and their utilization in the report, the nature and treatment of the problems involved, the main conclusions, and such other information as in their opinion would serve to determine the suitability of the report for publication in accordance with the principles of the National Bureau.

5. A copy of any manuscript proposed for publication shall also be submitted to each member of the Board. For each manuscript to be so submitted a special committee shall be appointed by the President, or at his designation by the Executive Director, consisting of three Directors selected as nearly as may be one from each general division of the Board. The names of the special manuscript committee shall be stated to each Director when the summary and report described in paragraph (4) are sent to him. It shall be the duty of each member of the committee to read the manuscript. If each member of the special committee signifies his approval within thirty days, the manuscript may be published. If each member of the special committee has not signified his approval within thirty days of the transmittal of the report and manuscript, the Director of Research shall then notify each member of the Board, requesting approval or disapproval of publication, and thirty additional days shall be granted for this purpose. The manuscript shall then not be published unless at least a majority of the entire Board and a two-thirds majority of those members of the Board who shall have voted on the proposal within the time fixed for the receipt of votes on the publication proposed shall have approved.

6. No manuscript may be published, though approved by each member of the special committee, until forty-five days have elapsed from the transmittal of the summary and report. The interval is allowed for the receipt of any memorandum of dissent or reservation, together with a brief statement of his reasons, that any member may wish to express; and such memorandum of dissent or reservation shall be published with the manuscript if he so desires. Publication does not, however, imply that each member of the Board has read the manuscript, or that either members of the Board in general, or of the special committee, have passed upon its validity in every detail.

7. A copy of this resolution shall, unless otherwise determined by the Board, be printed in each copy of every National Bureau book.

(Resolution adopted October 25, 1926,
as revised February 6, 1933, and February 24, 1941)

To Jeanne, Laura, Jonathan, and Andrew

CONTENTS

Contents

TABLES

Tables

Tables

CHARTS

ACKNOWLEDGMENTS

IN CARRYING out this study I have been helped by many people.

Lawrence H. Seltzer and C. Harry Kahn advised me from start to completion and made available materials developed for the National Bureau's Personal Income Tax Study.

I have benefited from searching criticisms and numerous suggestions by W. Leonard Crum, Geoffrey H. Moore, Joseph Pechman, and Willard L. Thorp. Also, for a critical reading of the manuscript at one stage or another of its development, I am indebted to Richard A. Easterlin, Solomon Fabricant, M. Slade Kendrick, Oswald W. Knauth, Morris Mendelson, and Carl Shoup.

In the work incorporated in Chapter 2, Edwin Kuh and Jacob Mincer advised on statistical problems, Milton Leontiades and Stan West on data sources and estimating procedures, and Ernest Engquist, Jr., on the sampling variabilities of *Statistics of Income* and how to interpret them.

The criticisms and suggestions of all these men have improved the study. But the responsibility for errors and conclusions is solely mine.

Jacob Silverman handled the computations and carried out the estimates for the first draft of the manuscript. Massimo Brighi and Robert Hamada performed a similar service at a later stage. I am grateful to the Sloan Research Fund of the School of Industrial Management at the Massachusetts Institute of Technology for financial assistance which made Messrs. Brighi and Hamada's help possible.

H. Irving Forman's skill is evident in the charts. Carolyn Stone and Marie-Christine Culbert edited the manuscript more than capably.

xv

PREFACE

THE individual income tax levied by the Federal Government has since the war become by far the most important single source of governmental revenue in the United States. In 1958, an aggregate tax liability of $34.3 billion was reported on 45.7 million taxable income tax returns. Over 85 per cent of the estimated total of adjusted gross income received by all individuals now appears on taxable returns.

Because of the fiscal and the broader economic importance of the individual income tax, the National Bureau of Economic Research has sponsored quantitative and analytical studies of various aspects of the tax and their changes over time. One of these studies, *Interest as a Source of Personal Income and Tax Revenue,* written by me, was published by the Bureau in 1955 as Occasional Paper 51. Another, entitled *Personal Deductions in the Federal Income Tax* by C. Harry Kahn, appeared in 1960. The present report on dividend income is the third.

LAWRENCE H. SELTZER

DIVIDENDS UNDER
THE INCOME TAX

Introduction and Summary

THIS book describes and analyzes some of the more important developments in dividend taxation and the role of dividends in the tax structure. Many of these stand out in sharp relief against the historical background of almost half a century of personal income taxation, as shown primarily by the Treasury's annual tabulations of tax data, *Statistics of Income*. Part of the report concerns income tax history, with attention centered on dividends; part of it is concerned with special features of dividends and the laws under which they have been taxed. The book is organized around the following four topics:

1. The importance of dividends in personal and taxable income.
2. The extent to which dividend receipts have shown up on tax returns.
3. Tax liability traceable to dividends.
4. The "double taxation" of dividends and, more generally, the differential taxation of corporate earnings, as well as recent methods designed to provide income tax relief for stockholders.

In seeking a full answer to some of the questions raised in this study, it will be necessary to look beyond dividends per se to the corporate earnings that occasioned their payment, whether they were distributed to stockholders, paid as taxes to government, or retained in the corporate till.

Some of the data presented here go through 1958, some through 1957, and some stop even earlier, depending on the information available at the time of writing.

It may be helpful at this point to set forth our main findings in order to give the reader a sense of the scope of the study. The brief summary which follows is necessarily oversimplified, and presents the results without the qualifications that are necessary in interpreting them.

3

Dividends Under the Income Tax

Importance of Dividends in Personal and Taxable Income

Throughout the history of the income tax a high percentage of personal dividend receipts can be traced to taxable returns. The percentage ranged between 60 and 90, even though the income tax did not become a mass levy until World War II, because dividends have always gone in large part to the upper income groups. For this reason also, aggregate dividends reported on tax returns have generally moved with total dividend payments despite sharp changes in exemption levels.

Until World War II dividends characteristically constituted a much higher percentage of taxpayers' adjusted gross income than of their total personal income. Since the wartime extension of the income tax to cover most of the population, however, the two percentages have been very close.

In every year the percentage of taxpayers' income represented by dividends rose with income class. For all income classes, the first years of World War II mark the beginning of a period of sharp decline in the importance of dividends as a component of taxpayers' income, not because dividends fell in size but because the amount of wages and salaries and entrepreneurial income subject to tax increased greatly.

The major part of dividends reported on taxable returns has gone to taxpayers with over $5,000 of income (net income through 1943, adjusted gross from 1944 on)—between 69 and 97 per cent without correction of income for changes in the value of money, and between 77 and 99 per cent when real income (i.e., income levels adjusted for changes in purchasing power) is used to mark off the income classes.

In general the number of taxable dividend returns has increased over 1934–1957, which is consistent with other evidence of growth in the number of stockholders. But in the more recent years of our study, the number of dividend returns shows a much slower growth than the estimates of stockowners.

Almost all dividend recipients had incomes of under $50,000. In all the years for which the information could be obtained, never more than 2.5 per cent and frequently less than 1 per cent had incomes greater than this. Despite their small *number,* taxpayers in income classes of $50,000 and over received a sizable proportion of total dividends. In 1956, for example, they comprised 2.5 per cent of all taxable dividend returns and received 36 per cent of the dividends reported on such returns.

4

Similarly, concentration shows up when dividend recipients are arrayed by size of dividend receipts. In 1950, for example, only 6 per cent of all dividend recipients reported $5,000 or more of dividends, but they received 65 per cent of all dividends reported by individuals on tax returns. No other type of income was distributed in such a concentrated fashion.

Extent to Which Dividends Have Shown Up on Tax Returns

In every year of the period 1936–1958, total dividends paid to individuals and fiduciaries (estates and trusts) exceeded the amount of dividends that could be traced to tax returns. The difference between the two is called here the dividend gap. A review of the gap over the twenty-three-year period did not disclose a tendency for the underreporting of dividends to correct itself over time. During these years, which witnessed a revolutionary conversion of the income tax from a levy on a few citizens to one that reaches almost every income recipient, the gap trended upward in absolute terms and relatively was about as important near the end of the period as at the start.

An examination of the year-to-year changes in the dividend gap suggests that its relative size roughly reflects taxpayer response to variations in tax rates, especially tax rate increases. However, the evidence on this point is not clear-cut from 1950 on.

Estimates from a sample audit by the Bureau of Internal Revenue of personal income tax returns for 1948 and from sample surveys by the Internal Revenue Service of 1958 and 1959 tax returns suggest that dividend underreporting is most serious among dividend recipients of less than $25,000.

In the most recent year for which systematic estimates could be made, 1958, it appears that the Federal Government's revenue loss due to dividend underreporting was between $200 and $240 million. (This may be too high; see section in chapter 2 on 1959 survey.) This figure is small relative to total personal income tax collections, but that does not mean the problem is unimportant. A widespread feeling that some taxpayers are not bearing their share of the tax load might undermine the zeal with which many taxpayers police themselves. Thus, the importance of dividend underreporting could transcend the revenue loss directly associated with it.

Dividends Under the Income Tax

Tax Liability Traceable to Dividends

In order to determine how heavily dividends have been taxed under the personal income tax alone, the aggregate tax liability of personal income taxpayers was allocated among the components of their income for every year, 1918–1957. Here we are concerned only with the personal income tax liability on dividends. The broader problem of the taxation of corporate earnings will be taken up in the next section.

Two factors have dominated the weighted average effective rate on dividends: the size of the dividend flow and its distribution, and the progressivity of the personal income tax rate schedule. The special tax provisions pertaining to dividends (their exemption from normal tax through 1935 and the exclusion and tax credit introduced in 1954) had only a slight effect.

Because dividends have always gone in large part to stockholders in the upper income brackets, the proportion of tax liability attributable to them has always been higher than the dividend share of adjusted gross income on taxable returns. Characteristically this ratio has been two to one.

Through 1941 a large fraction of total personal income tax liability —between one-fifth and one-half—was due to dividends. Since that date, with the extension of the income tax to cover most income recipients, dividend tax liability accounted for a smaller share, typically about 7 per cent of total tax liability.

In every year we observe successively higher values in going from dividends as a fraction of personal income to dividends as a fraction of adjusted gross income on taxable returns and, finally, to dividend tax liability as a fraction of total tax liability. This has imparted some revenue flexibility to the income tax, since the dividend tax liability has varied more markedly than dividends themselves. Since dividends were a much more important component of the tax base before 1941, the revenue flexibility they imparted was more significant in this earlier period.

From 1940 on, between 15 and 25 per cent of dividends paid out to individuals and others treated as such in the national income accounts went into tax payments to the Federal Government. Before 1940 the percentage was 10 or less.

We found a large difference between the average effective tax rates on dividends and the marginal rates (those that would have applied on the average to a small increment in dividends proportionately distributed among all stockholders). As a rule, marginal rates were about twice as high as effective rates. In 1929 the effective rate was 6.1 per cent, the marginal rate 13.2 per cent; in 1952, they were 28.9 and 55.6, respectively. Thus both rates increased substantially, the marginal somewhat more than the average. In view of this, it is a puzzling financial fact that corporations tended to pay out about the same proportion of after-tax earnings in the 1950's as in the 1920's. One would expect, if tax considerations were a strong influence, that dividend pay-out rates would be lower in the more recent period.

Income tax liability may be defined to cover corporate as well as personal taxation. In this context, the personal income tax liability on dividends should be added to the corporate tax on corporate earnings to obtain the total tax liability on the earnings of corporate enterprises. In this view, the income taxes on corporate earnings make up a sizable proportion of total income taxes: in recent years, 40 per cent; in the earlier period of our study, well over 50 per cent, sometimes as much as 75 or 80 per cent. This represents, of course, a much higher fraction of income tax liability than corporate earnings represent of national income. But these figures do not necessarily mean that corporate earnings are "overtaxed." For a judgment on this matter, the earnings of corporations must be related to the income class status of the claimants thereof, i.e., the stockholders. It is to this range of questions that the next few paragraphs are directed.

The Differential Taxation of Corporate Earnings and Stockholders

In the early years of the personal income tax, corporate rates were set and dividends treated in such a manner that the corporate tax could be viewed as a withholding appendage of the personal income tax, for distributed earnings at least. Since 1919, for a number of reasons this has not applied to distributed earnings. And from its very inception, the tax treatment of retained earnings was not directly related to the income circumstances of the stockholders on whose behalf the retention took place.

The fact that the two income taxes have not been integrated has led variously to charges of "double taxation of dividends," unfairly high or unjustly low taxation of retained earnings, or, more generally, differential (unequal) taxation of corporate earnings. These and similar charges mirror one or another aspect of a multifaceted problem which has been analyzed in successive steps. It is important to note that these charges and our analysis both assume that the corporate tax is not shifted and that present stockholders have not bought shares "free of tax," i.e., that the selling price of shares has not been lower by the present value of all expected future tax payments. (Or, perhaps, that the stream of expected future tax payments has been finite and limited to a small number of periods.)

As to distributed earnings and the problem somewhat inaccurately designated as the "double taxation" of dividends, it is important to recognize that the requirement that a corporation pay some tax to the government before it distributes the rest to stockholders does not mean that stockholders have been deprived by the full amount of the corporate income tax payment. For had it not gone to the government but to the stockholders instead, some fraction of the corporate tax would have been paid out as personal tax. The "extra" burden, then, is the corporate tax minus the personal tax that would have been due on the corporate tax. Since, for a given amount of earnings for distribution (the pre-corporate-tax counterpart of dividends), the same corporate tax applies no matter what the tax bracket (income level) of the personal income taxpayer is, and since, also, the personal tax rate that would have applied rises with the stockholder's income, the "extra" burden *falls* as shareowner income *rises*. But there will always be some extra burden because the personal rates that would have applied never equal or exceed 100 per cent.

As a numerical illustration of the "extra" burden, assume for simplicity that the corporate tax rate is 50 per cent. Thus for every $1 of dividends, there are $2 of earnings for distribution. On this $2 the 20 per cent bracket stockholder would be taxed $1.20 ($1.00 of corporate tax and 20 cents of personal tax on the dividend he received). Had all the $2 been distributed to him with no corporate tax intervening, he would have paid 40 cents of tax. Hence his "extra" burden is 80 cents. Similar calculations for a stockholder in the 90 per cent bracket give an "extra" burden of 10 cents. All other doubly taxed stockholders fall between these extremes, with their "extra" burden declining as their tax rate bracket rises. (The highest "extra" burden falls on those not subject to the personal income tax who, in this context, can be considered to fall in the zero rate bracket.)

In 1954, income tax relief for stockholders was provided by the exclusion of the first $50 of dividends ($100 for joint returns) and 4 per cent of additional dividends as a credit against tax. Per dollar the exclusion clearly affords the greatest relief to those who are in the highest marginal rate brackets, and least to those in the lowest. (And, paradoxically, none at all to those in the zero bracket.) The credit is more democratic; it involves an equal *amount* of relief for all stockholders (except that, again, no relief is provided those who pay no personal income tax). To return to our numerical example, the credit applies 4 cents of relief to each stockholder. The 20 per cent bracket stockholder has his "extra" burden cut 5 per cent from 80 to 76 cents; the 90 per cent bracket stockholder ends up with an extra burden of 6 cents whereas it was 10 cents before the credit relief, thus experiencing a 40 per cent cut in his "extra" burden. A 10 per cent credit would completely relieve the high income stockholder, but would leave the stockholder in the 20 per cent bracket with 70 cents of overtaxation for each $2 of earnings for distribution generated on his behalf. There is no need to belabor the point further. But it is appropriate to explain why the credit works in this way.

If double taxation exists, then it could be remedied completely, definitionally and arithmetically, in one of two ways: by removing either the corporate tax on earnings or the personal tax on dividend income. Removing the personal tax would leave all stockholders subject to the flat rate corporate tax, a rate divorced from their personal income ("ability to pay"). The same consideration applies to the partial alleviation of double taxation effected via the dividend credit, since it is a step toward removal of the personal tax. If the credit were sufficient to do this fully for one particular personal income tax marginal rate bracket, it would leave all stockholders at rates above this undertaxed and all those at rates below this overtaxed compared with the rates they pay on income from other sources. However, if the credit were applied not as a fixed proportion (4 per cent) of dividends, but as a fixed fraction of the extra burden, relief would, of course, be in the same proportion for all stockholders. In terms of the illustrative figures used earlier, a credit of 10 per cent of the extra burden would cut the differentially heavier tax load for the stockholder in the 20 per cent bracket from 80 to 72 cents; for the 90 per cent bracket stockholder, the decline would be from 10 to 9 cents. A reduction in the corporate tax rate is the equivalent of a credit of this kind. For example, lowering the corporate rate from 50 to 45 per cent would cause the same change in the extra burden as a tax credit of 10 per cent of the extra burden.

9

As for the trend in overtaxation measured by the extra burden computed as an incremental rate on earnings for distribution, we found pronounced and continuous growth over the whole period under study for low income stockholders, a sizable but less pronounced rise for those in the middle income brackets, and a very moderate increase for those at the highest income levels (say $500,000) for whom, indeed, overtaxation is currently smaller than in 1925–1931.

We stress that this conclusion applies to the differentially heavier tax on corporate earnings. It does *not* mean that current tax rates are lower than in 1925–1931; on the contrary, they are much higher now. But the absolute increase in personal income tax rates were not as heavy for the lower and middle income stockholders as for those in the top income brackets. And this is the clue to the difference in the trend in overtaxation at the different income levels. In the most recent years of the period under study, corporate and personal rates were both higher than in 1925–1931. Other things unchanged, the higher corporate rate would mean greater overtaxation; also, other things equal, the higher personal rate would mean less overtaxation, because the higher the personal rate that would have applied, the less the stockholder is deprived when his corporation pays a tax on its earnings. At the lower and middle income levels, the rise in personal rates was not large enough to overcome the effect of the rise in the corporate rate; hence *overtaxation* increased. At the upper income levels, however, personal rates rose sufficiently to decrease overtaxation by more than it was increased by the rise in the corporate tax rate; therefore, on net balance, overtaxation decreased.

Another way to measure the degree of overtaxation of earnings for distribution is to determine how much a stockholder has left after the corporate tax on earnings plus the personal tax on dividends, compared with how much he would have had after tax if his earnings for distribution had been taxed in full by the personal income tax alone. On this basis, overtaxation has tended to increase markedly over the period studied. But if the beginning and end of the period are compared, the increase has been sharpest for the lowest tax bracket stockholders, not as sharp for those in the middle tax brackets, and even less pronounced for those at the top of the income range. (See Chapter 4 for a more detailed discussion of this point.)

Of course, more than the tax treatment of distributed earnings is involved in the extra burden on stockholders. The portion of corporate earnings which is retained can be handled in much the same way as

10

distributed earnings. On $2 of earnings for retention (the pre-corporate-tax counterpart of retained earnings), $1 is paid in corporate tax, while 40 cents would have been paid by the 20 per cent bracket investor had he been taxed currently on this $2, and $1.60 by the 90 per cent bracket shareowner. Here, then, we can say the "extra" burden is not the corporate tax, but the difference between the corporate tax and the personal tax that would have applied. The "extra" burden declines with stockholder income level and after a point will become negative. That is to say, the "extra" burden is positive when the corporate rate exceeds the personal rate; it is zero when the two are equal; and it is negative when the corporate rate falls short of the personal rate that would have applied. This formulation neglects the complication of capital gains taxation, which is discussed in Chapter 4. No change in principle is introduced but it does mean that the change from over- to undertaxation of earnings for retention comes at a rate greater than the actual corporate tax rate.

So far this summary has dealt with marginal dollars, but equally interesting is what happens when we take account of the aggregate amounts of earnings for distribution and earnings for retention. To do this, we imputed corporate earnings and tax payments to stockholders and compared this with what they would have paid on these imputations under the personal income tax alone, the difference between the actual and hypothetical tax burdens being the "extra" burden, or benefit, as the case may be. A quick summary for a representative year (before any account has been taken of the exclusion and credit) appears in Chart 9. As would be expected, the differential ("extra" burden computed as a rate) against earnings for distribution declines with stockholder income but is always positive; the differential against earnings for retention likewise falls with stockholder income, and changes from positive to negative. The weighted average of these two measures, the differential against net corporate earnings, follows the same pattern as the differentials that comprise it. Reflecting the greater absolute magnitude in 1951 of earnings for retention, it lies closer to that differential than the one on earnings for distribution. It too turned negative after a point.

Applying the provisions of the Internal Revenue Code of 1954 to the data for 1950 provides a picture of the relief granted average stockholders at selected income levels. The absolute amount of relief declines with income. The relative degree of relief is U-shaped with income, being higher at both the lower and upper ends of the stockholder income scale than in between. This seems to run counter to the findings noted above, but the reconciliation is simple. At the lower stockholder income where the average amount of earnings for distribution is small, the exclusion (which gives more relief per $1 of dividends) far outweighs the credit; hence the heavy degree of relief here. Moving up the income scale, the exclusion fades in importance, and the amount of relief in absolute terms tends to approach the constant represented by the credit. With the differential declining with rising stockholder income, after a point, once more the higher the average stockholder income, the greater is the relative degree of relief.

CHAPTER 1

The Importance of Dividends in Personal and Taxable Income

Taxable Dividends and Aggregate Personal Dividend Receipts

OVER the period 1918–1957 personal dividend receipts traced out cyclical patterns broadly similar to those of the general economy. (See Table 1 and Chart 1.) The dividend component of personal income increased from year to year through 1929; fell through 1933; then commenced a gradual rise, unbroken (except for a sharp acceleration in dividend payments in 1936 and 1937 in response to the undistributed profits tax) through 1949; declined slightly between 1950 and 1952; and rose from year to year through 1957 where this study stops.[1]

A somewhat different pattern, however, characterized the relative importance of dividends in personal income. From 1919 through 1929 dividends grew more rapidly than total personal income; their proportion increased from 4.6 per cent of the total to over 7.9 per cent (or 7.2 per cent according to the adjusted personal income figure for 1929 of the National Income Division of the Department of Commerce Office of Business Economics). The 1929 and 1930 proportions represent a peak never again achieved; the trend since is toward a general,

[1] There is a correspondence between the level of economic activity and aggregate dividend receipts with both measured on an annual basis, but it is loose. Annual dividend receipts did not decline in any of the milder business cycle contractions since 1920, namely, 1923–1924, 1926–1927, 1945–1946, 1953–1954. A closer examination based on monthly data discloses that dividends typically lag behind aggregate economic activity. See Daniel Creamer, *Personal Income During Business Cycles,* Princeton University Press for the National Bureau of Economic Research, 1956, p. 65.

Dividends Under the Income Tax

TABLE 1

TOTAL PERSONAL DIVIDEND RECEIPTS AND DIVIDENDS REPORTED ON
TAXABLE RETURNS, 1918–1957

(dollars in billions)

Year (1)	Personal Dividend Receipts (2)	Personal Income Receipts (3)	Dividends as a Percentage of Personal Income Receipts (4)	Dividends on Taxable Returns [a] (5)	Adjusted Gross Income on Taxable Returns (6)	Dividends as a Percentage of Adjusted Gross Income (Taxable Returns) (7)	Dividends on Taxable Returns as a Percentage of Personal Dividend Receipts (8)
1918	$ 3.5	$ 55.2	6.3%	$ 2.3	$ 15.5	14.8%	66%
1919	3.2	63.1	5.1	2.3	20.1	11.4	72
1919	2.9	63.7	4.6				79
1920	3.2	66.9	4.8	2.5	22.9	10.9	78
1921	3.0	53.3	5.6	2.1	15.7	13.4	70
1922	3.0	57.3	5.3	2.3	17.3	13.3	77
1923	3.8	66.5	5.8	2.7	20.3	13.3	71
1924	3.8	66.9	5.7	2.8	22.2	12.6	74
1925	4.4	70.8	6.2	3.1	20.0	15.5	70
1926	4.7	73.7	6.4	3.5	19.8	17.7	74
1927	5.0	74.1	6.7	3.8	20.3	18.7	76
1928	5.5	75.9	7.2	4.1	23.7	17.3	75
1929	6.3	80.2	7.9	4.3	23.1	18.6	68
1929	5.8	80.1	7.2				74
1930	5.5	71.0	7.7	3.9	16.0	24.4	71
1931	4.1	60.3	6.8	2.6	10.5	24.8	63
1932	2.6	45.6	5.7	1.6	8.7	18.4	62
1933	2.1	44.2	4.8	1.3	8.1	16.0	62
1934	2.6	50.3	5.2	1.7	9.6	17.7	65
1935	2.9	56.9	5.1	1.9	11.4	16.7	66
1936	4.5	65.1	6.9	3.5	16.0	21.9	78
1937	4.7	70.2	6.7	3.8	17.4	21.8	81
1938	3.2	64.6	5.0	2.5	14.5	17.2	78
1939	3.8	69.1	5.5	3.0	17.9	16.8	79
1940	4.0	74.8	5.3	3.5	26.2	13.4	88
1941	4.5	92.6	4.9	4.0	49.9	8.0	89
1942	4.3	118.9	3.6	3.5	73.2	4.8	81
1943	4.5	145.3	3.1	3.5	105.2	3.3	78
1944	4.7	137.4	3.4	3.7	115.4	3.2	79
1945	4.7	162.0	2.9	3.7	118.4	3.1	79

(continued)

14

TABLE 1 (concluded)

Year (1)	Personal Dividend Receipts (2)	Personal Income Receipts (3)	Dividends as a Percentage of Personal Income Receipts (4)	Dividends on Taxable Returns [a] (5)	Adjusted Gross Income on Taxable Returns (6)	Dividends as a Percentage of Adjusted Gross Income (Taxable Returns) (7)	Dividends on Taxable Returns as a Percentage of Personal Dividend Receipts (8)
1946	5.8	174.6	3.3	4.6	119.1	3.9	79
1947	6.5	186.6	3.5	5.3	136.3	3.9	81
1948	7.2	203.6	3.5	5.9	143.0	4.1	82
1949	7.5	199.7	3.7	6.3	139.5	4.5	84
1950	9.2	220.6	4.2	7.5	159.8	4.7	81
1951	9.0	247.2	3.6	7.4	186.3	4.0	82
1952	8.9	262.0	3.4	7.3	199.8	3.7	82
1953	9.2	276.2	3.3	7.2 [b]	213.7 [b]	3.4	78
1954	9.8	276.8	3.5	7.6	211.5	3.6	77
1955	11.2	296.4	3.8	8.4	231.5 [b]	3.6	75
1956	12.1	318.2	3.8	9.4	252.1	3.7	78
1957	12.6	334.4	3.8	9.9	264.7 [b]	3.7	79

SOURCE: Column 2, 1918–1929: Simon Kuznets, *Shares of Upper Income Groups in Income and Saving*, New York, NBER, 1953, p. 571; 1929–1955: *U.S. Income and Output, 1958*, line 13, Table II-1, p. 145; 1956–1957: *Survey of Current Business*, July 1960, p. 8. Column 3, 1918–1929: Kuznets, *Shares of Upper Income Groups*, p. 571; 1929–1945: Lawrence H. Seltzer, *Interest as a Source of Personal Income and Tax Revenue*, Occasional Paper 51, New York, NBER, 1955, p. 1250; 1946–1957: See *ibid.*, p. 1250, footnote, for computation approach; data for 1946–1955, from *U.S. Income and Output;* data for 1956–1957, from *Survey of Current Business*, July 1959. Column 5: *Statistics of Income.* Column 6: Data computed for NBER Personal Income Tax Study. Double values in columns 2 and 3 for 1919 and 1929 provide overlap when one series is replaced by another.

NOTE: This table (and a number of others in this report) incorporates data prepared for the National Bureau's Personal Income Tax Study under the direction of Lawrence H. Seltzer.

[a] Includes dividends reported on taxable returns of individuals and fiduciaries (estates and trusts); from 1936 through 1953 includes also an estimate of the dividend component of individual's income from estates and trusts.

[b] Total income and dividends of fiduciaries, not tabulated in 1953, 1955, and 1957, are assumed to be the same as in 1952, 1954, and 1956, respectively.

CHART 1

**Personal Dividend Receipts and Dividends Reported on Taxable Returns,
1918–1957**

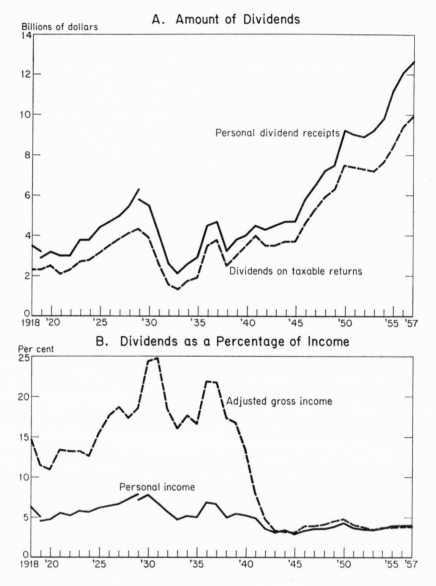

A. Amount of Dividends

Billions of dollars

Personal dividend receipts

Dividends on taxable returns

B. Dividends as a Percentage of Income

Per cent

Adjusted gross income

Personal income

16

although interrupted, decline in the importance of dividends as a component of personal income through 1945, and stability at about 3.5 per cent thereafter.

Several factors other than the aggregate total of dividends might be expected to affect the amount of dividends reported on taxable returns. For one thing, the level of exemptions and credits for dependents, being a determinant of the number of taxable returns, might be important here. For another, the figures on taxable returns could reflect taxpayer resistance in reporting income receipts.

In general, however, these influences have not been as important as another factor—the high degree of concentration [2] that characterizes the dividend distribution. Therefore, even in the years before World War II, a major fraction of aggregate dividends showed up on taxable returns although only a minor segment of the income-receiving population paid any personal income tax (or even had to file a tax return).[3] And so over the whole period under study, dividends reported on taxable returns have tended to move with the total of personal dividend receipts. Starting with 1918, dividends reported on taxable returns generally increased from year to year to a peak in 1929, decreased yearly to a trough in 1933, and then tended to rise, although not without exception, for the remainder of the period (see Table 1, column 5).

Since the personal income tax was a minority levy up to about 1940, dividends were much more important in the income of taxpayers than in total personal income. Until 1929 they accounted for between 4.5 and 7.8 per cent of personal income, but they comprised between 10 and 20 per cent of taxpayers' adjusted gross income.[4] Over the ensuing ten years they became even more important. In 1930 and 1931, for example, almost one-fourth of taxpayers' income came from dividends. With the rapid extension of the scope of the personal income tax, taxable income more closely approximated personal income, and dividends reported for tax purposes constituted about the same proportion of taxable income as of personal income. The relative importance

[2] In this study concentration means predominance at the high end of some distribution—in this case the high end of the income scale.

[3] In 1920, for example, 78 per cent of aggregate personal dividend receipts showed up on taxable returns; in 1957, about 79 per cent. Variations in this ratio did occur in the years between, and they suggest that taxpayers' reporting zeal may have fluctuated too. This matter is explored in Chapter 2, where we develop data more directly appropriate to the dividend "gap."

[4] Adjusted gross income, the net sum of income from all sources reported on tax returns (including only 50 per cent of net long-term capital gains) has been chosen as the most appropriate tax return counterpart of personal income.

of dividends in taxable income declined sharply. (Compare columns 4 and 7 of Table 1.)

In every year of the study period, dividends were larger than any of the other property income components of taxpayers' incomes.[5] (The one exception to this statement occurred in 1946 when net capital gains, with long-term gains included at 100 per cent rather than the 50 per cent required for tax purposes, exceeded dividends.) Over the span 1927 through 1939 they also totaled more than entrepreneurial income on taxable returns. Wages and salaries of taxpayers, of course, have always amounted to a much larger figure than dividends. But through the thirties, their preponderance over dividends was not so marked in adjusted gross income on taxable returns as it was in aggregate personal income. For example, in 1929, the tax return tabulations show wages and salaries to have been about five times as large as dividends while the employee compensation component of personal income was about nine times the dividend item. By 1941 with the scope of the income tax sharply extended and more of wages and salaries subject to tax, this gap had narrowed considerably: for taxable returns the wages and salaries were 12½ times dividends; for personal income the ratio was 14:1. And by 1953, the ratio of 24:1 for taxable returns was only slightly higher than the ratio of 23:1 for personal income.

Patterns in Income Class Distribution of Taxable Dividends

In discussing the picture that emerges when a breakdown of dividends among income classes is undertaken, we should bear in mind some of the serious qualifications that reduce the value of the data. First, they are classified by income per return not income per family or spending unit. Therefore individuals, families, taxpayers who report the family's income as a whole, and taxpayers who report only their own share of the family income are thrown together indiscriminately. Second, whatever picture we get is, to some extent, affected by the choice of income groupings—refined classes will, in general, exhibit a more volatile pattern than data arrayed by broad groupings. Third, a taxpayer falling in a given money income range was a substantially different economic entity at 1932 levels of incomes and prices than, say, at those prevailing in 1947. In addition to these difficulties there is a break in our annual series in 1944: Before this year the data were

[5] These other components are interest, net realized capital gains, rents and royalties, and annuities.

arrayed by the net income class of the taxpayer; after it, by adjusted gross income.[6] Since the latter is less net than the former, taxpayers in the net income class $6,000–$7,000, for example, represent a higher average adjusted gross income level than taxpayers in the adjusted gross income class $6,000–$7,000.[7] Finally, of course, the results obtained depend on how the income range is chopped up.

It is not possible to make effective adjustments for most of these difficulties. They qualify the results and inject an element of vagueness. They suggest that faith be placed only in discovered relationships pronounced enough to rise above statistical ambiguities.

For these reasons it has seemed more appropriate to work with broader income ranges than with narrow classes. This procedure irons out some of the irregularities due to shifts in amounts and shares between adjacent classes and reveals only very broad and pronounced results. The data upon which the summary is based appear in Table 2 and Chart 2. (Those who are interested in more detailed data will find tabulations by finer income classes in Tables 7, 8, and 9, at the end of this chapter.) But the use of broad income classes does not remove two difficulties noted above—changes in income levels due to both inflation and growth in real income, and the shift from a net income base to an adjusted gross income base in 1944. The next part of this chapter attempts an adjustment on both scores.[8] Finally, the potential difficulty in interpreting our data that arises from the possibility that high income stockholders may hold shares with low dividend pay-outs and low income stockholders may have shares with high dividend pay-outs is discussed in the note at the end of this chapter.

When the absolute amount of dividends reported on taxable returns is considered, three income class patterns are discernible:

1. In the income class under $5,000 the amount of dividends reported seems over most of the period to have been primarily a function of

[6] In computing net income all deductions—both those attributable to specific income sources, e.g., partnership losses, etc., and those allowed against income in general, e.g., charitable contributions, etc.,—are subtracted from total income. In computing adjusted gross income, only specific income source deductions are subtracted.

[7] In 1945, for instance, of the 168,200 taxpayers who reported adjusted gross incomes of over $6,000 and under $7,000, only 27,000 had net incomes this high; the rest had net incomes lower than $6,000, most of them (108,000) being in the $5,000-to-$6,000 net income range; see *Statistics of Income for 1945*, Part 1, pp. 173–174.

[8] The necessity for some such adjustment and, in general, for a greater emphasis on the effect of price and income level changes in vitiating the meaning of income class comparisons over long periods of time has been stressed by Professor Willard Thorp who read an earlier draft of this study.

19

TABLE 2

Summary Data for Dividends Reported on Taxable Returns Arrayed in Three Broad Income Classes, 1918–1957

YEAR	ABSOLUTE AMOUNT OF DIVIDENDS a — Income Class			DIVIDENDS AS A PER CENT OF ADJUSTED GROSS INCOME — Income Class			SHARE OF DIVIDEND RECEIPTS REPORTED ON TAXABLE RETURNS — Income Class			SHARE OF TOTAL PERSONAL DIVIDEND RECEIPTS b — Income Class		
	Under $5,000	$5,000 to $50,000	$50,000 and over	Under $5,000	$5,000 to $50,000	$50,000 and over	Under $5,000	$5,000 to $50,000	$50,000 and over	Under $5,000	$5,000 to $50,000	$50,000 and over
	(thousand dollars)			(per cent)			(per cent)			(per cent)		
1918	187,844	1,234,496	898,713	2.4	21.7	45.2	8.1	53.3	38.7	5.3	35.2	25.5
1919	175,781	1,248,641	879,648	1.8	16.0	35.2	7.7	54.2	38.1	5.5	39.0	27.4
1919										6.1	42.8	30.1
1920	184,946	1,520,999	842,879	1.5	18.2	42.0	7.2	59.7	33.0	5.6	46.6	25.7
1921	134,894	1,286,914	628,224	1.7	19.7	45.6	6.6	62.7	30.6	4.6	43.9	21.4
1922	144,151	1,324,537	814,483	1.8	18.4	39.5	6.3	58.0	35.6	4.9	44.7	27.4
1923	272,696	1,502,441	913,592	2.6	19.4	42.7	10.2	55.9	33.9	7.2	39.7	24.1
1924	296,553	1,439,813	1,113,034	2.7	16.8	42.0	10.4	50.6	39.1	7.7	37.4	28.9
1925	160,358	1,571,137	1,373,904	3.0	15.2	32.8	5.1	50.6	44.2	3.6	35.4	29.4
1926	139,454	1,729,411	1,664,004	2.8	16.4	39.1	4.0	49.0	47.1	3.0	36.2	34.9
1927	113,941	1,914,779	1,816,816	2.5	17.7	36.8	3.0	49.8	47.2	2.3	37.8	35.9
1928	112,569	1,939,322	2,042,050	2.4	16.3	29.0	2.7	47.4	49.9	2.0	35.6	37.4
1929	106,843	2,136,324	2,074,123	2.4	17.9	30.9	2.5	49.6	48.1	1.7	33.7	32.7
1929										1.9	36.7	35.6
1930	211,073	2,096,335	1,553,420	4.8	23.7	55.7	5.5	54.3	40.3	3.9	38.5	28.6
1931	78,996	1,553,505	969,003	2.7	25.2	71.2	3.0	59.7	37.2	1.9	37.6	23.4

1932	108,174	969,258	562,265	2.6	24.8	95.9	6.6	59.1	34.3	4.1	36.6	21.3
1933	91,462	739,754	455,307	2.5	20.1	59.1	7.2	57.5	35.4	4.5	35.7	21.9
1934	89,338	1,011,436	569,424	2.4	20.8	58.1	5.3	60.5	34.1	3.4	39.3	22.2
1935	96,241	1,114,407	695,797	2.2	19.5	53.4	5.1	58.4	36.5	3.4	38.5	24.1
1936	501,915	1,814,118	1,160,565	8.5	22.9	52.9	14.5	52.2	33.4	11.3	40.7	26.1
1937	610,686	1,986,514	1,192,388	8.5	24.3	59.2	16.1	52.4	31.4	13.0	42.4	25.4
1938	574,351	1,310,249	596,289	8.6	19.8	46.8	23.2	52.9	24.0	18.1	41.2	18.7
1939	643,054	1,552,789	807,738	7.3	20.3	55.6	21.4	51.6	26.9	16.9	40.8	21.3
1940	858,095	1,708,242	905,407	5.4	19.8	53.5	24.8	49.2	26.0	21.8	43.3	22.9
1941	1,234,798	1,781,446	946,245	3.3	16.7	41.8	31.1	45.0	23.9	27.7	40.0	21.3
1942	1,090,784	1,641,792	798,736	1.9	12.4	28.5	30.9	46.6	22.7	25.0	37.7	18.4
1943	974,956	1,733,396	827,931	1.2	9.9	24.2	27.6	49.1	23.4	21.5	38.3	18.3
1944	878,544	1,877,040	917,131	1.0	8.2	25.1	23.9	51.1	24.9	18.9	40.4	19.7
1945	798,155	1,966,978	961,361	0.9	7.7	22.8	21.5	52.8	25.7	17.0	41.7	20.3
1946	869,861	2,397,902	1,293,360	1.1	7.6	25.7	19.1	52.5	28.4	15.1	41.5	22.4
1947	896,878	2,792,546	1,607,257	0.9	7.9	32.2	16.9	52.7	30.4	13.7	42.7	24.6
1948	695,620	3,039,785	2,187,813	0.8	6.0	31.4	11.7	51.3	37.0	9.6	42.1	30.3
1949	915,727	3,242,979	2,156,939	1.1	6.4	35.5	14.5	51.3	34.2	12.2	43.1	28.7
1950	785,413	3,831,080	2,927,672	0.9	6.1	33.4	10.4	50.8	38.8	8.4	41.1	31.4
1951	781,847	3,954,384	2,709,287	0.8	4.8	30.5	10.5	53.1	36.4	8.6	43.5	29.8
1952	758,721	4,016,034	2,505,040	0.8	4.1	30.7	10.4	55.2	34.4	8.5	45.3	28.2
1953 e	800,359	4,125,814	2,281,771	0.9	3.6	30.7	11.1	57.2	31.7	8.7	44.6	24.7
1954	672,404	4,309,341	2,680,301	0.8	3.7	29.4	8.7	56.4	34.9	6.7	43.4	26.9
1955	668,905	4,352,950	3,397,175	0.8	3.2	32.7	7.9	51.7	40.4	5.9	38.8	30.3
1956	720,763	5,211,764	3,494,093	0.9	3.3	30.1	7.4	55.4	37.2	5.8	43.2	29.0
1957	738,682	5,568,539	3,562,344	0.9	3.2	30.4	7.4	56.5	36.1	5.8	44.6	28.5

(continued)

TABLE 2 (concluded)

YEAR	NUMBER OF TAXABLE RETURNS REPORTING DIVIDENDS [c] Income Class				SHARE OF TOTAL TAXABLE DIVIDEND RETURNS Income Class			AVERAGE DIVIDENDS PER TAXABLE DIVIDEND RETURN [d] Income Class		
	Under $5,000	$5,000 to $50,000	$50,000 and over	Total	Under $5,000	$5,000 to $50,000	$50,000 and over	Under $5,000	$5,000 to $50,000	$50,000 and over
						(per cent)			(dollars)	
1934	258,735	257,827	7,660	524,222	49.4	49.2	1.4	345	3,923	74,338
1935	312,478	301,302	10,135	623,915	50.1	48.3	1.6	308	3,699	68,653
1936	658,011	437,522	17,740	1,113,273	59.1	39.3	1.6	763	4,146	65,421
1937	795,455	453,805	16,468	1,265,728	62.8	35.9	1.3	768	4,377	72,406
1938	741,731	377,156	9,460	1,128,347	65.7	33.4	0.9	774	3,474	63,033
1939	973,027	429,447	11,920	1,414,391	68.8	30.4	0.8	661	3,616	67,763
1940	1,579,232	471,244	13,753	2,064,229	76.5	22.8	0.7	543	3,625	65,833
1941	2,360,374	510,839	17,504	2,888,717	81.7	17.7	0.6	523	3,487	54,059
1946	1,945,397	1,130,344	42,665	3,118,406	62.4	36.2	1.4	447	2,121	30,314
1947	1,938,302	1,226,376	41,955	3,206,633	60.4	38.3	1.3	463	2,277	38,309
1948	1,377,252	1,455,598	59,219	2,892,069	47.6	50.3	2.1	505	2,088	36,944
1949	1,537,634	1,543,972	53,062	3,134,668	49.1	49.2	1.7	596	2,101	40,649
1950	1,440,847	1,742,596	73,314	3,256,757	44.2	53.5	2.3	545	2,198	39,933
1951	1,464,464	2,082,320	76,689	3,623,473	40.4	57.5	2.1	534	1,899	35,328
1952	1,455,820	2,291,287	73,420	3,820,527	38.1	60.0	1.9	521	1,753	34,119
1953 [e]	1,476,108	2,481,489	67,919	4,025,516	36.7	61.6	1.7	542	1,663	33,595
1954	1,144,974	2,434,727	82,206	3,661,907	31.3	66.5	2.2	587	1,769	32,605
1955 [e]	1,167,620	2,669,721	92,843	3,930,184	29.7	67.9	2.4	573	1,631	36,590
1956	1,181,583	3,011,752	106,488	4,299,823	27.5	70.0	2.5	610	1,730	32,812
1957 [e]	1,166,498	3,316,520	109,529	4,572,547	25.5	72.5	2.0	633	1,679	32,524

Dividends in Personal and Taxable Income

certain features of the tax law (particularly the level of exemptions) rather than of the total of corporate net dividend payments. The absolute amount of dividends reported was low over the first half of the period covered by the personal income tax. It rose quite sharply in 1936 due to a combination of factors; among them were increased dividend payments resulting from the undistributed profits tax, increased coverage of the tax system, and a change in the method of tabulating the data for fiduciary returns. Up to 1946, lower exemptions kept the amount of dividends in this class larger than it was in the twenties even though dividends on taxable returns (as well as personal dividends) lay below the 1929 level over these years.

2. In the income class between $5,000 and $50,000, where half or more of all taxed dividends were received, changes in the tax system had a relatively minor effect. The pattern of dividend reporting essentially mirrored the pattern of the aggregate net dividend flow—peaks in the late twenties, 1937, and 1941, troughs in the early thirties, 1938, and 1942, and a continual rise since that date (relatively slight during the war, and more rapid in the postwar years).

3. At the top of the income range, in the income class of $50,000 and over, a similar pattern emerged. Parenthetically, we note that in the over-$500,000 class, on a more refined class breakdown, dividends did not reach their 1929 total until 1955, although aggregate dividend payments had, of course, been above the 1929 figure since 1946, and 50 per cent higher than in 1929, in each of the years 1950–1954.

Concerning the importance of dividends as a component of taxpayers' adjusted gross income, several broad features are apparent:

23

CHART 2

Income Class Distribution of Dividends on Taxable Returns, 1918–1957

A. Amount of Dividends

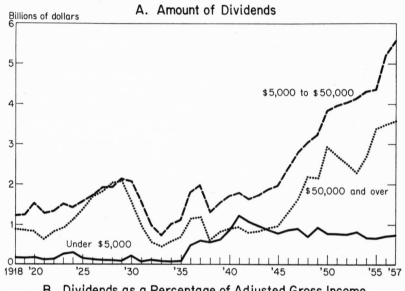

B. Dividends as a Percentage of Adjusted Gross Income

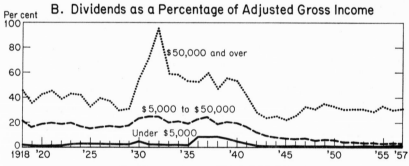

C. Percentage of Total Dividends

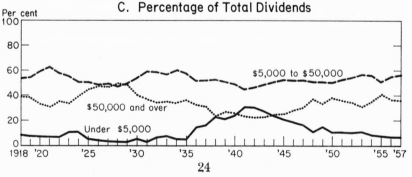

Dividends in Personal and Taxable Income

1. In every year the percentage of taxpayers' adjusted gross income attributable to dividends increased with income class. (Had we used finer income class breakdowns a few exceptions would have been found. But they are minor except for this one: at the very bottom of the income scale dividend receipts sometimes weigh more heavily because the taxpayers there include a higher proportion of widows and retired individuals to whom dividends are an important source of income. In Table 8, compare the under-$2,000 class with the immediately adjacent two classes, particularly for the more recent years.)

2. From 1936 through 1940 in the lowest of our summary income classes (under $5,000) dividends were five to ten times as important a component of taxpayers' income as they were before or after these dates. The growth in their importance during these years can be explained, in part at least, by the acceleration of dividend payments that accompanied the undistributed profits tax. Their ensuing decline in importance may be traced to the great increase in the early forties in the number of taxpayers, for the most part wage and salary recipients, as a result of lowered exemptions and the rapid rise in labor and entrepreneurial incomes relative to dividends (which also tended to push taxpayer recipients thereof, along with their dividends, into higher income classes).

3. For all income classes, the decade of the forties marks a sharp decline in the importance of dividends as a component of taxpayers' incomes. This did not happen because, over this period, the amount of dividends reported fell. On the contrary they increased, but an even more pronounced increase occurred in the wages and salaries and entrepreneurial components of adjusted gross income.[9]

[9] Between 1943 and 1944 particularly, and between the early forties and the later forties generally, even if all other factors had remained unchanged we should expect to find a fall in the proportion of dividends to adjusted gross income because of the change in the income concept by which the basic data were classified: the change in 1944 from net to adjusted gross. Average adjusted gross income is larger than average net income in any income class. With a change in the basis of classification, and with everything else remaining unchanged, some taxpayers in the old under-$5,000 net income class would move out of it when classified on the basis of adjusted gross income. Since dividend receipts typically comprise a higher proportion of income the higher a taxpayer's total income, those who leave the class will have a higher proportion of dividends than those who remain. Hence the proportion of dividends to adjusted gross income would tend to fall. The same reasoning applies to all the other classes too. For, although in the case of all but the highest class there will be movement in as well as movement out upon reclassification, those who leave will be likely to have a higher proportion of dividends to adjusted gross income than those who enter from below. Similarly in the highest class those who

Regarding the distribution of the total of taxable dividend receipts among income classes, the following observations can be made:

1. Taxable dividends were very clearly concentrated, over the whole of our period, in income classes above $5,000. Through 1935, stockholders in the income classes of $5,000 and over received between 90 and 98 per cent of all dividends reported by taxpayers. From 1936 through 1949 their share fluctuated between 70 and 85 per cent, and since 1950 it has been 90 per cent or higher.

2. Over the period under review long swings in the income class distribution of dividends on taxable returns can be discerned.

In general, the middle ($5,000-to-$50,000) classes of our summary income brackets had a fairly stable share of dividends, the range running between limits of 50 to 60 per cent of the total. Greater relative variations over time characterized the shares of the under-$5,000 and the $50,000-and-over classes.

Starting at 14 per cent, the under-$5,000 income group's share moved gradually downward to a low of 2.5 per cent of total dividends reported on taxable returns in 1929, then slowly upward to a high of over 30 per cent in 1941 and 1942, followed by a gradual drift downward once more to about 7.5 per cent by 1957.

High exemptions and the consequent restriction of the income tax primarily to the upper rung of the ladder of income recipients, the heavy concentration of dividends in the upper income classes, and the generally rising income levels over the period 1918 through 1929 all help to explain the low and declining share of the under-$5,000 class in the total of dividends reported on taxable returns. The rise in this class' share from 1929 through 1942 can be attributed to the decline in incomes that occurred after 1929, particularly up through the middle thirties, and the decline in exemptions (which made for more taxpayers in this lower income class) in 1932 and 1940–1942. Finally, stable and then rising exemptions plus an upward movement in incomes account for the general downward drift of this lowest income class' share from 1942 on.

The long swings in the share of dividends going to the $50,000-and-over class have, as a rule, been in the opposite direction from those for the lowest summary income class. To a large degree the reasons are simply the reverse of those just noted for the under-$5,000 income

---

enter from below will bring proportionately more to the adjusted gross income total than to aggregate dividends; the proportion of dividends to adjusted gross income will therefore fall.

class. Thus we find an upward movement from 39 per cent in 1918 to a high of almost 50 per cent in 1928 and 1929, then a downward drift to less than 23 per cent by 1942, and a movement upward once more to between 35 and 40 per cent in recent years.

An Attempt to Correct for Price Level Changes

Needless to say, the generalizations made here and in the rest of this brief review relate to a specific set of income class arrangements of the aggregate data. All such income class comparisons are rendered ambiguous by the shift from net income to adjusted gross income as the basis of classification for *Statistics of Income* tabulations that took place in 1944. A more serious qualification to income class comparisons lies in the variations in the economic significance of any given set of money income classes over a forty-year period in which pronounced changes in price levels have occurred.

It is not possible to correct precisely for either of these factors. But neither is it realistic to neglect them entirely. Therefore for one measure, an adjustment for changing price levels and income concepts has been attempted in order to furnish the reader with some sense of how different the findings would be.

Table 3 shows the percentage share of total dividends on taxable returns reported by taxpayers in three broad income classes after adjustment for these two considerations. These data are the "real" net income counterparts of the three columns headed "Share of Dividend Receipts Reported on Taxable Returns" in Table 2.[10]

The pattern of relative shares described earlier in money terms still stands for the adjusted data; but in real terms, it is pitched at a lower level for the under-$5,000 group, at roughly the same level for the middle income group, i.e., $5,000 to $50,000, and at a higher level for the $50,000-and-over class. For every class, of course, the discrepancy between real and money percentage shares is smallest since 1947.

What this adjustment accomplishes, in effect, is to get rid of some

[10] The under-$5,000 class, for example, now has a different money income boundary in every year, as determined by the Consumer Price Index, with 1947–1949 as the base. The boundary then represents the same amount of purchasing power as $5,000 did in the period 1947–1949, and varies from $2,765 of money income in 1933 to $6,010 in 1957. The other money income classes have been similarly determined, and, from 1944 on, an additional adjustment (always downward) has been made to convert the bounding lines from an adjusted gross income to a net income basis.

27

TABLE 3

SHARE OF DIVIDEND RECEIPTS REPORTED ON TAXABLE RETURNS, BY
"REAL" NET INCOME CLASSES, 1918–1957

(per cent)

| | | "*Real*" Net Income Class | |
Year	Under $5,000	$5,000 to $50,000	$50,000 and over
1918	2.8	47.5	49.7
1919	4.0	50.3	45.7
1920	5.4	57.3	37.3
1921	3.8	58.0	38.2
1922	3.1	51.6	47.3
1923	5.2	52.0	42.8
1924	5.4	46.6	48.0
1925	2.8	44.5	52.7
1926	2.4	43.0	54.6
1927	1.6	43.4	55.0
1928	1.4	41.0	57.6
1929	1.3	43.1	55.6
1930	3.3	53.3	43.4
1931	1.2	51.5	47.2
1932	2.2	51.1	46.7
1933	2.3	48.0	49.7
1934	1.6	49.4	49.0
1935	1.5	47.9	50.6
1936	6.0	48.4	43.6
1937	7.4	49.9	42.7
1938	12.0	53.9	34.1
1939	10.5	51.5	38.0
1940	14.3	49.3	36.4
1941	19.7	47.9	32.4
1942	23.1	47.3	29.6
1943	21.3	49.3	29.4
1944	14.8	51.6	33.6
1945	13.8	51.9	34.3
1946	13.0	49.9	37.1
1947	13.6	51.9	34.5
1948	10.1	50.3	39.6
1949	12.3	50.7	37.0
1950	8.9	49.7	41.4
1951	10.1	52.8	37.1
1952	10.4	55.2	34.4
1953	11.2	57.3	31.6
1954	8.8	56.5	34.8
1955	8.0	51.7	40.3
1956	7.6	55.8	36.8
1957	8.2	57.7	34.9

of the factors—those associated with price level changes—that helped to determine the pattern marked earlier. Thus, for example, on a real basis the share of the lowest income group in total dividends on taxable returns remained insignificant until the middle thirties when exemptions were lowered. But the rough generalizations based on the money income classes still stand. Only between the middle thirties and early forties was a sizable share reported by the under-$5,000 class. The over-$50,000 class' share declined over the period of our study, although the decline appears to have tailed out in about 1946. The share of the middle income group has fluctuated within fairly narrow bounds.

Shifts in Distribution of Taxable Dividends Among Income Classes

To end this discussion after covering the totals and shares of *amounts* of dividends would leave an important part of the story untold. For it is clearly important to know something about the *number* of dividend recipients as well. But for this purpose, unfortunately, the ground is much weaker in terms of the available information. Data are lacking on number of dividend returns for the earlier part of the period under study. Tabulations start in 1934 and, with some estimates and guesses, figures can be pieced together for a run of years through 1941. (In particular, the estimates in the under-$5,000 class for a number of years in this period are shaky.) For several reasons (nontabulation in 1942 and 1943 and tabulation combined with interest returns in 1944 and 1945) the thread cannot be picked up again until 1946, but then it can be carried forward in a fairly straightforward fashion. The figures on number of dividend returns should be viewed as incomplete and subject to a fairly wide margin of error in most of the period 1934–1941; as substantially correct (but not strictly comparable with the earlier period because of the change in 1944 from net income to adjusted gross income as the basis of tabulation) from 1946–1953; and as somewhat different starting in 1954 because from that year on dividends received as part of income from estates and trusts were reported under the heading of dividends, whereas from 1936 through 1953 they were reported as income from estates and trusts.

The remarks that follow cover the last three sections of Table 2, and are based on money income classes.

1. The number of taxable dividend returns tended to increase (albeit interruptedly and at uneven rates) over the whole of the period

for which the data are available—the more recent half of the span of years covered by this study.

Several causes lie behind this result: lowered exemptions and rising incomes with an increase in the number of taxable returns as a consequence, a growth in dividend payments, and, in the latter part of the period, an increase in the number of stockholders. Specific factors can be cited to explain particular changes over this period. For instance, the large increase in number of taxable dividend returns between 1935 and 1936 can be explained in part, at least, by the spurt in dividend payments induced by the undistributed profits tax. The decline between 1947 and 1948 is related to the granting in 1948 of the privilege of income-splitting (without the assignment of assets) in general, rather than just for residents of community property states, for joint returns of husband and wife. Husband and wife split-ups of dividend receipts no longer meant a lower combined tax liability. Many dividend recipients who had formerly reported separately began in 1948 to report jointly and were counted as one. This seems corroborated by the sharp fall between 1947 and 1948 in the number of taxable dividend returns in the under-$5,000 income class, although the increase in personal exemptions between 1947 and 1948 (from $500 to $600), which removed some returns from the taxable category, was another factor in the fall of returns in this class.

2. The broad factors—lowered exemptions, rising incomes, and increased dividends—explain the rise in taxable dividend returns from 1934 through 1941. The latter two apply to some degree to the earlier years of the period 1946–1957. The years 1950–1953, however, show no change in exemptions and a virtually constant total of personal (or taxable return) dividend receipts (see columns 2 and 5 of Table 1). While incomes continued to rise over these four years, no sizable number of returns moved out of nontaxable into taxable categories on this score. What then, accounts for the continued growth in the number of taxable dividend returns between 1950 and 1953? Apparently there was a real increase in the number of dividend recipients because of an increase in the number of stockholders. The data of the last three columns of Table 2 substantiate this conjecture. In the under-$5,000 income class, dividends per taxable dividend return stayed about the same over the four years 1950–1953; in the other two classes, the average amount of dividends on taxable returns reporting them fell sharply. Since total dividends received by individuals was fairly constant from 1950–1953, and since the pressure to split stock ownership and dividend

income between husband and wife was removed in 1948, it is reasonable to infer that the number of stockholders went up over these four years.

3. This same inference cannot be drawn unambiguously from the data for the years following 1953, because rising dividend payments are associated with the annual increase in the number of taxable returns reporting dividends. However other evidence suggests a further increase in the number of stockholders.[11] An examination of these estimates shows an impressive growth in the number of stockholders between 1952 and 1956. The total number of individual shareowners increased by 82 per cent; those in households whose income was under $5,000 numbered 56 per cent more in 1956, while the number of shareowners in households whose income equaled or exceeded $5,000 more than doubled (see Table 4).

But the evidence drawn from tax return data shows nothing like this order of volatility. Here, for comparison with the Stock Exchange estimates, the focus must be on the returns of individuals alone, both taxable and nontaxable.[12] Thus the tax return data are not the same as in Table 2, which covered taxable returns of individuals and fiduciaries.

Between 1952 and 1956 the number of tax returns reporting dividends increased by only 21 per cent. With due recognition of the pitfalls in comparing income classes where definitions of income differ—household income in the one case and adjusted gross income in the other—it is possible to spot the income range where the greater discrepancy occurs. In sharp contrast to the shareowner rise of 56 per cent in the under-$5,000 class already noted, there is a *decline* of 10 per cent in the number of tax returns with under $5,000 of adjusted gross income reporting dividend receipts. Dividend tax returns in the $5,000-and-over adjusted gross income class rose by 28 per cent between 1952 and 1956, but this is much less than the doubling found from the shareowner estimates. Shareowners and dividend recipients are, of course, different categories. One would expect fewer dividend recipients than shareowners because some companies do not pay dividends, and

[11] Lewis H. Kimmel, *Share Ownership in the United States,* Washington, 1952, and New York Stock Exchange, *Who Owns American Business, 1956 Census of Shareowners,* New York, 1956. (I have used the revised income class breakdown as given for 1956 in the 1959 Census. See the source note for Table 4.)

[12] The Brookings study and the *Census of Shareowners* give an income class breakdown only for individuals. Taxable and nontaxable returns have been combined to ensure that the results are not due to the movement of some dividend recipients from the taxable to nontaxable category or vice versa.

TABLE 4

COMPARISON OF NUMBER OF STOCKHOLDERS AND NUMBER OF DIVIDEND RECIPIENTS ON TAX RETURNS, 1952 AND 1956

Household or Adjusted Gross Income Class	1952			1956			Percentage Change Between 1952 and 1956 in	
	Number of Stockholders (thousands) (1)	Number of Dividend Recipients (thousands) (2)	Col. 2 as a Per Cent of Col. 1 (3)	Number of Stockholders (thousands) (4)	Number of Dividend Recipients (thousands) (5)	Col. 5 as a Per Cent of Col. 4 (6)	Number of Stockholders (7)	Number of Dividend Recipients (8)
Under $5,000	2,050	1,897	93	3,195	1,698	53	56	−10
$5,000 and over	2,700	2,322	86	5,435	3,071	57	101	28
Total	4,750	4,219	89	8,630	4,769	55	82	21

SOURCE: Column 1: Lewis H. Kimmel, *Share Ownership in the United States*, p. 95. Column 2: *Statistics of Income for 1952*, Part 1, p. 21. Column 3: New York Stock Exchange, *Share Ownership in America, 1959*, p. 15. Column 4: *Statistics of Income, Individual Income Tax Returns for 1956*, p. 40.

because many households with several shareowners would lump their dividend receipts for tax reporting. But with dividend payments rising as they did between 1952 and 1956, the numbers under these two classifications should, if anything, come closer together. Moreover, some slight increase in the number of tax returns reporting dividends can be expected since 1954, for, with the exclusion and credit introduced in that year, part of what was formerly reported as income from estates and trusts would be reported as dividends.

It is not hard to suggest why, at any given time, there should be a greater discrepancy between shareowners and dividend tax returns in the under-$5,000 income class. Some dividend recipients did not need to file; others who would be nontaxable might not file even if legally required to do so; record-keeping is probably poorer in this group; the likelihood of being detected if dividends were not reported is not as great; employees who have obtained small amounts of stock under company saving plans who are uncertain about whether they received (or were credited for) dividends on them, or whose right to the stock has not been vested, would not report dividends, etc.

But all this, while it may explain in small part what has been observed, does not get very far in explaining this puzzle—the *growing* shortfall between the estimates of stockholders and the estimates of dividend recipients. The puzzle can be summarized in another way. Why did the individual tax returns which reported dividends amount to 89 per cent of the estimated number of individual stockholders in 1952 and only 55 per cent in 1956? It is possible and, indeed, as Chapter 2 shows, very likely that some persons do not report their dividend receipts. And, again as the data of Chapter 2 will indicate, it appears that the practice of under- or nonreporting became more widespread between 1952 and 1956. It is possible also that the tax return estimates or the shareowner estimates or both are subject to error more serious than has been suspected on the basis of their sampling design. The data available do not permit a test of this hypothesis.[13]

[13] Data made available very recently indicate that the question raised concerning the difference between the 1952 and 1956 results applies also to 1959. For in that year there were, according to the preliminary release of *Statistics of Income, 1959*, dated June 29, 1961, some 5.9 million returns that reported dividends, and this represents only 47 per cent of the 12,490,000 individuals owning shares in publicly held corporations in early 1959. (See *Share Ownership in America, 1959*, published by the New York Stock Exchange.) Between 1956 and 1959 about 1 million people became new shareholders through participation in company saving plans, and until the stock vests to them, the dividends may go to a trust and not to them at all.

4. The vast mass of dividend recipients fell in the income classes under $50,000. In all the years for which we could obtain data, not more than 2.5 per cent and frequently less than 1 per cent had incomes higher than $50,000. So between them, the two broad income classes below $50,000 accounted for almost all the dividend returns. Since net income was used in tabulating the 1934–1941 data, while adjusted gross income was the basis for 1946–1957, the number of returns could not be treated as a continuum. But broad comparisons are not precluded. In the earlier period, 1934–1941, a major and growing fraction of all taxable dividend returns fell in the under-$5,000 class. In 1934 the under-$5,000 and the $5,000-to-$50,000 classes each contained about 49 per cent of all taxable dividend returns; by 1941 the corresponding percentages were almost 82 and just under 18. The later period—1946–1957—shows a different trend. The share of the lowest group in total taxable dividend returns started at over 60 per cent, but fell continually to 25.5 per cent by 1957. Just the opposite was true of the $5,000-to-$50,000 class, as indeed it must be since between them these two classes encompass about 98 per cent of all taxable dividend returns. It is appropriate to remind the reader at this point that these results, based on the data for given income-size classes, are strongly affected by the upward movement in prices and incomes since the end of World War II.

5. The data on number of dividend returns, in conjunction with the evidence presented earlier on amounts of dividends, point up the high degree of concentration in the income-class distribution of dividends. In 1957, for example, the 2.0 per cent of taxable dividend recipients in the income class $50,000 and over received 36 per cent of the dividends reported on taxable returns.

Distribution of Dividends by Dividend Size Classes

Data are also available on the distribution of dividends per se, i.e., by size classes of dividend receipts.[14] The more recent figures—1946–1952 [15]

Therefore, it might be more appropriate to relate the 5.9 million dividend recipients on tax returns to 11.5 million stockholders; with this adjustment, the tax return figure comes to 51 per cent of the Stock Exchange estimate.

[14] For all returns filed from 1946–1952 (with the exception of 1951) and for taxpayers with net incomes of $5,000 and above for 1936–1941.

[15] For 1953 a comparable tabulation was not made, and comparisons involving 1954 and later years are rendered ambiguous by the fact that the data for these years are tabulated net of exclusions.

—may be summarized this way. The vast majority of dividend recipients had "small" incomes from this source. Over one-third had less than $100 of dividends, about one-half had less than $200, and around two-thirds less than $400 of dividends annually. On the other hand, a mere 4 to 6 per cent received $5,000 or more of dividends (see Table 5 for more detail). Small in number, this latter group was, however, rich in dividends. In 1950, for example, the 6 per cent of all dividend recipients with dividends of $5,000 or more received an estimated 65 per cent of all dividends reported by individuals on tax returns. The lowest third of dividend receivers had about 1 per cent of the total, the lowest two-thirds under 7 per cent. (Only income from estates and trusts appears to approach the concentration shown by dividends. But this income, of course, is heavily weighted with dividends; well over 50 per cent of the income of fiduciaries comes from dividends.)

Of all the sources of income specified on tax returns, dividends have been most concentrated in their distribution. The 1950 data summarized in Table 6 show this clearly. Compared with the upper 10 per cent of the dividend recipients' share of almost three-fourths of dividends, the top decile of recipients of wages and salaries showed a figure of only 26 per cent of total wages and salaries; for entrepreneurial income the comparable figure was 42 per cent; for rents and royalties, 54 per cent; for interest, 57 per cent; for capital gains, 64 per cent; and 67 per cent of income from estates and trusts went to the upper 10 per cent of the recipients of this income source. The Gini coefficient has been used as a single summary measure of the degree of concentration of each income type's distribution by recipients thereof. It ranges between 0 and 1, with 0 being the figure that would be obtained if all dividend recipients had the same amount of dividends, and 1 the value that would characterize a distribution in which one person received all the dividends reported on tax returns. This measure makes it clear that dividends stand alone in degree of inequality. The only two income types that approach this degree of concentration—income from estates and trusts and capital gains—are, of course, closely related to dividends (see column 6 of Table 6); dividends, as already noted, account for a high proportion of income from estates and trusts,[16] while capital gains arise to a large extent from trading in assets, ownership of which is the source of dividend income.

[16] In 1950 dividends represented about 60 per cent of the total income of taxable estates and trusts, and, presumably, therefore, some percentage on this order of the income received by individuals from estates and trusts.

TABLE 5

DISTRIBUTION OF DIVIDEND RECEIPTS BY DIVIDEND SIZE CLASSES, 1946–1952

(taxable and nontaxable returns, individuals only, number of returns in thousands)

Dividend Size Class (dollars)	1946			1947			1948		
	Number of Returns	Per Cent of Total	Cumulative Per Cent of Total	Number of Returns	Per Cent of Total	Cumulative Per Cent of Total	Number of Returns	Per Cent of Total	Cumulative Per Cent of Total
Under 100	1,250.0	37.78%	37.78%	1,257.0	36.45%	36.45%	1,100.0	33.12%	33.12%
100 to 200	490.0	14.81	52.59	515.0	14.93	51.38	500.0	5.06	48.18
200 to 300	276.0	8.35	60.94	293.0	8.50	59.88	278.0	8.37	56.55
300 to 400	179.0	5.40	66.34	187.0	5.42	65.30	189.0	5.69	62.24
400 to 500	134.0	4.05	70.39	141.0	4.09	69.39	145.0	4.36	66.60
500 to 1,000	368.0	11.13	81.52	383.0	11.10	80.49	399.0	12.01	78.61
1,000 to 1,500	174.0	5.26	86.78	186.0	5.39	85.88	181.0	5.45	84.06
1,500 to 2,000	99.0	2.99	89.77	103.0	2.99	88.87	109.0	3.28	87.34
2,000 to 2,500	65.0	1.97	91.74	71.0	2.06	90.93	74.0	2.23	89.57
2,500 to 3,000	47.0	1.42	93.16	49.0	1.42	92.35	51.0	1.54	91.11
3,000 to 4,000	59.0	1.78	94.94	64.0	1.86	94.21	68.0	2.05	93.16
4,000 to 5,000	35.0	1.06	96.00	41.0	1.19	95.40	45.0	1.36	94.52
5,000 to 10,000	74.0	2.24	98.24	88.0	2.55	97.95	97.0	2.92	97.44
10,000 to 25,000	43.0	1.30	99.54	50.0	1.45	99.40	59.0	1.78	99.22
25,000 to 50,000	10.4	0.31	99.85	13.2	0.38	99.78	16.8	0.51	99.73
50,000 to 100,000	3.7	0.11	99.96	4.7	0.14	99.92	6.4	0.19	99.92
100,000 or more	1.6	0.05	100.01	2.2	0.06	99.98	3.0	0.09	100.01
Total	3,308.7			3,448.1			3,321.2		

(continued)

TABLE 5 (concluded)

Dividend Size Class (dollars)	1949			1950			1952		
	Number of Returns	Per Cent of Total	Cumulative Per Cent of Total	Number of Returns	Per Cent of Total	Cumulative Per Cent of Total	Number of Returns	Per Cent of Total	Cumulative Per Cent of Total
Under 100	1,160.0	31.73	31.73	1,183.0	32.25	32.25	1,447.0	34.30	34.30
100 to 200	519.0	14.20	45.93	508.0	13.85	46.10	621.0	14.72	49.02
200 to 300	314.0	8.59	54.52	307.0	8.37	54.47	346.0	8.20	57.22
300 to 400	209.0	5.72	60.24	194.0	5.29	59.76	234.0	5.55	62.77
400 to 500	165.0	4.51	64.75	161.0	4.39	64.15	185.0	4.38	67.15
500 to 1,000	457.0	12.50	77.25	431.0	11.75	75.90	477.0	11.31	78.46
1,000 to 1,500	222.0	6.07	83.32	232.0	6.32	82.22	236.0	5.59	84.05
1,500 to 2,000	133.0	3.64	86.96	135.0	3.68	85.90	150.0	3.56	87.61
2,000 to 2,500	95.0	2.60	89.56	88.0	2.40	88.30	99.0	2.35	89.96
2,500 to 3,000	61.0	1.67	91.23	65.0	1.77	90.07	66.0	1.56	91.52
3,000 to 4,000	87.0	2.38	93.61	86.0	2.34	92.41	89.0	2.11	93.63
4,000 to 5,000	51.0	1.39	95.00	55.0	1.50	93.91	50.0	1.19	94.82
5,000 to 10,000	100.0	2.74	97.74	115.0	3.13	97.04	118.0	2.80	97.62
10,000 to 25,000	58.0	1.59	99.33	75.0	2.04	99.08	71.0	1.68	99.30
25,000 to 50,000	16.4	0.45	99.78	21.3	0.58	99.66	19.5	0.46	99.76
50,000 to 100,000	6.0	0.16	99.94	8.0	0.22	99.88	6.7	0.16	99.92
100,000 or more	2.8	0.08	100.02	3.8	0.10	99.98	3.0	0.07	99.99
Total	3,656.2			3,668.1			4,218.2		

SOURCES: 1946: *Statistics of Income*, Part 1, pp. 152, 153.
1947: *Statistics of Income*, Part 1, pp. 106, 107.
1948: *Statistics of Income*, Part 1, pp. 102, 103.
1949: *Statistics of Income*, Part 1, pp. 98, 99.
1950: *Statistics of Income*, Part 1, pp. 56, 57.
1952: *Statistics of Income*, Part 1, p. 26.
NOTE: 1951 data not tabulated.

TABLE 6

Shares of Selected Percentile Bands of Recipients
of Specified Income Types, 1950

(per cent)

Type of Income	Share of Lower 25% (1)	Share of Lower 50% (2)	Share of Lower 75% (3)	Share of Lower 90% (4)	Share of Upper 10% (5)	Gini Coefficient of Inequality (6)
Dividends	0.74%	2.78%	10.60%	25.60%	74.40%	.86
Income from estates and trusts	0.94	4.97	15.25	32.77	67.23	.78
Capital gains	1.12	5.40	18.27	35.77	64.23	.76
Interest	3.32	7.63	20.98	43.22	56.78	.70
Rents and royalties	2.13	8.48	25.32	45.94	54.06	.70
Partnership income	2.46	10.69	28.69	48.75	51.25	.65
Business and professional income	3.95	14.94	35.53	57.97	42.03	.56
Annuities and pensions	2.41	13.56	40.64	66.42	33.58	.53
Salaries and wages	6.54	24.03	50.94	73.79	26.21	.38

Data cover all those who filed tax returns. In each case the percentiles are determined on the basis of receipts from this particular source. Partnership income and business and professional income do not include reported losses from these sources.

A Note on Possible Variation of Pay-Out Ratios with Tax Bracket of Stockholders

In commenting on the income class distribution of dividends in an earlier draft of this study, Professor Willard Thorp wondered whether "stocks with lower pay-outs might not have gravitated to high bracket holders and those with high dividend yields gone to the lower classes."

His question raises a possibility that is important both for the discussion just completed, and for the analysis of Chapter 4 of our study. For essential to the analysis in this later chapter is the imputation of pro rata shares of corporate earnings—dividends plus retained earnings plus corporate income tax—on the basis of dividend receipts.

Over almost the whole of the period in which we have had a personal income tax, it has "paid" all taxpayers to get, if they could, a given amount of income to be cast up in a form that would be treated as a capital gain rather than in a form that would be considered ordinary income for tax purposes. Moreover, as a general rule, in any particular year, the worth of such a conversion, i.e., the net tax saving it represented, rose with the stockholder's tax rate bracket. The tax advantage of capital gains vis à vis dividend income increased most when the exemption of dividends from normal tax was removed in 1936; bracket rates rose in the ensuing years and a ceiling rate was imposed on capital gains. See Table 10 for the relevant data and differential worth of a capital gain.

Would it not be sensible to think, then, that higher income investors would seek out in particular the stock of corporations with low dividend pay-out ratios, hoping thereby to take out what might otherwise have been dividends taxed at regular rates, in the form of capital gains that would be taxed at lower rates? To the degree that this occurred, since all the shares outstanding must have holders, we could infer that low income taxpayers ended up with stock whose pay-out ratio was above average. A significant difference in pay-out ratios of stockholding among income classes would distort any income-class comparison of dividend receipts, especially if, as seems possible, the differences became more pronounced at some time or times in the period over which the income class distribution was being compared.

This is a complicated problem, and cannot be settled on an a priori basis. The behavior posited by Professor Thorp's question is rational, and there are numerous allegations that it does exist. On the other hand, no one would deny that some high income individuals do seek heavy current income, widows perhaps or persons more interested in spending than in further accumulation. Some data relevant to this problem appear in Table 11. These are based on answers to questions in interviews undertaken in 1949. The elusiveness of replies to interview questions is well known, and the categories of investment objective are not mutually exclusive. But these data show that the proportion of capital appreciation seekers and of those who desire both income and capital appreciation increases with income class. Capital appreciation seems to weigh more heavily in the decisions of high income investors. This would appear to support the possibility that dividend pay-out of stockholdings and tax-bracket of stockholder are inversely related.

On the other hand it is sometimes asserted for reasons not clearly specified that higher dividend pay-outs will cause stock to rise in price, so even investors interested in capital gains could very well hold high pay-out stock and be undertaking an action consistent with their objectives.

TABLE 7

Dividends ᵃ Reported on Taxable Returns, by Income Classes, 1918–1957

(thousands of dollars)

Year	Under $2,000	$2,000 to $3,000	$3,000 to $5,000	$5,000 to $10,000	$10,000 to $25,000	$25,000 to $50,000	$50,000 to $100,000	$100,000 to $500,000	$500,000 and over	Total
					Income Class					
1918	14,551	38,535	134,758	326,430	507,262	400,804	324,561	381,269	192,882	2,321,053
1919	13,579	35,964	126,238	322,226	526,813	399,602	328,075	380,577	170,996	2,304,072
1920	15,319	38,802	130,825	384,902	647,572	488,525	377,785	334,139	130,955	2,548,826
1921	14,419	24,358	96,117	349,231	541,211	396,472	295,338	253,077	79,809	2,050,032
1922	15,504	25,516	103,131	321,841	562,752	439,944	352,045	324,481	137,961	2,283,173
1923	28,445	48,854	195,397	321,231	660,270	520,940	398,552	371,408	143,628	2,688,729
1924	31,462	53,647	211,444	227,081	657,661	555,071	468,736	457,117	187,182	2,849,400
1925	13,767	30,318	116,273	220,964	731,865	618,308	512,534	597,335	264,032	3,105,399
1926	12,519	33,999	92,936	247,360	815,445	666,606	578,784	723,617	361,599	3,532,869
1927	9,940	23,607	80,394	400,306	834,567	679,906	623,864	781,120	411,742	3,845,536
1928	8,887	24,846	78,836	409,829	835,312	694,181	641,315	887,476	513,259	4,093,941
1929	7,596	22,442	76,805	469,533	930,662	736,129	645,814	883,823	544,486	4,317,290
1930	46,625	44,631	119,817	514,253	932,635	649,447	527,776	647,516	378,128	3,860,828
1931	6,177	18,234	54,585	424,590	715,012	413,903	338,381	396,566	234,056	2,601,504
1932	14,337	22,807	71,030	309,663	394,962	264,633	232,224	224,448	105,593	1,639,697
1933	13,909	19,953	57,600	227,611	297,176	214,967	181,420	178,830	95,057	1,286,523
1934	11,501	17,170	60,667	284,161	421,446	305,829	222,509	228,001	118,914	1,670,198

Year										
1935	11,808	18,301	66,132	303,958	462,011	348,438	266,836	289,169	139,792	1,906,445
1936	99,504	109,776	292,635	478,360	757,888	577,870	473,665	488,940	197,960	3,476,598
1937	135,939	130,207	344,540	547,080	823,452	615,928	493,966	504,756	193,666	3,789,588
1938	177,863	117,386	279,102	408,821	547,439	353,989	248,128	256,289	91,872	2,480,889
1939	187,097	131,924	324,033	457,454	649,713	445,622	336,803	332,507	138,428	3,003,581
1940	272,660	220,896	364,539	506,915	709,043	492,284	364,935	389,563	150,909	3,471,744
1941	413,222	334,254	487,322	543,071	729,124	509,251	383,706	407,554	154,985	3,962,489
1942	433,214	294,381	363,189	471,648	690,369	479,775	362,735	331,796	104,205	3,531,312
1943	384,070	249,142	341,744	511,253	720,682	501,461	373,081	343,847	111,003	3,536,283
1944	265,146	218,776	390,936	569,380	787,347	520,322	395,898	383,628	137,604	3,672,713
1945	231,995	214,130	348,903	574,419	836,633	555,937	418,003	403,857	139,499	3,726,498
1946	215,368	235,846	418,647	667,556	1,023,637	706,709	536,267	558,910	198,183	4,561,123
1947	223,695	234,742	438,441	757,160	1,190,636	844,750	651,803	701,982	253,472	5,296,681
1948	124,631	168,407	402,582	785,101	1,247,402	1,007,282	862,428	1,012,467	312,918	5,923,218
1949	153,743	237,980	524,004	893,481	1,324,907	1,025,584	856,143	969,167	331,624	6,316,633
1950	118,134	195,694	471,585	947,976	1,584,164	1,298,940	1,109,285	1,321,394	496,993	7,544,165
1951	128,685	183,984	469,178	1,039,390	1,617,925	1,297,069	1,075,556	1,212,921	420,810	7,445,518
1952 b	126,385	188,901	443,435	1,029,347	1,269,955	1,716,732	1,041,432	1,089,204	374,404	7,279,795
1953 b	135,126	203,226	462,007	1,115,515	1,300,658	1,709,641	962,201	956,331	363,239	7,207,944
1954 b	90,163	133,955	448,286	1,074,783	1,862,954	1,371,604	1,111,845	1,132,919	435,537	7,622,046
1955	88,580	147,037	433,288	1,102,878	1,972,810	1,277,262	1,509,707	1,340,411	547,057	8,419,030
1956	98,435	147,009	475,319	1,163,322	2,294,211	1,754,231	1,425,856	1,457,764	610,473	9,426,620
1957	107,389	157,732	473,561	1,350,545	2,427,507	1,790,487	1,477,526	1,494,561	590,257	9,869,565

SOURCE: Annual volumes of *Statistics of Income*, Part 1. See note to Table 1.

a Includes dividends reported on taxable returns of individuals and fiduciaries (estates and trusts); from 1936–1953 includes also an estimate of the dividend component of individuals' income from estates and trusts.

b In this year the data were tabulated by income classes different from those usually employed. The $20,000-to-$30,000 class total was allocated between the $10,000-to-$25,000, and the $25,000-to-$50,000 class amounts on the basis of the 1951 ratios.

41

TABLE 8

Year	Under 2	2 to 3	3 to 5	5 to 10	10 to 25	25 to 50	50 to 100	100 to 500	500 and over
					Income Class (thousands of dollars)				
1918	0.9	1.5	3.7	12.9	25.1	35.4	40.7	44.1	59.4
1919	0.6	1.3	2.6	9.2	18.7	26.5	31.0	34.9	49.0
1920	0.5	0.9	2.5	10.6	20.7	29.9	36.3	44.0	63.3
1921	0.6	1.5	2.6	12.2	22.2	32.0	39.3	50.0	66.9
1922	0.6	1.6	2.5	10.5	20.9	30.1	36.3	40.9	46.2
1923	1.1	2.3	3.4	10.4	21.7	31.9	39.3	44.9	47.8
1924	1.3	2.4	3.4	6.7	19.6	30.3	38.4	43.0	51.2
1925	1.3	2.7	3.6	5.8	17.5	26.2	31.8	34.0	32.1
1926	1.1	2.9	3.4	6.1	19.2	29.6	27.2	40.8	39.8
1927	1.0	2.1	3.2	9.6	19.3	29.0	35.8	37.6	37.4
1928	1.0	2.1	2.9	8.9	18.0	26.2	30.5	29.7	26.2
1929	0.9	2.0	3.1	9.9	19.9	29.4	34.5	31.8	26.3
1930	4.8	4.3	5.1	13.4	27.4	40.8	50.7	58.5	59.0
1931	0.9	2.6	3.4	14.9	30.3	43.8	60.0	76.1	85.0
1932	1.2	2.5	3.4	15.9	29.0	44.2	74.4	113.0 [a]	139.5 [a]
1933	1.2	2.6	3.2	12.8	23.1	34.3	51.2	65.4	66.4
1934	1.0	2.8	3.0	12.7	23.7	36.7	46.5	63.1	84.4
1935	0.9	2.4	2.8	11.7	21.9	34.0	42.7	57.8	78.1
1936	5.9	10.1	9.4	14.2	25.4	36.3	45.2	56.0	72.2
1937	6.3	10.4	9.1	15.1	27.1	40.3	50.8	63.1	79.6
1938	8.7	10.0	8.1	12.8	23.0	34.1	43.2	53.6	41.5
1939	6.9	8.1	7.3	12.5	23.5	36.0	47.0	60.4	74.2
1940	5.4	4.4	6.3	12.5	22.5	34.5	44.6	58.8	70.9
1941	3.3	2.1	5.6	11.3	18.3	27.3	34.6	45.3	60.1
1942	2.1	1.3	2.7	8.1	14.0	19.8	24.8	30.4	42.6
1943	1.3	0.8	1.4	6.4	11.4	15.9	20.3	26.3	40.1
1944	1.1	0.8	1.1	4.8	10.5	14.9	19.8	28.3	47.7
1945	0.9	0.7	1.0	4.6	9.3	13.3	17.9	26.1	40.8
1946	1.1	0.8	1.2	4.3	9.1	14.0	19.7	30.6	40.9
1947	1.3	0.7	0.9	4.1	10.1	16.6	24.6	38.1	50.7
1948	1.1	0.7	0.8	2.6	8.8	15.7	23.6	37.6	50.0
1949	1.4	1.0	1.1	2.9	9.8	17.3	26.8	42.1	56.7
1950	1.1	0.9	0.8	2.4	10.0	17.0	25.4	38.5	51.7
1951	1.2	0.9	0.8	1.9	8.7	15.4	23.1	35.2	53.1
1952	1.2	1.0	0.7	1.5	7.3	14.2	23.1	36.8	54.0
1953	1.3	1.1	0.7	1.4	6.5	13.9	23.1	36.8	55.7
1954	1.1	0.8	0.7	1.3	7.4	14.6	22.8	35.3	41.9
1955	1.0	0.9	0.7	1.2	6.5	11.9	28.1	36.1	41.9
1956	1.2	1.0	0.8	1.1	6.2	14.6	22.9	36.5	43.7
1957	1.4	1.1	0.8	1.1	5.9	14.3	22.9	37.4	46.4

[a] Net capital losses experienced in these income classes; hence a value of over 100 per cent for dividends.

TABLE 9

Income Class Shares of Dividends Reported on Taxable Returns, 1918–1957

(per cent)

					Income Class (thousands of dollars)					
Year	Under 2	2 to 3	3 to 5	5 to 10	10 to 25	25 to 50	50 to 100	100 to 500	500 and over	Total
1918	0.6	1.7	5.8	14.1	21.9	17.3	14.0	16.4	8.3	100.0
1919	0.6	1.6	5.5	14.0	22.9	17.3	14.2	16.5	7.4	100.0
1920	0.6	1.5	5.1	15.1	25.4	19.2	14.8	13.1	5.1	100.0
1921	0.7	1.2	4.7	17.0	26.4	19.3	14.4	12.3	3.9	100.0
1922	0.7	1.1	4.5	14.0	24.6	19.3	15.4	14.2	6.0	100.0
1923	1.1	1.8	7.3	11.9	24.6	19.4	14.8	13.8	5.3	100.0
1924	1.1	1.9	7.4	8.0	23.1	19.5	16.5	16.0	6.6	100.0
1925	0.4	1.0	3.7	7.1	23.6	19.9	16.5	19.2	8.5	100.0
1926	0.4	1.0	2.6	7.0	23.1	18.9	16.4	20.5	10.2	100.0
1927	0.3	0.6	2.1	10.4	21.7	17.7	16.2	20.3	10.7	100.0
1928	0.2	0.6	1.9	10.0	20.4	17.0	15.7	21.7	12.5	100.0
1929	0.2	0.5	1.8	10.9	21.6	17.1	15.0	20.5	12.6	100.0
1930	1.2	1.2	3.1	13.3	24.2	16.8	13.7	16.8	9.8	100.0
1931	0.2	0.7	2.1	16.3	27.5	15.9	13.0	15.2	9.0	100.0
1932	0.9	1.4	4.3	18.9	24.1	16.1	14.2	13.7	6.4	100.0
1933	1.1	1.6	4.5	17.7	23.1	16.7	14.1	13.9	7.4	100.0
1934	0.7	1.0	3.6	17.0	25.2	18.3	13.3	13.7	7.1	100.0
1935	0.6	1.0	3.5	15.9	24.2	18.3	14.0	15.2	7.3	100.0
1936	2.9	3.2	8.4	13.8	21.8	16.6	13.6	14.1	5.7	100.0
1937	3.6	3.4	9.1	14.4	21.7	16.3	13.0	13.3	5.1	100.0
1938	7.2	4.7	11.3	16.5	22.1	14.3	10.0	10.3	3.7	100.0
1939	6.2	4.4	10.8	15.2	21.6	14.8	11.2	11.1	4.6	100.0
1940	7.9	6.4	10.5	14.6	20.4	14.2	10.5	11.2	4.3	100.0
1941	10.4	8.4	12.3	13.7	18.4	12.9	9.7	10.3	3.9	100.0
1942	12.3	8.3	10.3	13.4	19.6	13.6	10.3	9.4	3.0	100.0
1943	10.9	7.0	9.7	14.5	20.4	14.2	10.6	9.7	3.1	100.0
1944	7.2	6.0	10.7	15.5	21.5	14.2	10.8	10.5	3.8	100.0
1945	6.2	5.8	9.4	15.4	22.5	14.9	11.2	10.8	3.7	100.0
1946	4.7	5.2	9.2	14.6	22.4	15.5	11.8	12.3	4.3	100.0
1947	4.2	4.4	8.3	14.3	22.5	15.9	12.3	13.3	4.8	100.0
1948	2.1	2.8	6.8	13.3	21.0	17.0	14.6	17.1	5.3	100.0
1949	2.4	3.8	8.3	14.1	21.0	16.2	13.6	15.3	5.3	100.0
1950	1.6	2.6	6.2	12.6	21.0	17.2	14.7	17.5	6.6	100.0
1951	1.7	2.5	6.3	14.0	21.7	17.4	14.5	16.3	5.6	100.0
1952	1.7	2.6	6.1	14.1	17.5	23.6	14.3	15.0	5.1	100.0
1953	1.9	2.8	6.4	15.5	18.0	23.7	13.4	13.3	5.0	100.0
1954	1.2	1.7	5.8	14.1	24.3	18.0	14.5	14.8	5.6	100.0
1955	1.1	1.7	5.1	13.1	23.4	15.2	17.9	15.9	6.6	100.0
1956	0.9	1.5	5.0	12.4	24.3	18.7	15.2	15.4	6.6	100.0
1957	1.2	1.6	4.6	13.8	24.3	18.2	14.9	15.2	6.0	100.0

Dividends Under the Income Tax

TABLE 10

EFFECTIVE RATE ON AN ADDED DOLLAR OF DIVIDEND INCOME AND ON AN ADDED DOLLAR OF
NET LONG-TERM CAPITAL GAINS FOR SELECTED STATUTORY NET INCOMES [a] AND YEARS, 1936–1960

(per cent)

| Year | Net Income | | | | | | | | | | | |
| | \$5,000 | | \$10,000 | | \$25,000 | | \$50,000 | | \$100,000 | | \$1,000,000 | |
	(1)	(2)	(3)	(4)	(5)	(6)	(7)	(8)	(9)	(10)	(11)	(12)
1936–1937 [b]	4.0	2.4	9.0	5.4	19.0	11.5	31.0	18.6	59.0	35.4	76.0	45.6
1938–1939 [c]	4.0	2.0	9.0	4.5	19.0	9.5	31.0	15.0	59.0	15.0	76.0	15.0
1940 [d]	4.4	2.2	11.0	5.5	34.1	16.5	48.4	16.5	66.0	16.5	78.4	18.5
1941	13.0	6.5	21.0	10.5	48.0	15.0	59.0	15.0	68.0	15.0	78.0	15.0
1942	22.0	11.0	34.0	17.0	58.0	25.0	69.0	25.0	83.0	25.0	88.0	25.0
1943 [e]	24.8	11.0	36.8	17.0	60.8	25.0	71.8	25.0	88.0	25.0	90.0 [f]	25.0
1944–1945	25.0	12.5	37.0	18.5	62.0	25.0	75.0	25.0	90.0	25.0	90.0 [f]	25.0
1946–1947	20.9	10.5	32.3	16.2	56.1	25.0	68.4	25.0	82.7	25.0	86.5	25.0
1948–1949	16.6	8.3	19.4	9.7	33.4	16.7	51.9	25.0	63.4	25.0	82.1	25.0
1950	17.4	8.7	20.0	10.0	34.6	17.3	53.7	25.0	65.5	25.0	84.4	25.0
1951	20.4	10.2	22.4	11.2	39.0	19.5	60.0	25.0	73.0	25.0	91.0	25.0
1952–1953	22.2	11.1	24.6	12.3	42.0	21.0	66.0	26.0	75.0	26.0	92.0	26.0
1954 [g]	18.0	10.0	20.0	11.0	36.0	19.0	57.0	25.0	70.0	25.0	89.0	25.0
1955–1960 [h]	16.0	10.0	18.0	11.0	34.0	19.0	55.0	25.0	68.0	25.0	87.0	25.0

NOTE: Odd-numbered columns show effective rate on added dollar of dividend income and even-numbered columns show rate on added dollar of net long-term capital gains.

SOURCE: For 1936–1950, Lawrence H. Seltzer, *The Nature and Tax Treatment of Capital Gains and Losses*, New York, National Bureau of Economic Research, 1951, pp. 523–524; for 1951 on, Internal Revenue Code.

[a] Married person, two dependents, maximum earned income credit.

[b] Rates on gain from sale of capital assets held over two, but not over five years.

[c] Rates on gain from sale of capital assets held more than two years.

[d] Includes Defense Tax.

[e] Includes Victory Tax.

[f] Takes account of maximum effective rate limitation of 90 per cent.

[g] Assumes exclusion exhausted and 4 per cent credit taken only in latter half of year (i.e., credit of 2 per cent).

[h] Assumes exclusion exhausted and 4 per cent credit taken over the whole year.

A stockholder in a major corporation explained it this way: [17]

One of the main factors that enters into the market value of stock is the dividend it pays.

To show how dividends affect prices, I have tried to find a parallel example with which to compare Jersey, and I believe that American Can fills the bill. Both are fine companies; their stocks are really "prime." They are rated equally by Fitch. In 1947 they closed within a half point of each other, around 81. Their high prices of 1948 were within one-eighth point, around 93. The book value of Can is

[17] From a statement by Mr. Wolf, a stockholder, at the 1949 Annual Meeting of Standard Oil Company, New Jersey, pp. 20–21 of a transcript published by the company for its stockholders, July 18, 1949.

Dividends in Personal and Taxable Income

TABLE 11

INVESTMENT OBJECTIVES OF A SAMPLE OF ACTIVE INVESTORS INTERVIEWED IN 1949

(percentage of spending units)

Income Class (*thousand dollars*)	Number of Cases	Capital Preservation	Security and Income	Income	Income and Capital Appreciation	Capital Appreciation	All
Under 7.5	201	4%	42%	26%	20%	8%	100
7.5 to 12.5	182	5	41	17	28	9	100
12.5 to 25	160	8	32	20	31	9	100
25 to 50	121	6	24	19	42	9	100
50 to 100	46	20	18	13	33	16	100
100 and over	26	12	7	9	46	26	100
Not ascertained	10	—	—	—	—	—	100

SOURCE: J. Keith Butters, Lawrence E. Thompson, and Lynn L. Bollinger, *Effects of Taxation: Investments by Individuals*, Boston, 1953, p. 37.

$10 or so less than that of Jersey, yet Can sold at 91⅜ yesterday, and Jersey sold at 64⅜. Why? Perhaps because Can, while earning only $9.71 a share in 1948 increased its dividends from $3 to $4, while Jersey, earning over $12 in 1948, decreased its dividends from $4 to $2. I venture the theory that if Jersey had paid us $4 last year the stock would now be selling right up where Can is, perhaps even higher.

We may also cite the conclusion of Butters, Lintner, and Cary: [18] "It is entirely conceivable that Ashland's policy of paying out a larger percentage of earnings as dividends would increase the market value of its securities more than a policy of negligible distributions; the market value of listed securities—as contrasted with closely held, un-traded securities representing a controlling interest in a company—depends in considerable part on their dividend records."

From the standard texts in finance and investments one gets the view that among the numerous factors that may affect the price of stock, dividends are important. How important varies from the most

[18] J. Keith Butters, John Lintner, and William L. Cary, assisted by Powell Niland, *Effects of Taxation: Corporate Mergers*, Boston, 1951, p. 49.

important to more important than some people think. A sampling of opinion follows:

"The considered and continuous verdict of the stock market is overwhelmingly in favor of liberal dividends as against niggardly ones. The common-stock investor and the security analyst must take this judgment into account in the selection of stocks for purchase. It is now becoming standard practice to evaluate common stocks by applying one multiplier (or 'capitalization rate') to that portion of the earnings paid out in dividends and a much smaller multiplier to the undistributed balance." [19]

"One thing is clear and that is that the market does not uniformly accept the line of reasoning we suggested at the outset which implied that the more paid out in dividends, the less the value of what remained in the business. On the contrary, observation suggests that an increase in the dividend payment normally acts to raise market price rather than lower it, and there are several reasons why this should be expected. . . . " [20]

"Generally, earnings per share have the greatest influence on valuations of stocks and a widely used method is that of capitalizing earnings. However, we observed that many analysts take dividends into account along with earnings in developing their ideas of value. And we went on to suggest that perhaps dividends are a more logical basis than earnings for valuation of stocks." [21]

No definitive analysis of this question has been made to date, although much has been written on it. Some investigators hold in theory —and claim to have established in fact—a positive association between the size of the dividend paid on a share of stock and its price. Others assert that if these results are valid—and they are not sure this is the case—it is only because dividends are a good proxy measure for the really relevant variable, viz., expected earnings. To cite a few examples:

David Durand has investigated the effects of book value, earnings, and dividends on the price of common stock of banks. In general, but with exceptions, he found the price of bank stock to be positively associated with their dividend payments. But he warns the reader:

[19] Benjamin Graham and David L. Dodd, with the collaboration of Charles Tatham, Jr., *Security Analysis: Principles and Techniques*, 3rd ed., New York, 1951, p. 432.

[20] Pearson Hunt, Charles M. Williams, and Gordon Donaldson, *Basic Business Finance*, Homewood, Ill., 1958, pp. 648–649.

[21] Harry Sauvain, *Investment Management*, 2nd ed., Englewood Cliffs, N. J., 1959, p. 312.

"Generalizations, moreover, may be misleading unless very carefully drawn. From the frequency with which dividends takes first place among the weights, one might be tempted to conclude that this factor is the most important one affecting bank stock prices in general; but one should not lose sight of the presence of exceptions among the 117 stocks from 1946 to 1953 or of the possibility that other factors might take first place for other groups of stocks or for other periods of time." [22]

Myron Gordon holds, on the basis of econometric tests of a model of stock price behavior using cross-sectional data for 1951 and 1954 for four industries—chemicals, foods, steel, and machine tools—that dividend pay-out and stock price are positively associated, although the degree of association is subject to wide variations, and there are exceptions.[23]

On the other hand, Franco Modigliani and Merton Miller have argued, after developing and testing a model of the cost of capital, that as long as investment policy is optimal, stockholders, in theory, should be indifferent to pay-out policy. (They go on to assert that considerations of control or convenience for management may affect pay-out ratios, but this is not because the pay-out rate per se will affect the prices of shares.) In a more recent, as yet unpublished, paper, the same authors after analyzing the data for over sixty electric utilities for 1954, 1956, and 1957 concluded that in the latter two years current earnings and growth of earnings were the variables that "explained" the price of common stocks; only in 1954 did dividends have an effect on stock prices.[24]

In a similar vein, Haskel Benishay in a cross-sectional multiple regression analysis of fifty-six companies for four years, 1954, 1955, 1956, and 1957, finds indications that "the higher is the pay-ratio the higher is the value of the firm." But having "rejected as an interpretation of this result that, ceteris paribus, investors prefer distribution to retention of earnings," he feels that "Instead the pay-out ratio may

[22] In his study, *Bank Stock Prices and the Bank Capital Problem,* Occasional Paper 54, New York, NBER, 1957, p. 16.

[23] M. J. Gordon, "Dividends, Earnings, and Stock Prices," *Review of Economics and Statistics,* May 1959, pp. 99–105.

[24] Franco Modigliani and Merton H. Miller, "The Cost of Capital, Corporation Finance and the Theory of Investment," *American Economic Review,* June 1958, reprinted in Ezra Solomon (ed.), *The Management of Corporate Capital,* Glencoe, Ill., 1959, pp. 150–181, especially footnote 53 on p. 177. Also, Modigliani and Miller, "Leverage, Dividend Policy, and the Cost of Capital," a paper presented at the meeting of the Econometric Society, December 1960, in St. Louis, Missouri.

represent, in the capacity of an instrumental variable, the extent of error in the measurement of expected income." [25]

That the question is still open is all that one can firmly conclude from the studies cited and other similar ones. But I think this review of the literature also suggests that the path to capital gains is not strewn solely with low-yielding stock, and we know that the really low-yielding stock is small in amount, while the holdings of "high-bracket" taxpayers are large. This leaves open the possibility, at least, that the income class figures of Chapter 1 and our procedure for imputing corporate earnings in Chapter 4 may not be seriously in error.

We have saved the most "direct" evidence for the end of the discussion. This indicates something about its nature. For if it were really both direct and conclusive, it would not have been necessary to examine, as we have done so far, opinions, conjectures, and the results of research all of which have some relevance for the problem of this note but none of which singly or together settle the problem.

The data we have that relate to Professor Thorp's query are fragmentary, not directly focused on the question, and inconclusive. Yet to my mind (to put the conclusion before the evidence) they suggest that, all things considered, the drift of high-bracket and low-bracket taxpayers to low pay-out and high pay-out stock respectively—if it has occurred—has not, in the aggregate, been powerful enough to cause us to view income class distributions of dividends and stock ownership imputations based on dividends with real skepticism. But this conclusion is putting the cart before the horse. What are the data? I have been able to find two sets of evidence.[26]

First, there is available for 1936 a cross-tabulation which gives the asset size of dividend-paying corporations and the net income class of dividend recipients filing income tax returns for that year.[27] The dividends received by shareholders, tabulated by twenty-seven net income classes, are classified on the basis of asset size (ten in all) of the originating corporations. For instance, stockholders in the net income class $70,000 to $80,000 received 0.37 per cent of their dividends from corporations with assets of less than $50,000; they received 0.52

[25] Haskel Benishay, "Variability in Earnings-Price Ratios of Corporate Equities," *American Economic Review*, March 1961, p. 90.

[26] What follows, i.e., the rest of this note, is taken in large part from Daniel M. Holland, *The Income-Tax Burden on Stockholders*, Princeton for NBER, 1958, pp. 106–114.

[27] *Bulletin of the Treasury Department*, January 1943, pp. 3–6.

per cent from corporations with assets of $50,000 to $100,000, etc. These data, more refined than those available for any other year, can be used to estimate differences in average distribution ratios associated with the dividend receipts of taxpayers in the various net income classes, because, on the average, corporations in each asset size class had different distribution ratios. These ratios tend to increase with the asset sizes of the dividend distributing corporations [28] (see Table 12). Note that these ratios at best only approximate the information relevant to the problem posed in this note. Directly relevant would be data derived from an array in which the distribution ratio itself constituted the basis for classifying the data. Use of an approximation qualifies the result of the test (summarized in Table 13) and tends to damp the figures finally obtained compared with the results that would have been obtained from data classified directly by dividend distribution ratios. Basically, the test involved computing a distribution ratio for each net income class, by weighting each asset size distribution ratio (Table 12) by the proportion that dividends paid by corporations

TABLE 12

RATIO OF NET DIVIDENDS PAID OUT TO NET CORPORATE EARNINGS FOR NET INCOME CORPORATIONS, BY ASSET SIZE CLASSES, 1936

(dollars in thousands)

Asset Size Class	Net Dividends Paid Out	Net Corporate Earnings	Distribution Ratio
Under $50	$ 79,902	$ 148,818	0.5369
$50 to 100	93,349	154,577	0.6039
100 to 250	218,687	349,336	0.6260
250 to 500	238,476	374,159	0.6374
500 to 1,000	272,306	453,423	0.6006
1,000 to 5,000	718,404	1,234,418	0.5820
5,000 to 10,000	343,452	567,963	0.6047
10,000 to 50,000	902,773	1,334,255	0.6766
50,000 to 100,000	414,546	548,464	0.7577
100,000 and over	1,280,608	1,531,202	0.8363
All net income corporations	4,562,500	6,696,613	0.6813

SOURCE: *Statistics of Income for 1936, Part 2.*

[28] Cf. George E. Lent, *The Impact of the Undistributed Profits Tax,* New York, 1948, p. 43.

TABLE 13

NET INCOME CLASSES' WEIGHTED-AVERAGE DISTRIBUTION RATIOS, 1936

Net Income Class (thousand dollars)	Weighted-Average Distribution Ratio
Under 1	0.730
1 to 2	0.737
2 to 3	0.729
3 to 4	0.720
4 to 5	0.710
5 to 10	0.701
10 to 15	0.691
15 to 20	0.686
20 to 25	0.685
25 to 30	0.682
30 to 40	0.682
40 to 50	0.678
50 to 60	0.679
60 to 70	0.683
70 to 80	0.690
80 to 90	0.689
90 to 100	0.696
100 to 150	0.693
150 to 200	0.695
200 to 250	0.710
250 to 300	0.735
300 to 400	0.726
400 to 500	0.734
500 to 750	0.735
750 to 1,000	0.754
1,000 and over	0.775
Total	0.701

in this asset size class comprised of the total dividend receipts in each net income class. The relevant values for all net income classes appear in Table 13. The pattern of deviations from the over-all average distribution ratio is surprisingly regular.[29] Starting with the lowest net income class and moving up, we find distribution ratios above the over-all average, but the extent of departure from the general average tends to decline. Dividends representing distribution ratios below average were received by all classes from $10,000 up to $200,000. The lowest ratio was reached in the $40,000-to-$50,000 net income class;

[29] The deficit income class is neglected for purposes of this discussion because the calculations covered taxpayers only. Moreover, purposeful conduct cannot be inferred from the deficit class since, presumably, deficits are involuntary.

above this class the extent of departure from the over-all average distribution ratio becomes gradually less until at the $200,000-to-$250,000 net income level a distribution ratio above average is once more reached. This above-average ratio is characteristic of the rest of the income distribution, with the extent of departure from the average increasing steadily as the income level increases, and reaching its maximum in the $1,000,000-and-over class. If the behavior of these divergences in distribution ratio were plotted with income on the horizontal axes, above-average distribution ratios on the vertical axis above the origin, and below-average distribution ratio below the origin, then a plot of the net income class distribution ratios would be U-shaped.

How important are these differences in the distribution ratios characterizing the investments of the various net income classes? They are really very small. It is only at the extreme levels that the divergence from the average for all classes is over 5 per cent. But, as pointed out above, if the data were classified by the distribution ratio of each dividend-paying corporation, relatively greater differences would probably have been obtained. An interesting feature of this pattern of the distribution ratio is its regularity. With only a few minor exceptions, it varies smoothly from one income class to the next, falling constantly to a minimum and thereafter rising constantly. This pattern is not exactly what would have been expected solely on personal income tax minimization grounds. It is true that over a significant range the distribution ratios for the higher net income receivers are below average and this is reasonable. But if it is rational for a $45,000 net income shareholder to seek to hold personal taxes down more than average, via corporate saving, is not the pressure to do this even greater on the $450,000 net income stockholder? But the latter typically received dividends representing a distribution ratio higher than average.

The results of this test do not permit positive generalizations for 1936 for a reason beyond the lack of precise and suitable data: uncertainty arises because the undistributed profits tax, instituted in 1936, stimulated dividend distribution and changed the relative pattern of distribution ratios of different asset size class corporations.[30]

---

[30] Cf. Lent, *Undistributed Profits Tax.* According to Lent, while all but one of the asset size classes were induced by the undistributed profits tax to distribute more liberally, the greatest relative increase was made by corporations in asset size classes in which a higher proportion of stock was held by taxpayers in the middle range of net income classes. Over this income interval the test disclosed distribution ratios below average—despite the influence of the new tax. Therefore in the absence of the

There is certainly no basis for concluding that many higher income class taxpayers did not choose investments in companies with very meager distribution policies in order to forestall high personal surtaxes. But, in 1936 at least, this tendency appears to have been almost completely counterbalanced and even swamped (in the case of top income classes) by the opposite choice of stock in corporations with distribution ratios above average. In that year, considerations other than corporate saving rates evidently affected the relationship between size of personal income, including dividends, and distribution ratios of corporations from which the dividends were received.

While the above test, fragmentary though it is, suggests that there was on net balance no pronounced tendency in 1936 for the rich to seek investment in high-saving corporations, it is possible that in the years after 1936, when opportunities for tax saving on capital gains increased, such a tendency became marked.

The second set of evidence is data for 1949 on the patterns of financial asset holdings of individuals in Wisconsin, developed by Thomas R. Atkinson, which permit inferences to be drawn as to whether high-income taxpayers, as a group, take advantage of the preferential tax rate on capital gains by concentrating their holdings in corporations with low distribution ratios. Wisconsin law requires reporting on state income tax returns not only dividend receipts but also stock holdings. Having access to the returns, Atkinson was able to estimate the value of the stock from which a sampled group of taxpayers received dividends in 1949.[31] For this purpose he divided common and preferred stocks into two categories—traded and untraded. Stock issues for which dividend and price quotations were available in investment manuals fall in the traded category and the rest are classified as untraded. The value of traded stock holdings was determined by multiplying the average number of shares of the particular issue held by the individual in 1949 "by the unweighted mean between the high and low 1949 market price." For untraded stock Atkinson used book value.[32] His estimates for all Wisconsin taxpayers are presented in Table 14 (columns 1 and 2).

---

undistributed profits tax, the over-all average distribution ratio of Table 13 would have been higher and, for each income class, the extent of the deviation from this average would have been greater (but in the same direction as the table shows).

[31] Thomas R. Atkinson, *The Pattern of Financial Asset Ownership: Wisconsin Individuals, 1949*, Princeton for NBER, 1956.

[32] Atkinson, *Financial Asset Ownership*, p. 49.

Dividends in Personal and Taxable Income

TABLE 14

YIELD ON TRADED AND UNTRADED COMMON STOCK HELD BY WISCONSIN
INDIVIDUALS, ARRAYED BY INCOME CLASSES, 1949

(per cent)

	Yield on Common Stock		Weighted-Average Distribution Ratio [c] (3)
Income Class	Traded [a] (1)	Untraded [b] (2)	
$0 to $5,000	7.3	3.2	55.7
$5,000 to $6,000	6.8	3.1	51.2
$10,000 to $20,000	6.7	4.3	53.7
$20,000 to $50,000	6.5	4.9	49.3
$50,000 and over	7.3	5.1	50.4

SOURCE: Atkinson, *Financial Asset Ownership*, p. 131.
[a] Based on market value.
[b] Based on book value.
[c] For traded stock.

Atkinson has this to say about his data.[33]

It has been suggested that the liberal provisions regarding taxation of long-term capital gains will encourage high income individuals to purchase the stocks of corporations which retain most of their earnings. . . . If the tax treatment of capital gains were important, as has been suggested, in determining the behavior of investors, one would expect yields figured as the ratio of dividends to the value of stock held to decline for successively higher income groups. . . . [The data of Table 14 appear] to confirm that thesis except in the case of individuals with incomes of $50,000 or over, for whom the yield on traded stocks is higher than for any other group. One would expect persons in the top income group to be benefited most by the provisions of the capital gains tax; accordingly, the presence of extremely high yields on the marketed stocks held by that group casts doubt upon the validity of the thesis as a sole explanation of investor behavior.

I think his skepticism is justified, but his data do not conclusively establish the point. For it is not the yield, i.e., D/M (where D = dividends and M = market value) but D/Y (where Y = corporate earnings)

[33] Atkinson, *Financial Asset Ownership*, p. 130.

53

that is the relevant figure here. It is true that $(D/M)(M/Y) = D/Y$, but this means we would need to know something about the behavior of M/Y, the price-earnings ratio, by income class of stockholders to be certain that the product of $(D/M)(M/Y)$, i.e., D/Y, moved with income class the same way as D/M itself.

Column 3 of Table 14 gives weighted-average distribution ratios, D/Y, for the traded stockholdings in each of his income classes. These were computed by applying to Atkinson's industrial breakdown for traded stockholdings, the dividend distribution ratios appropriate to each industry sub-group.[34] Data from column 3 appear to show that there is some tendency for high income and high corporate saving rates to be associated, but the relation is uneven indeed, and reverses at just the point where one would expect it to be most pronounced, i.e., at the highest income class tabulated. Thus the conclusion is equivocal. But we hasten to note that this, just like our earlier test, is inconclusive. For the variation that the weighted-average distribution ratio measures is merely the variation *between* industry groups; it fails to get at what may very well be equally or more important—the variation in dividend pay-out rate *within* each industry group. That is to say, we assumed in constructing our index that all chemical industry stockholdings, for example, were characterized by the same pay-out ratio, and the only factor making for a difference among income classes would be the differential proportions that each industry and its pay-out ratio play in each income class' portfolio. But certainly within the chemical industry there are sharp variations in pay-out rates, and high bracket stockholders could seek out those firms with low dividend rates. Our procedure has no way of adjusting for this possibility. Adding to the inconclusiveness of the results is the fact that these data cover a single year, and one that was not "typical."

But traded stocks, with which our discussion has hitherto been concerned do not exhaust Atkinson's evidence. Indeed, there are good grounds for holding that the hypothesis that the stock investments of high-bracket investors are characterized by a lower pay-out percentage

[34] The distribution ratios, D/Y, come mainly from Sidney Cottle and W. Tate Whitman, *Corporate Earning Power and Market Valuation, 1935–1955*, Durham, 1956, but some were computed by me from samples of prominent firms in a few industries. For one reason or another, usually broadness of industrial classification or the inappropriateness for the problem at hand of individual holdings of mutual investment trust shares, which distribute all their earnings, some industrial groups in the table on pp. 155–156 of Atkinson's book were left out in constructing the weighted-average distribution ratio. They accounted for only a small fraction of stock, however.

than the average percentage for stockholdings of all dividend recipients can be tested most straightforwardly by the data for untraded corporations. For these companies are more typically small and closely held, and the operations of such enterprises can be more easily geared to the owners' personal requirements than is the case for widely owned corporations. Moreover, with traded stock, a low dividend pay-out policy might lead to a fall in the value of the stock (or prevent a rise); therefore the ratio of dividends to stock value, i.e., the yield, would not be useful data for testing the hypothesis. Book valuation would not be affected in this way.

An examination of the data most relevant here (column 2, Table 14) shows that in general the higher the income class, the greater the dividend return in proportion to stockholders' equity. On the face of it, these figures appear to contradict the hypothesis under test, but such a direct conclusion is not warranted. It is not the ratio D/B (D = dividends and B = book value) which is relevant evidence in this connection, but more properly it is D/Y (Y = earnings) which is the product of D/B and B/Y. Only if B/Y is constant or rises from one stockholder income class to another can the pattern of movement of the values of D/B be taken definitely to indicate the direction of the ratio D/Y. In other words, since D/B increases reading up the stockholder income scale, if B/Y rises or remains constant then D/Y will increase with stockholder income. Without evidence on the behavior of B/Y by stockholder income classes, the argument must be inferential. For income corporations (responsible for almost all corporate net dividend payments in the years covered) W. L. Crum has demonstrated that the rate of return on net worth, Y/B, tends to fall as asset size rises.[35] This means that its inverse, B/Y, rises with asset size. And since the 1936 data suggest a loose correlation between corporate asset size and dividend recipient income class, the D/B ratios in the untraded column of the table can be taken to indicate a D/Y that moves in the same direction, rising with stockholder income class. The same result would follow if it were the case that corporations whose stock is untraded tend to fall within a narrow asset size range, with B/Y roughly constant for all relevant corporation asset size and stockholder income classes.

Thus, the analysis apparently ends with the conclusion that the

[35] William Leonard Crum, *Corporate Size and Earning Power*, Boston, 1939, pp. 27–30. Crum's findings are for each of the years 1931 through 1936. Similar computations for 1944, 1947, and 1952 confirm the occurrence of this pattern over the period of this investigation.

data do not support the hypothesis that high income stockholders, as a group, tend to invest proportionately more heavily than lower income stockholders do in corporations that save a higher than average proportion of their earnings. But this is not a conclusion to be pressed strongly. The chain of argument is not complete; some links are missing. In particular, the transition from corporation asset size to stockholder income classes is a rather rough and ready procedure. Moreover, data for one state in one year are obviously not a valid basis for generalization.[36] The data are too tangential to the problem at hand and generally too imperfect to sanction a firm conclusion that, in fact, personal income tax relief via the route of retained earnings is not sought to a greater relative extent by stockholders in the higher income classes. But they do suggest that the effect, if it exists, is not very "strong."

[36] Indicative of the need for caution in interpreting these data is the following information supplied by Atkinson in a letter dated February 25, 1951.

"Finally I did some investigating on the reason that the per cent return on closely held stocks behaves in an opposite manner than your thesis would require. I broke the tabulation down into holdings of stocks in corporations from which the holder also received wages, and stocks in corporations from which they did not. No luck there. The ratios continued to rise for each type of holding. However, the proportion of low yielding bank stock out of the total closely held stocks owned by each income group falls as income rises which may account for some of it. Similarly, the holdings of stock in personal holding companies rise percentage-wise as income increases and these stocks have an extremely large rate of return when computed on book value basis as the underlying assets, real estate and stocks for the most part, are carried on the books, for the most part, at purchase price. For instance, the Able Company is a holding company whose principal assets consist of Baker Company stock. The Baker stock must have been valued at the original cost for Able paid out almost as much in dividends as its total book value in 1949. Thus, even if the operating company retained a high percentage of earnings, the per cent return on the book value of the holding company would be very high.

"These factors may account for some of the reasons that the ratios rise. However, I think the more important reasons have to do with the character of the closely held corporations the stock of which is held by people in different income groups. Low income groups hold closely held stock of banks, retail and wholesale concerns and service concerns, all of which are small businesses which have extremely low earnings after payment of the wages of the manager who is probably also the principal stockholder. Their earnings would be much smaller both absolutely and relative to book value than some larger closely held corporations. Furthermore, undoubtedly the larger closely held corporations are owned somewhat more widely, i.e., outside of management and family circles, and there is a pressure to distribute dividends to the outsiders, perhaps due to mistrust, and also due to the inability in many cases for capital gains to be taken by the outsiders because of lack of market or a market composed only of 'insiders.' Finally, perhaps unions will accept a six per cent return on investment more easily than high salaries to management in their bargaining considerations." Able and Baker are substituted for the names of specific companies in this quotation.

CHAPTER 2

Dividend Underreporting on Tax Returns

High Fraction of Total Dividends Traced to Tax Returns

IT has already been noted that because their distribution is so highly concentrated, a significant proportion of aggregate personal dividend receipts can be traced to tax returns even in those years when the personal income tax did not reach most of the population. Thus, as summarized in Table 15, over the four decades of our study the percentage of total dividends found on taxable returns was never lower than 60, and most frequently ran over 75.[1]

Yet a closer look at Table 15 indicates that some of the variations in this coverage ratio are not of the kind one would expect and may therefore be significant. Why, with exemptions lowered, incomes rising, and the number of taxpayers increasing greatly from 1941 on, did the fraction of total dividends traceable to taxable returns decline noticeably?

Although the figures for taxable returns in Table 15 suggest this question, they are not the most germane or convenient for attacking it directly. Therefore, in what follows, the data for all returns will be used—nontaxable as well as taxable—and the data on tax returns and on aggregate dividends will be adjusted to make them comparable. To this end also, the dividends received by fiduciaries and those paid out to their beneficiaries will be handled differently and more precisely than heretofore.[2] For these reasons, items 4 and 13 of Table 16 below

[1] The data in Table 15 are from Table 1, and appear here for the reader's convenience.

[2] Before 1936, these adjustments were either unnecessary or impossible.

57

TABLE 15

AGGREGATE PERSONAL DIVIDENDS AND DIVIDENDS REPORTED ON
TAXABLE RETURNS, 1918–1957

(dollars in millions)

Year (1)	Aggregate Personal Dividends (2)	Dividends on Taxable Returns (3)	Col. 3 as a Per Cent of Col. 2 (4)
1918	$ 3,518	$2,321	66.0%
1919	2,882	2,304	79.9
1920	3,211	2,549	79.4
1921	2,959	2,050	69.3
1922	3,044	2,283	75.0
1923	3,837	2,689	70.1
1924	3,811	2,849	74.8
1925	4,421	3,105	70.2
1926	4,721	3,533	74.8
1927	5,046	3,846	76.2
1928	5,485	4,094	74.6
1929	5,813	4,317	74.3
1930	5,490	3,861	70.3
1931	4,088	2,602	63.6
1932	2,565	1,640	63.9
1933	2,056	1,286	62.5
1934	2,587	1,670	64.6
1935	2,863	1,906	66.6
1936	4,548	3,477	76.5
1937	4,685	3,790	60.9
1938	3,187	2,481	77.8
1939	3,788	3,004	79.3
1940	4,043	3,472	85.9
1941	4,458	3,962	88.9
1942	4,289	3,531	82.3
1943	4,484	3,536	78.9
1944	4,673	3,669	78.5
1945	4,691	3,723	79.4
1946	5,784	4,561	78.9
1947	6,521	5,297	81.2
1948	7,243	5,923	81.8
1949	7,473	6,317	84.5
1950	9,208	7,544	81.9
1951	9,029	7,446	82.5
1952	8,954	7,280	81.3
1953	9,225	7,208	78.1
1954	9,839	7,622	77.5
1955	11,215	8,419	75.1
1956	12,132	9,427	77.7
1957	12,588	9,869	78.4

SOURCE: Col. 2: Table 1; col. 3: *Statistics of Income.*

Dividend Underreporting on Tax Returns

TABLE 16

Derivation of Dividends Not Accounted for on Tax Returns, 1958

(million dollars)

	Source of Dividends	Amount
	1. Dividends reported by individuals on tax returns, including dividends received from fiduciaries (estates and trusts)	9,058
Plus	2. Estimated dividends in "other income," 1040A returns	3
Plus	3. Dividends retained by fiduciaries and dividends included in the charitable contributions of fiduciaries	375
Equals	4. Dividends of individuals and fiduciaries accounted for on tax returns	9,436
	5. Dividends paid by domestic corporations	14,952
Minus	6. Intercorporate dividends	2,829
Plus	7. Dividends received by individuals from abroad	179
Minus	8. Dividends paid to foreigners	413
Minus	9. Dividends received by nonprofit organizations	501
Minus	10. Dividends received by noninsured pension funds	402
Minus	11. Capital gains dividends paid out by investment trusts	327
Minus	12. Nontaxable dividends	230
Equals	13. Maximum estimate of dividends reportable by individuals and fiduciaries	10,429
	14. Dividend "gap" (line 13 minus line 4)	993
	15. Relative dividend "gap" (line 14 ÷ line 13 times 100)	9.5%

NOTE: Source and methods of estimation appear in the notes to Table 23.

differ, respectively, from the dividends on taxable returns and aggregate personal dividends in Table 15.

The difference between the aggregate amount of specific types of income generated in the productive process and the totals of such types of income traceable to tax returns has been a subject of interested speculation over the years, particularly since the "democratization" of the income tax. The reasons for this interest are obvious: the possible poor record-keeping, faulty memory, and dishonesty of taxpayers and the potential revenue losses of the Federal Government on these counts. Work on this problem has, of course, gone beyond speculation: estimates of the gap have been made.[3] And additional estimates for

[3] Pioneering work has been done by Selma Goldsmith (cf. her "Appraisal of Basic Data for Constructing Income Size Distribution," pt. VI, *Studies in Income and Wealth*, 13, New York, National Bureau of Economic Research, 1951, and "Relation of Census Income Distribution Statistics to Other Income Data," in *An Appraisal*

dividends will be set forth in this section. But it is necessary to note at the outset that some measure of speculation and uncertainty will always surround such estimates. The author has essayed this task twice before, and a good deal of the framework and language of this section is taken from these earlier efforts, particularly the more recent of them.[4] But the estimates that follow, and the conclusions based on them, differ from those in the two earlier efforts, in part because one learns by doing, and in part because one learns from others. Other investigators have noted and corrected errors and oversights in my earlier procedures.[5]

The fact that the estimates change each time they are undertaken and are considerably lower than in my two previous attempts suggests an imprecision which it would be foolish to deny. Undoubtedly there is still an intractable hard core of error. But in my judgment the error is smaller than before, the present estimates are better than those made earlier, and, with appropriate qualifications, conclusions can be drawn from them. Moreover, as will be elaborated below, we are now in a position to judge, under restricted assumptions, whether a "real" change occurred in dividend-reporting propensities from year to year.

This chapter deals with a specific topic in a particular way. These limitations should be stressed. It is a particular concept of under-reporting which we seek to estimate, a concept which is several degrees removed from both dishonesty and revenue loss. Part of the job, then, is to make very clear what our measures mean or do not mean, and

---

of the 1950 Census Income Data, Studies in Income and Wealth, 23, Princeton for NBER, 1958). More recently the Treasury has released estimates of the dividend "gap" for 1955–1959. (See *President's Tax Message Along With Principle Statement, Detailed Explanation, and Supporting Exhibits and Documents*, Committee on Ways and Means, U.S. House of Representatives, May 3, 1961, p. 143.)

Unpublished estimates generously made available to the author have been undertaken for 1952, 1956, 1958, and 1959 by Stan West, Associate Director of the Department of Research and Statistics of the New York Stock Exchange.

[4] See Daniel M. Holland, "Dividend Underreporting on Tax Returns," *Journal of Finance*, May 1958, pp. 238–260, and *idem*, "Unreporting of Dividends and Interest on Tax Returns," in *Tax Revision Compendium*, Committee on Ways and Means, House of Representatives, 1959, Vol. 2, pp. 1397–1438. The estimates of this latter paper were partially revised in testimony given before that Committee on December 8, 1959; see *Panel Discussion before the Committee on Ways and Means*, House of Representatives, Eighty-Sixth Congress, First Session, p. 768.

[5] To the United States Treasury Department's Office of Tax Analysis staff, and to Stan West, and Milton Leontiades, both in the Department of Research and Statistics of the New York Stock Exchange, I am indebted for these corrections and an explanation of how they went about them. Neither they nor any one else but me is responsible for the errors of fact or interpretation that may still remain.

to provide some idea of the range of error that attaches to them. For it is only in the light of information of this kind that the findings can be interpreted. That is why the procedures and methods of estimating are spelled out in more detailed fashion than might seem necessary; and that is why, also, several estimates have been undertaken where there seemed to be legitimate grounds for alternative approaches.

The general question is the divergence between the total dividends paid out by corporations and the amount of this type of income reported on personal tax returns. This divergence is called the dividend gap which, as we measure it, is made up partly of dividends that were not and did not have to be reported under the revenue laws and partly of dividends that were not reported but legally should have been. As will be argued in greater detail below, while this latter category cannot be precisely broken out, inferences as to its size and growth or decline over time can still be made.

Specifically, this chapter covers three topics: (1) the size of the dividend gap in 1958 and the revenue loss associated with it; (2) changes in the gap over the last twenty-three years; and (3) evidence on the income class distribution of underreporting. It concludes with a note that explains our estimating procedures.

In discussing these topics, we depart from the measure of aggregate dividend receipts used in Table 15 and in Chapter 1—i.e., the dividend component of personal income as estimated by the National Income Division (NID) of the Office of Business Economics of the Department of Commerce—and substitute in its stead data directly from *Statistics of Income*. Although not important for the broad purposes of Chapter 1, this distinction is useful for the detailed scrutiny of a residual, which is our main concern in this chapter for a number of reasons. To the best of my understanding, in making their foreign dividend flows estimate the NID at several points used assumptions which involved an overstatement of personal dividend receipts from abroad. This means that in the aggregate individuals (and fiduciaries) are credited with "too much" in the way of pretax dividends. Although this is probably not a serious matter for the national income accounts, for our measure it would tend to overstate the dividend "gap." And since the gap is computed as a residual, this overstatement could be more serious. Moreover, for 1958, a *Statistics of Income* figure is to be preferred because we can expect the NID 1958 estimate to be revised once more, and it is better to use a consistent procedure for all years.

Dividend Gap in 1958

By way of introduction to our data, we first examine dividend under-reporting for one year, choosing the most recent year for which the requisite data have been published in detail, 1958. The approach is simple. By adding up various dividend amounts tabulated in *Statistics of Income* (Volume 1) or estimated therefrom, we obtain an estimate of the amount reported by individuals and fiduciaries on tax returns, called *R* here. Similarly, by adding to (or in most cases in subtracting from) the dividends paid out by corporations—again as published in *Statistics of Income* (Volume 2)—a number of categories of dividend flows that go to others than individuals and fiduciaries or that individuals and fiduciaries would not have to report, we arrive at a maximum amount that individuals and fiduciaries could be expected to report on tax returns, called *M* here. The difference between *M* and *R* is the gap, herein designated as *G*.

Table 16 shows the steps in our derivation of the gap.[6] The first step is to start with dividends received and reported as such by individuals on tax returns (including dividends received by individuals from estates and trusts). The next step is to add the small amount of dividends tabulated under "other income" on form 1040A returns, add also the dividends retained by estates and trusts (fiduciaries) to reach a figure of $9.4 billion of dividends of individuals and fiduciaries accounted for on tax returns (line 4). The next nine lines of Table 16 show the derivation of *M*. Here we start with dividends paid out in cash and assets other than own stock by domestic corporations, a total obtained from corporation income tax returns.[7] But some of this dividend flow took place between corporations and never reached individuals, and this (line 6) must be subtracted. Moreover, individuals

---

[6] For this purpose we use variant 2 (explained below) which in 1958 differed only slightly from variant 1.

[7] Note then that our derivation of *G* is not circular. *M* and *R* are in effect independent estimates from different statistical sources. The main item in both *M* and *R* is a tax return total, but in the one case (line 1) it is a total obtained from the personal income tax returns; in the others, the aggregate figure (line 5) comes from corporation income tax returns. Besides assuring that the measure of the gap is not circular, the fact that *M* and *R* are independently estimated, and more particularly the fact that their sampling variabilities are independent, permits us to set a confidence interval on the gap (once the sampling variabilities are known). And this, in turn, makes it possible to test for statistically significant changes in the gap from year to year (discussed later in this chapter).

received dividends from foreign corporations, which should show up on tax returns (line 7). But, on the other hand, the dividends paid by domestic corporations to foreigners would not be included in the data tabulated from personal income tax returns (line 8). Two sets of institutions that hold sizable amounts of stock but are not subject to personal income taxation—nonprofit organizations (universities, foundations, museums, hospitals, and the like) and noninsured pension funds—account for the subtractions of lines 9 and 10. The total on line 5 includes capital gains dividends paid out by investment companies. We know that they are to be reported as capital gains, and we assume they all went to individuals and fiduciaries. Therefore they are subtracted (line 11). Nontaxable dividends are, of course, not reported, and so must be subtracted (line 12).[8]

All these adjustments result in an estimate of $10.4 billion for the maximum amount of dividends that could possibly have been reported on individual tax returns (line 15). The difference between this total and the $9.4 billion on line 4 (dividends of individuals and fiduciaries accounted for on tax returns) we call the dividend "gap" (line 14).[9]

A detailed description of our procedures and the data for each year from 1936 through 1958, arranged as in Table 16, appears in the note at the end of this chapter.

In the main, our interest lies not in the amount of the gap for a single year, but in variations in the gap over time, since this may tell us something about possible changes in dividend-reporting propensities. But before turning to this, the meaning of the gap for 1958 (estimated at around $1 billion in Table 16) can be analyzed in detail, which will help prevent confusion that might otherwise arise. Also, of course, it is interesting to speculate on what might be the revenue implications of a gap of this size.

[8] Three types of dividends fall into this category—liquidating dividends; dividends of public utilities and, to a lesser degree, of real estate companies (primarily because of accelerated amortization and depreciation); and, since 1958, dividends of small business corporations which elected to be taxed as partnerships ("tax option" corporations). The first two categories are considered to be return of capital, not reportable as dividends. The third is included in the total on line 5, but would be reported along with the rest of each owner's aliquot share of the corporation's earnings and not as dividends.

[9] More appropriately, it should be called *a* dividend "gap," for as our table has already made clear and the discussion in the next few paragraphs to follow will amplify, there are numerous gap measures that could be devised. However, we shall call it *the* gap, meaning thereby not the only gap but the one we have chosen to use.

The first qualification, which although obvious is frequently overlooked, is that we should not present a single value for the gap but rather a range within which the true gap might fall were it estimated many times from different estimates of its component values. And for this range we could merely state the expectation that the "true" gap would be covered by the interval we set out, in nineteen cases out of twenty, or ninety-nine out of a hundred, etc. For the gap is a random variable and can take on a set of values different from the "true" value because of sampling variability. More precisely, G is a random variable because both M and R are random variables, and the sum (or difference) of random variables is itself a random variable. As noted in going through Table 16, M and R each are the net resultant of subtracting and adding estimated values. Sampling variabilities can be placed around most of these estimated values with some precision. This is because the sampling design of *Statistics of Income* is known.[10] Known sampling variabilities exist for the main components of M and R. For R we have estimates of the sampling variabilities of dividends reported by individuals and dividends reported by fiduciaries. We also have an estimate of the sampling variability of dividends paid by domestic corporations and intercorporate dividends, which is the main component of M. We can go further and assign sampling errors to the remaining components of M and R, and since these are almost pure guesses we make them "large." As a matter of fact, the relevant magnitudes are such that, even though $\sigma_G^2 = \sigma_M^2 + \sigma_R^2$,[11] it turns out that σ_R^2 dominates the results. Therefore, σ_G is very close

[10] This does not mean that the desired or necessary sampling variability is easily obtainable. The author is grateful to Ernest Engquist of the Internal Revenue Service who gave general counsel and advice on this matter as well as estimates of sampling variabilities of the main components of M and R.

[11] σ^2 = variance; σ = standard deviation. We have this expression for the variance of the gap because the variance of a sum (or difference) of independently estimated random variables is the sum of the variances. More specifically, our "model" in principle is this:

1. $M = M' + \epsilon$, where M is the observed value, M' is the true value, and ϵ is a sampling error with mean 0 and σ^2 given by our sampling variability.

Similarly, we have

2. $R = R' + \nu$ and with $G = M - R$

3. $\sigma_G^2 = \sigma_M^2 + \sigma_R^2 = \sigma_{M'}^2 + \sigma_\epsilon^2 + \sigma_{R'}^2 + \sigma_\nu^2$

However we know that M' and R' are the true values. Thus each has a $\sigma^2 = 0$. Therefore we can rewrite (3) simply as:

3. $\sigma_G^2 = \sigma_\epsilon^2 + \sigma_\nu^2$ and

4. $\sigma_G = \sqrt{\sigma_\epsilon^2 + \sigma_\nu^2}$

Actually, in addition to sampling errors the data reflect biases, i.e., nonrandom errors of measurement. A little more is said about this later.

to σ_R. For 1958 we estimate σ_G to have been about ±$41 million. Thus the .99 confidence interval (which is set by a range of about ±2½σ_G around the measured gap) for the gap would be $900 million to $1.1 billion. The odds are 99 to 1 that this confidence interval covers the "true" gap, if no bias is present or if biases cancel out.

Now for the second main qualification. The gap, as we define it, is *not* a direct measure of dishonesty or evasion in the reporting of dividends, nor is it the base to which to apply a marginal rate to estimate the revenue loss due to the failure of taxpayers to report all of their dividends. For, in addition to those dividends that should have been reported but were not, the gap includes the dividend receipts of those persons and estates and trusts who, because their adjusted gross income was below the filing requirement of $600, did not have to report for tax purposes.[12] It is not possible to determine with any precision the amount of this latter category of dividends, but a reasonable estimate would be about $150 million.[13]

We conclude, then, that in 1958 between $750 and $950 million of dividends (the gap of $1.0 billion plus or minus $0.1 billion minus the estimate of nontaxable dividends of $150 million) that should have been reported on tax returns were not.

[12] To go from the gap adjusted on this score to the tax base loss involves an additional subtraction—the dividends not reported by persons who had to report but would have been nontaxable anyway.

[13] This estimate was arrived at as follows: Dividends received by low-income individuals not required to file returns were estimated at $107 million by the U.S. Treasury for 1958 (see source cited in earlier footnote). In addition, some estates and trusts did not have to file tax returns because their income fell below the exemption levels. However, we are not interested in their dividend receipts per se, but only those that went to individuals who did not have to file. For otherwise the dividend receipts of such fiduciaries would show up on the tax returns filed by the individual beneficiaries thereof.

In connection with their work for the National Bureau's Postwar Capital Markets study, Eli Shapiro and Raymond Goldsmith have estimated the assets of fiduciaries not required to file, i.e., with a gross annual income of less than $600, as $6.3 billion in 1952. They consider this figure to be an overstatement rather than an underestimate. Assuming that stock comprised the same fraction of their assets as it did for the fiduciaries that did file (53.64 per cent), we get a figure of $3.4 billion of stockholdings for fiduciaries in this group. Using a yield of 4.76 per cent (the yield implicit in the Shapiro-Goldsmith multiplier of 21 by which dividend flows were capitalized to arrive at stockholdings), we estimate that $162 million of dividends were received by fiduciaries not required to file. Since net dividends (i.e., net corporate dividends plus dividends received from individuals abroad minus dividends paid to foreigners) in 1958 were about 30 per cent higher than in 1952, we may estimate that about $210 million of dividends were received in 1958 by fiduciaries not required to file. A generous guess is that between $40 and $50 million went to individuals not required to file.

To go from this figure to the amount of dividends directly related to revenue loss, however, requires some additional adjustments. For some of this underreporting is a venial sin, as far as tax revenue is concerned, since some taxpayers who are required to report their dividends but fail to do so would not be taxed on them anyway, because their exemptions and deductions exceed their adjusted gross income, or because of the exclusion from taxable income of the first $50 of dividends (on separate returns) or $100 of dividends (on joint returns). Without any firm basis for making these adjustments, it seems safe, i.e., more of an over- than an understatement, to put such dividends at $100 million in all.[14] This would mean an increment to the tax base of between $650 and $850 million if all unjustified nonreporting of dividends had been corrected in 1958. Using the estimates in Table 21 as a rough guide for the income class distribution of underreported dividends, and applying the marginal rates that follow from such a distribution, provides an estimated gain in income tax revenue falling in the interval (see note at end of this chapter for details). We conclude therefore that in 1958, the revenue loss from dividend underreporting was on the order of $200 to $240 million.

It may be of interest to place the dividend gap in perspective by comparing dividends with other types of income in this respect. For this purpose, variant 2 of Table 17 is most comparable with estimates for other sources of income. For 1957, we were able to trace 91.5 per cent of dividends to tax returns. This can be compared with the estimated coverage ratios for 1957 of 97 per cent for wages and salaries, 72 per cent for entrepreneurial income (a weighted average of 81 per cent for business and professional proprietors' income and 45 per cent for farm operators' income), and 42 or 63 per cent for interest.[15] Thus dividends are exceeded only by wages and salaries among the sources

[14] In the New York Stock Exchange estimates of the dividend gap prepared by Stan West and Milton Leontiades, dividends received by nonfiling, nontaxable individuals required to file are estimated at $50 million. Our estimate is large enough to cover both this and the $37 million they estimate for small, nontaxable estates and trusts.

[15] The wages and salaries and entrepreneurial income coverage estimates are from C. Harry Kahn, "Coverage of Entrepreneurial Income on Federal Tax Returns," in *Tax Revision Compendium,* Committee on Ways and Means, House of Representatives, 1959, Vol. 2, pp. 1443 and 1449. The lower interest estimate is from Holland "Unreporting of Dividends and Interest on Tax Returns," in same source, p. 1418; the higher coverage percentage for interest is an estimate of the U.S. Treasury Department and is more detailed and more accurate than mine. It can be found in *President's Tax Message,* 1961, p. 146.

of income in tax return coverage. That dividends should have a high coverage ratio is not surprising in view of their concentration in the upper portion of the income distribution. But one would not expect to find the proportion traceable to tax returns to be noticeably higher for wages and salaries than for dividends. This is undoubtedly partly explained by the fact that the tax liability on wages and salaries is withheld at the source.

As a necessary caution in interpreting what follows, we take this opportunity to point out the statistical hazards of our measure of the gap. Even after the gap has been expressed in terms of a confidence interval, it does not embody the "gospel" truth. For the statistical model is really more complicated than described above. In addition to sampling errors, the data also contain nonrandom errors, i.e., biases. All we can do is say that the biases may be large or small; they may cancel out or reinforce one another. (Whatever their size, they do not, of course, affect the variance of the gap.) It is our presumption, or perhaps hope, that they are small, since most of the numerical weight in our estimates comes from items subject to small or no bias, i.e., the items whose sampling variability we know. And we also assume that either they tend to cancel each other out or, if they reinforce each other, being small, the distortion introduced is not great. If these presumptions (or hopes) hold, the gap could be a reasonable approximation of the "truth," both as to level and variations in level for comparisons between years. In all honesty, I see no real basis for determining whether bias seriously affects the meaningfulness of changes in the size of the gap between given periods of time. (Remember, we have already taken account of random errors.) The difference between the values of the gap under variants 2 and 3 is due solely to different estimates of the dividends of nontaxable estates and trusts. In some years the difference between variants 2 and 3 was larger than the sampling errors, which suggests that sources of error other than sampling were important. Yet it is not the mere fact of bias that is damaging. For in comparisons over time a consistent bias is a virtue; absolute levels may be wrong, but meaningful conclusions can be drawn from changes in them if they are consistently wrong. Needless to say, since comparisons over time *are* undertaken, my judgment is that the bias is not strong enough and inconsistent enough to preclude comparisons over time.

Dividends Under the Income Tax

Changes in Gap over Last Twenty-Three Years

In addition to determining the present size of the dividend gap, it is also of interest to study the movement of the gap over time. In one sense this is essential since the gap is the residual of two sets of variables both subject to error and results for any one year must be viewed with scepticism. But more than that, by examining the data over a run of years, we can find out whether underreporting has become more or less significant. For if it has tended to dwindle over time, perhaps it is a problem that will correct itself; but if it has grown or remained at about the same level, perhaps more positive action than heretofore taken will be necessary to correct it. Also, an examination of the trends in underreporting may provide some insight into the factors that affect it. Has underreporting increased when the tax saving from not reporting increased (that is to say, when tax rates rose), and decreased as taxes became less severe? Although our data are not precise enough to provide an unequivocal answer to this question, they will, nevertheless, permit some inferences to be drawn.

With these considerations in mind, estimates of the dividend gap were prepared for 1936–1958. The results, summarized in Table 17, enable us to examine variations and trends in the size and relative importance of the gap. However, before turning to a discussion of these results, some general remarks are in order.

Although the gap is a residual made up both of dividends that should have been reported but were not and dividends that were not reported because they did not have to be, and although it is impossible to pinpoint these two components, nevertheless the data permit inferences about the zealousness of stockholders in reporting their dividend income. Thus, for example, if between two years the income above which filing was required was lowered and the gap (particularly in relative terms) rose, one can infer an increase in intentional underreporting (assuming, as seems reasonable, that memory lapse and poor records are stable factors not subject to sharp variations over short periods). For, other things being equal, the gap should have declined.

This same conclusion would follow if, with exemptions and filing requirements unchanged, dividends payments increased and the gap remained relatively as large or grew larger.[16] But such inferences

[16] In both this and the previous statement it is assumed that there were no startling changes from year to year in the way stock ownership and dividend receipts

Dividend Underreporting on Tax Returns

TABLE 17

Dividend Gap, 1936–1958

Year	Absolute Gap (million dollars)			Relative Gap (per cent) [a]		
	Variant 1	Variant 2	Variant 3	Variant 1	Variant 2	Variant 3
1936	519	272	—	12.0	6.3	—
1937	604	356	—	13.7	8.1	—
1938	325	150	—	10.9	5.0	—
1939	440	244	—	12.4	6.9	—
1940	130	−34	−24	3.5	−0.9	−0.6
1941	74	−107	−188	1.8	−2.6	−4.6
1942	412	141	299	10.4	3.6	7.6
1943	638	363	464	15.6	8.9	11.3
1944	670 [b]	400 [b]	575	15.6	9.3	13.4
1945	596	377 [b]	371	13.9	8.8	8.6
1946	836	498	527	15.8	9.4	10.0
1947	721	400	490	12.1	6.7	8.2
1948	628 [b]	260	434	9.5	3.9	6.6
1949	646 [b]	165 [b]	349	9.5	2.4	5.1
1950	863	489	607	10.3	5.9	7.3
1951	735 [b]	404 [b]	548	9.0	5.0	6.7
1952	782 [b]	523 [b]	—	9.7	6.5	—
1953	1,126	779	—	13.5	9.3	—
1954	971	934 [b]	—	11.3	10.9	—
1955	1,368	1,326	—	14.0	13.5	—
1956	1,202 [b]	1,154 [b]	—	11.6	11.1	—
1957	961	906	—	9.0	8.5	—
1958	1,051 [b]	993 [b]	—	10.0	9.5	—

Note: All changes in the gap for variants 1 and 2 between one year and the next are significant at the .01 level except where indicated by b. (Variant 3 was not tested for significant annual changes.) The test used is described in the note on procedures at the end of this chapter.

[a] The relative gap is the absolute gap computed as a percentage of the maximum estimate of dividends reportable by individual and fiduciaries (line 14 of Table 26).

[b] Change in gap between this and preceding year not significant at 0.1 level.

should be drawn only after due regard to the range of error that characterizes our estimates. Any pronounced changes shown up by the data are probably real, but the data will not support refined arguments based on relatively slight differences. In what follows, therefore,

are divided up within the family unit. This is a reasonable assumption, for it would have paid those rationally seeking to minimize taxes to make such arrangements before the start of our period.

we shall be concerned only with sharp and clear differences; small variations that cannot be dissociated from the imprecision of the estimates are neglected. To be more specific, in Table 17 the difference between 1943 and 1944 is not significant at the .01 level; the difference between 1941 and 1942 clearly is.

The presentation of three different estimates of the dividend gap in Table 17 is due to three things: legitimate differences in concept, the change in the way dividends were tabulated in *Statistics of Income* because of the tax relief provided this income share in the Internal Revenue Code of 1954, and my good fortune in having the advice of Dr. Joseph Pechman. Both the change in the tax law and a judgment that it was one sensible way of defining the gap explain the use of variant 1; Dr. Pechman's insight led to the development of variant 2, as an alternative to my original estimate, now called variant 3. The variants [17] differ among themselves only in the way in which the dividend component of the income of estates and trusts (fiduciaries) is accounted for. In variant 1 the dividend component of individuals' income from estates and trusts [18] and the dividends retained by fiduciaries are added to individuals' dividends reported as such. The sum of the dividend components of individuals' income from estates and trusts and the dividends retained by fiduciaries is a narrower base than that used in variants 2 and 3, as indicated by the bigger dividend gaps provided by variant 1. But for comparisons over time, it is not necessarily the level of the gap, but rather changes in the level, that is of prime importance. Moreover, variant 1 has its advantages: it is conceptually more appropriate for a comparison over time that includes the years 1954–1958, and its estimates of fiduciary dividends, while more narrowly based, are probably more accurate than those of variants 2 and 3 from 1940 through 1951.[19] Variants 2 and 3 account for the dividends of estates and trusts on the basis of what these entities per se, whether

[17] Details on the values used in their derivation appear in the note at the end of this chapter.

[18] From 1954 on, to get the benefit of the exclusion and credit, dividends received from estates and trusts were broken out and reported and tabulated as dividends. For the years 1936–1953 we had to estimate the dividend component of what was reported under the heading of income from estates and trusts.

[19] These are the years in which dividends of nontaxable estates and trusts were not tabulated and had to be estimated for variants 2 and 3. But in all years individuals reported income from estates and trusts whether the estate or trust was taxable or not, and while the dividend component of this income, as noted above, had to be estimated up through 1953 for variant 1, this estimate is probably less subject to error.

taxable or not, reported on the returns they filed. Because they account for the dividends when received by the fiduciaries rather than when some beneficiary of the trust reports having received them, variants 2 and 3 will show larger dividends associated with fiduciary income than variant 1. Variants 2 and 3 will, and variant 1 will not, include dividends paid out by fiduciaries to individuals not required to report and to tax-exempt organizations. Since they will also include dividends paid out by fiduciaries to individuals who, although required to report, fail to do so, variants 2 and 3 overstate the degree of reporting. Also, to the extent that estates and trusts not required to report for tax purposes pay out dividends to individuals who report them on their tax returns, variant 1 includes something not covered by 2 and 3. The failure of variant 1 to include dividends paid by fiduciaries to tax-exempt organizations is trivial. I estimate it for 1958, for example, at under $60 million; in earlier years it was presumably less.

The difference between variants 2 and 3 originates in the method of estimating the dividends of nontaxable fiduciaries in the years in which only the data for taxable fiduciaries were published—1936, 1937, and 1940–1951. For variant 2, dividends of nontaxable fiduciaries were estimated by using the ratios (or interpolating between them) of fiduciary dividends to total personal dividends in the years for which both taxable and nontaxable fiduciary data were tabulated—1939, 1952, 1954, and 1956. For variant 3, it was the ratio of taxable fiduciary dividends to dividends of nontaxable fiduciaries in 1939 and 1952 that was used as the basis of estimation. In developing these estimates, I had initially used variant 3, but at the suggestion of Joseph Pechman, tried the method incorporated in variant 2. While there is no way of establishing which of these two variants, 2 or 3, is more nearly correct, the variant 2 values appear more "reasonable," and I shall, therefore, refer to them and the variant 1 values in discussing changes in the dividend gap. In any event, the differences among all three annual measures concern levels of the gap and not its pattern of movement over time. When it comes to year-to-year changes (not levels), variants 1 and 2 tend to give the same picture, as can be seen from Chart 3. By way of comparison, the coverage percentages for wages and salaries are also plotted on the chart.[20]

---

[20] The percentage of wages and salaries accounted for on tax returns comes from C. Harry Kahn, "Coverage of Entrepreneurial Income on Federal Tax Returns," in *Tax Revision Compendium*, Vol. 2, p. 1443.

With this run of estimates numerous comparisons are open to us, and we start with a comparison that in one particular aspect is the least equivocal. In 1937, 1938, and 1939 and again in 1952, 1954, and

CHART 3

Percentage of Dividends and Wages and Salaries Accounted for on
Tax Returns, 1936–1958

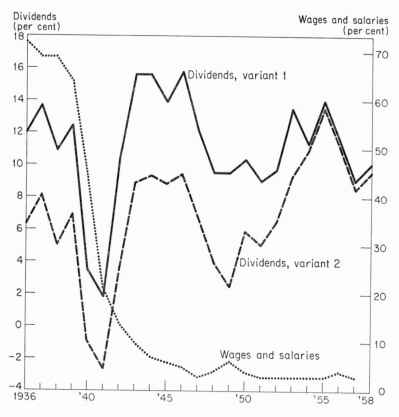

1956, the dividends of all fiduciaries, i.e., both taxable and nontax-able, were tabulated and published. Special features of the 1954 data make it inappropriate for the purpose at hand,[21] so it is excluded in what follows. For these five years, then, the variant 2 values are less

[21] Adjustments would be needed because the dividend exclusion and credit were in effect for only part of the year.

open to question since the dividends of nontaxable fiduciaries did not have to be estimated.

The early set of years (1937–1939) may be compared with the more recent ones (1952 and 1956) first in terms of the scope and coverage of the income tax, using 1939 specifically to represent the earlier years and 1952 the more recent period. In 1939, filing requirements were $2,500 or $1,000 of net income for married or single taxpayers respectively, or $5,000 of gross income regardless of net; less than 2 million dividend returns and less than 8 million returns in all (both individual and fiduciary) were filed; and about 40 per cent of total adjusted gross income was reported on tax returns. In 1952, filing requirements were $600 of adjusted gross income (whether married or single); well over 4 million dividend returns and just under 57 million returns in all were filed; and about 92 per cent of total adjusted gross income appeared on tax returns.[22] Then 1937–1939 should be compared with 1952 and 1956 in terms of the coverage of dividends on tax returns. For earlier years, the gap is between $150 and $350 million, or between 5 and 8 per cent of total dividends; for the more recent two years, the gap is about $523 million in 1952, about 6.5 per cent of total dividends, and $1.2 billion, or 10 per cent of total dividends, in 1956.

Here and in the rest of this chapter, as a general rule, we discuss the gap as a single number instead of a range because the ranges are clearly different, i.e., they do not overlap. For example, the average gap for 1937–1939 is significantly different from that in 1952 and 1956, by the test explained in the note appended to this chapter.

From what is known about the extension of the scope and coverage of the tax system between the earlier and later periods, one would expect, other things unchanged, that the gap should have become less pronounced. But a gap in absolute magnitude several times as large as the earlier one and in relative terms substantially the same if not larger strongly suggests that, in fact, something did change. It is hard to resist concluding that in these two later years dividend recipients were not reporting their dividends as fully as in earlier years.[23] A

[22] Filing requirements and number of returns are from *Statistics of Income for 1939*, Part 1, pp. 122 and 298; *Statistics of Income for 1952*, Part 1, pp. 18, 70, and 89. Adjusted gross income percentages are estimated by C. Harry Kahn.

[23] There is no intention here of claiming specifically that those who reported in 1937–1939 *and* in 1952 and 1956 reported less fully in the later period. The statement applies simply to dividend recipients in general at these two sets of dates.

Dividends Under the Income Tax

TABLE 18

EFFECTIVE RATES OF INDIVIDUAL INCOME TAX FOR A MARRIED PERSON WITH TWO DEPENDENTS AND A SINGLE PERSON, AT SELECTED LEVELS OF NET INCOME, 1940–1954

Net Income Level (dollars)	1936–1939	1940	1941	1942	1943	1944 and 1945	1946 and 1947	1948 and 1949	1950	1951	1952 and 1953	1954–1960
MARRIED, TWO DEPENDENTS												
3,000	—	—	1.9	6.4	8.9	9.2	6.3	3.3	3.5	4.1	4.4	4.0
5,000	1.0	1.5	5.4	11.8	14.6	15.1	11.8	8.6	9.0	10.6	11.5	10.4
10,000	3.4	4.4	11.2	19.1	22.1	22.5	18.6	13.6	14.2	16.2	17.7	15.9
50,000	17.2	27.5	39.9	49.7	52.8	53.7	48.2	33.2	34.3	38.5	42.2	37.8
100,000	32.0	42.9	52.2	63.5	67.8	68.6	62.3	45.6	47.2	52.6	56.0	51.9
500,000	60.7	65.9	68.9	82.7	88.0	88.6	81.3	71.7	73.9	80.7	82.2	80.5
SINGLE PERSON, NO DEPENDENTS												
3,000	2.3	2.8	7.4	15.7	19.1	19.5	16.2	13.6	14.3	16.6	18.1	16.3
5,000	2.8	3.4	9.7	18.4	22.1	22.1	18.4	16.2	16.9	19.3	21.0	18.9
10,000	5.6	6.9	14.9	23.9	27.8	27.6	23.5	21.2	22.0	24.9	27.2	24.4
50,000	18.7	29.4	41.8	51.6	56.1	55.9	50.3	46.4	48.0	53.5	56.9	52.8
100,000	33.0	44.3	53.2	64.6	69.7	69.9	63.5	58.0	60.8	67.3	69.7	66.8
500,000	61.0	66.2	69.1	82.9	88.4	88.9	81.6	77.0	79.2	86.0	87.2	85.9

SOURCE: *The Federal Revenue System: Facts and Problems*, Materials Assembled for the Subcommittee on Tax Policy, Joint Committee on the Economic Report, 1959, p. 192.

ready explanation for the decline in reporting zeal lies in tax rates, which of course were much higher in 1952 and 1956 than in 1937–1939. Changes in tax rates over this period are summarized in Table 18. At the lower income levels, effective rates rose by multiples of 5 to 10. For the higher income levels the severity of the rise may be more appropriately judged by the percentage decrease in income after tax as shown in Table 19.

Persons in doubt as to whether to report dividends or not might be more directly influenced by marginal rates. But these in general tell much the same story. For example, a married man with two dependents failing to report a dollar of dividend receipts at the $5,000 net income level would have saved 4 cents in 1939, but over 22 cents in 1952; at $10,000, the tax saving would have been 9 and 25 cents, respectively; at $50,000, it would have been 31 and 66 cents; while at $500,000 it would have been 62 and 92 cents. Even more pronounced at most income levels are the differences between 1939 and 1952 rates for separate returns.

Parenthetically it may be observed from Chart 3 that the coverage percentage for wages and salaries behaved in a fashion consistent with (1) the pronounced decline in exemptions starting with the war, (2)

TABLE 19

PERCENTAGE INCREASE IN EFFECTIVE RATES AND PERCENTAGE DECLINE IN INCOME
AFTER TAX, AT SELECTED NET INCOME LEVELS, BETWEEN 1939 AND 1952

Net Income Level (dollars)	Percentage Increase in Effective Rates	Percentage Decrease in Income After Tax
MARRIED, TWO DEPENDENTS		
3,000	a	4
5,000	1,050	11
10,000	421	15
50,000	145	30
100,000	75	35
500,000	35	55
SINGLE, NO DEPENDENTS		
3,000	687	16
5,000	650	19
10,000	386	23
50,000	204	47
100,000	111	55
500,000	43	67

a No tax in 1939.

the general increase in income from 1936 on, and (3) the institution of withholding of almost all of the wages and salary tax liability in 1943.

In my judgment, this evidence on the change in the dividend "gap" between 1937–1939 and 1952 and 1956 suggests that one response to high tax rates has been an increase in the amount of dividends stockholders fail to report.[24] Yet stockholders should not be singled out on

[24] One rational response to increased tax rates would be the splitting up of stock ownership and dividend income within the family unit to minimize tax liability. This could be done by giving stock to minors or to a spouse. The tax advantage of arrangements that change stock ownership from husband to wife or vice versa was substantially removed by the introduction of income splitting in 1948. It is not likely that to get a relatively small amount of dividends down to a nontaxable level, the advantages of income splitting would be foregone. What happened between 1947 and 1948 suggests that, prior to general income splitting where there was a parceling out of stock ownership within the family, the primary effect was to get dividends down lower in the tax schedule, but not down so low that they did not have to be reported. For while the number of taxable returns reporting dividends (see Chapter 1) fell between these years by about 300,000, the increase of $760 million between 1947 and 1948 in dividends reported as such on tax returns in relation

this score. We concentrate on them because this study happens to be concerned with dividends. But, there are good reasons to think that underreporting also increased (or reporting failed to increase as much as it should have) for some other sources of income.[25]

POSITIVE ASSOCIATION BETWEEN UNDERREPORTING AND LEVEL OF TAX RATES

It seems possible to go beyond the comparison based on two sets of widely separated years and discover a more general association between variations in tax rates and the size and relative importance of the dividend gap, but with qualifications and exceptions. If, as already noted, a decline in exemptions or filing requirements is not accompanied by a constant or falling gap as we measure it, or if a rise in exemptions or filing requirements is not accompanied by a constant or rising gap,[26] then other factors must explain variations in the gap. Variation in tax rates is one such factor. Another possible explanatory variable to be discussed later is the relative change in aggregate dividend payments.

The basis for judging that the change in tax rates has had an effect lies in a review of the change in the gap from 1936 to 1958. It makes little difference for this purpose whether we use variant 1 or 2, although the timing of effects will, on occasion, show up differently under each variant. For convenience again, a single value will be used rather than the conceptually more appropriate confidence interval. But we will only draw conclusions about changes in the gap

---

to the $650 million increase in total personal dividends is very much the same as the $750 million increase in dividends reported as such on tax returns between 1946 and 1947 in relation to the $660 million change in total personal dividend payments between these two years. Therefore we can infer that transfer of stock ownership (and, hence, dividends) between married partners may have put some dividends into lower tax brackets, but freed only a relatively small amount of dividends from the necessity of having to be reported. As regards gifts to minors, over the span of years under discussion here this had to be effected via a trust arrangement. To the extent that such trusts had enough income to be required to file, their dividend receipts are included in our estimates via dividends of fiduciaries. Recent legislation, starting in 1954, has simplified this procedure, and currently in all fifty states transfer of stock to minors is permitted without the necessity of setting up a trust. Another possibility, giving stocks to charities and foundations, if availed of, would show up in our estimates in the dividend receipts of nonprofit organizations.

[25] See, for example, the two articles by Selma Goldsmith cited earlier; Holland's "Unreporting of Dividends and Interest on Tax Returns" and C. Harry Kahn's "Coverage of Entrepreneurial Income on Tax Returns," both in *Tax Revision Compendium*, Vol. 2, pp. 1439–1459.

[26] The expectation of a constant gap is a possibility under both these conditions because of the high concentration of the dividend distribution.

that stand up under the significance test described in the note at the end of this chapter. Thus, we shall speak about a "sharp" fall in the gap between two years only when a difference of this magnitude could not be due to random variability in the data more than one time in a hundred. We stress once more that it is only the distortions of random errors of measurement that we eliminate in our significance test. The biases could still *affect* the results, although it is our judgment that they are not strong enough to *determine* the results. But there is no way to prove this.

The initially high coverage of dividends on tax returns and the tendency for the gap to decline from 1936 through 1941 follow from the relatively small number of persons who received relatively large amounts of dividends, and the sharp decline in exemptions and filing requirements in 1940 and 1941. This latter can be summarized simply by noting that in 1939 about 40 per cent of total adjusted gross income could be traced to tax returns, and by 1942 the percentage was 81.[27] As evidence of the increased scope of the income tax, we find the percentage of dividends not traceable to tax returns declining, under variant 1, by over 70 per cent between 1939 and 1940 and to slightly below zero, according to variant 2. And we find the relative gap further below zero by 1941 if we follow variant 2; under variant 1, it is cut in half between 1940 and 1941. In absolute terms, too, of course, dividends not reported on tax returns underwent a pronounced decline, under both variants. The negative gap in variant 2 for 1940 and 1941 is not as remarkable as it may seem. It should be recalled that we take as accounted for the dividends reported by fiduciaries whether distributed or retained. Since we also estimate the dividend component of the fiduciary income of individuals, some double counting that leads to an overstatement of coverage (an understatement of the gap) is involved here. In view of the general lack of precision of our estimates, the negative gap should be taken to indicate no more than that dividend receipts not traceable to tax returns came to a very small total. In a sense, the 1941 results constitute a rock bottom figure for the gap, the coverage of dividends on tax returns being so high that one would not expect a decrease in the gap despite the further lowering of filing requirements and the upward movement of incomes, both of which led to a higher fraction of the population and its income receipts coming under the personal income tax. Nor would it be sur-

[27] In 1939, less than 8 million returns were filed; in 1942 the number of returns exceeded 36 million.

prising, given the roughness of our estimates, if the gap increased slightly under these conditions.

But it did not remain substantially unchanged. On the contrary, the amount and relative degree of noncoverage on tax returns increased substantially in 1942 and again in 1943. Compared with the dividend gap under variant 2 of minus $107 million in 1941, there was a gap of $141 million in 1942, and $363 million in 1943. (In variant 1 a similar rise occurred, from $74 million in 1941 to $412 million in 1942 and $638 million in 1943.) And all these changes in the gap are statistically significant. In relative terms, variant 2 shows in sharp contrast to a gap of below zero in 1941, a nonreported percentage of over 3.5 in 1942 and close to 9 in 1943; variant 1 gives a rise from under 2 to over 15 per cent. This does not square with the following evidence: Between 1941 and 1942, the number of returns filed increased by 11 million; between 1942 and 1943 there was an additional increase of 7 million. (All the data for 1942 and 1943 are as tabulated in *Statistics of Income,* rather than adjusted for withholding. But this does not affect their relevance for our purpose.)

Some of this rise in dividends not reported can be explained by the special tax provisions for military personnel, but in any reasonable estimate this could account for only a small part of the increase.[28] Nor

[28] Those serving abroad were permitted, beginning in 1941 and ending June 15, 1948, to defer filing until six months after their return to the United States (*Statistics of Income,* pt. I, 1948, p. 428). In 1942 an exclusion of $250 if single and $300 if married was permitted noncommissioned personnel. In 1943 this was raised to an exclusion of the first $1,500 of military pay for all members of the Armed Forces. But it is doubtful whether these provisions could explain much of the decline in dividend reporting. The following gives a rough idea of the relevant order of magnitude. In late 1951 or early 1952 when there were 1.8 million persons in the Armed Forces, it has been estimated that members of the Armed Forces who were "members of family groups" constituted 0.3 per cent of the total number of individual share-owners (Lewis H. Kimmel, *Share Ownership in the United States,* Brookings Institution, Washington, 1952, p. 98). This can be raised to 0.4 per cent to take account of those not members of family groups, and it can be assumed to apply to dividend receipts from both publicly (large and widely owned) and privately owned corporations as well as to stock ownership. We assume further that this same percentage held in 1941 when the average number in the Armed Forces was roughly comparable, and, finally, that new accretions to the military during 1942 and 1943 received 50 per cent more dividends than those in the Armed Forces in 1941, and that none of these additions filed tax returns. (All of these assumptions work toward overstating the dividends legitimately not reported by members of the Armed Forces. This last one, for example, implies they were all serving abroad.) Then we can attribute about 1 point of the 6.2-point rise of variant 2 in the nonreported percentage between 1941 and 1942 to dividends of members of the

is it realistic to expect that much of this increase in the gap can be explained by a sudden sharp increase in intrafamily shuffling of stock ownership to minimize tax liability.[29] Between 1941 and 1943 the rate increases were severe and concentrated, of course, in a short span of years.[30] Apparently more taxpayers were pushed below the margin of honesty as it became more profitable not to report dividend receipts (as well as other sources of income). But this should not be viewed as a purely mechanical response. In part it may be due to the shock effect of the rapidity of the rate rise. The increase in the gap over this period may also, in part at least, simply be one expression of the lower standard of conduct that characterized other areas as well during the war years.[31]

Armed Forces and between 1.5 and 2 points of the 5.3-point rise of variant 2 between 1942 and 1943 to this same factor. Thus, correcting for the Armed Forces, the 1942 percentage for dividends not reported would read 2.6 and the 1943 one between 7 and 7.5 (both as measured by variant 2). These are still very different from 1941. And our adjustment for dividends received by those in the Armed Forces is undoubtedly excessive.

29 To the extent that this took the form of trust arrangements, the dividends are in the main included in our figures. Other ways of arranging stockholdings probably were availed of earlier, since tax rates were by no means negligible before 1942. Moreover, much of the reshuffling to minimize taxes involved not taking dividend receipts out of the tax return population, but pushing them lower down the marginal rate schedule. That such had been the case is suggested by a comparison of the data immediately before and just after the introduction of income splitting for married persons in 1948, as noted in an earlier footnote.

30 Two factors are involved in the problem under discussion here. With everything else unchanged, an extension of the coverage of the tax system would tend to close the "gap," but an increase in rates would tend to open it by increasing the tax saving associated with underreporting. Thus, apparently, the increased scope of the tax system brought in more dividends between 1940 and 1941 than the rise in rates between these two years squeezed out. But by 1941 most of the tax base expansion had taken place, yet in the years that followed rates were raised further.

31 In reviewing an earlier draft of this manuscript, W. Leonard Crum pointed out an alternative to my explanation of this increase in the gap as a response to higher tax rates:

"Another 'ready explanation' is that the increased reach of the tax system brought in many new taxpayers, many of whom did not think they needed to 'bother' with reporting dividends, most of whom had not become over the years habituated to keep records and report income from a variety of sources, and some of whom regarded the new taxes thrust upon them as an undeserved burden which justified any sort of evasion which was likely to escape discovery (and such evasion *was* likely to escape discovery in a period when the Bureau was swamped with the huge increase in number of returns without a corresponding increase in the trained personnel for the enforcement of the act)."

(With the exception of this quotation and the question raised by Willard Thorp mentioned earlier, numerous suggestions from persons who read this study in draft

Yet, after the war was over, dividend reporting did not revert to its prewar level. In 1940, for example, with the income tax covering less than three-fifths of the income received by persons, almost all dividends showed up on tax returns; while in 1946, less than 91 per cent could be so traced by variant 2 (about 84 per cent under variant 1), although 90 per cent of all income was covered by the tax structure. In 1936, when the income tax was still a select levy, the gap constituted 6.3 per cent of total dividends as measured by variant 2, or 12 per cent under variant 1, although only little more than a third of the community's income was called to account for tax purposes. This contrasts with the experience ten years later—a gap of 9.4 per cent or 15.8 per cent for variants 2 and 1, respectively.

Effective tax rates at given income levels reached a peak in 1944–1945. Over the next four years, increases in exemptions, the lowering of rate schedules, and, most significantly for married persons, the extension of income splitting to all joint returns (in 1948), all led to a decline in effective rates. This decline was substantial; for married couples, at least, at most income levels, by 1948 legislated effective rates were somewhere between their 1941 and 1942 values; for separate returns the decline was not as pronounced. (Of course, to the extent that their incomes increased, taxpayers were subject to higher effective rates than a comparison of legislated rates at a given income level would indicate.) Along with this decline in effective rates we find that the dividend gap fell in absolute amount under both variants. With the aggregate flow of dividend payments increasing over time, there was a more pronounced decline in the *relative* importance of the gap. Between 1946 and 1949, the relative gap fell by more than 60 per cent under variant 2; from 15.8 to 9.5 per cent as measured by variant 1.[32]

Thus it appears, especially if we focus on the relative size of the gap, that the response to tax rates has been symmetrical—just as underreporting increased when rates rose, so it declined when tax rates fell. But the fall in underreporting was not as vigorous as its earlier rise. The gap remained relatively much larger than in 1940 or 1941.

Is this finding borne out from 1950 on? A glance at Table 18 shows

---

form have been adopted without specifically noting the suggestion or the person who made it.)

[32] The decline over this period is all the more noteworthy because the increase in exemptions and filing requirements from $500 of adjusted gross income to $600 in 1948 should, as we measure it, have led, other things equal, to a rise in the gap.

a slight rise in tax rates between 1949 and 1950, more severe increases in 1951, 1952, and 1953, and then a fairly pronounced fall in 1954, with a continuance of rates at the 1954 level up through the present. In general, the behavior of the dividend gap over this period does not strongly confirm our conclusion that there is a relation between the dividend gap and changes in tax rates. The relation is weak, and there was a lagged response. Thus it was not until 1953 that the variant 1 gap (on a relative basis) had become noticeably higher than in 1949; the evidence of variant 2, however, shows a more immediate response to tax rate increases.

The behavior of the gap between 1953 and 1955 does not support our generalization. Here reliance is placed on variant 1 because, with the change in tax treatment of dividends introduced in 1954 (the exclusion of $50 for separate returns and $100 for joint returns, and the credit against tax of 4 per cent of dividends above the excluded amount) the variant 2 values for 1954 are adjusted estimates and quite liable to be out of line with the run of years up to that time. If we examine the variant 1 gap, as measured in relative terms, we find it falling between 1953 and 1954, which is consistent with the sharp decline in tax rates. Surprising, however, is the rise in the gap between 1954 and 1955 (found also for variant 2) in the face of tax rates that did not vary between these two years. Moreover, in the face of constant tax rates there is a substantial decline between 1955 and 1957. Quirks in our data could, of course, be a possible explanation of the behavior of the gap over these years; so, too, could be some special feature of the data since 1954 that our method has not adequately adjusted for. Or it might be that taxpayers were reporting more thoroughly. But there is another possibility suggested by these results.

As an alternative to our hypothesis that changes in the gap are related to change in tax rates, or merely as another factor affecting the size of the gap, it could be that the dividend gap is positively associated with sharp increases in the total volume of dividends paid out, either because new people, unaccustomed to reporting (or even record-keeping) were receiving them, or because, with a large increase in dividend payments, the recipients thereof would have a higher tax liability and, particularly if pushed into a higher bracket, their incentive to underreport would be stronger.

But this simple conjecture is difficult to test, for to do so we would have to be able to remove the effects on the gap exercised by (1) the extension of the income tax to more income recipients and (2) changes in tax rates. We are able, however, to cite data that show a positive association between pronounced changes in dividend payments and percentage changes in the size of the relative dividend gap. From our data we have picked out the periods of "sharpest" year-to-year change in total dividend payments (our estimates of dividends adjusted for comparability with tax returns) and the change in the relative dividend gap, measuring both sets of changes as percentages. The results are summarized in Table 20, the first row of which shows, for example, that between 1938 and 1939 aggregate dividends increased by 18 per cent, the relative dividend gap went up some 35 per cent under variant 1 and 63 per cent under variant 2.

On first glance, the evidence does not seem to support the hypothesis that sharp increases in total dividends and increases in the dividend gap are associated. Under variant 1, in four of the eight periods of dividend increase the gap fell; for variant 2 this happened in three instances. But a closer look provides limited support for the hypothesis. The four periods of largest relative increase in aggregate dividends—

TABLE 20

COMPARISON OF PERCENTAGE CHANGES IN AGGREGATE PERSONAL AND FIDUCIARY
DIVIDENDS [a] AND IN DIVIDEND GAP FOR SELECTED TWO-YEAR PERIODS

(per cent)

Year (1)	Aggregate Dividends (2)	Relative Dividend Gap Variant 1 [b] (3)	Variant 2 [b] (4)
1938–1939	18	35	63
1940–1941	10	−43	215 [c]
1945–1946	23	40	32
1946–1947	12	−14	−20
1947–1948	11	−13	−35
1949–1950	23	34	196
1954–1955	14	41	42
1955–1956	6	−7	−46

[a] Adjusted for comparability with tax return data; see line 14 of Table 23 in note at end of this chapter.

[b] A minus sign in cols. 3 and 4 indicates that a decrease in the relative dividend gap was associated with an increase in aggregate dividend payments.

[c] The positive percentage in this case came from a negative numerator and denominator.

1938–1939, 1945–1946, 1949–1950, and 1954–1955—all showed a positive increase in the relative dividend gap.

In closing this portion of our discussion of the dividend gap, it is appropriate to repeat the need for caution in interpreting the results. Only those findings that seem to stand out despite the imprecision of our data and estimates have been set forth. Yet they remain more in the nature of personal judgments than established facts. That there are errors of estimate in our measure of the dividend gap cannot be denied. The random errors we have taken into account. That there are likely to be biases affecting the size of the gap cannot be denied either. Yet, there are good grounds for holding that the distortion would not be large enough to affect our conclusions on the behavior of the gap. Of the adjustments made in arriving at the estimates of the dividend gap (with the exception of fiduciary dividends which have already been discussed and for which alternative estimates have been made), the most sizable is dividend receipts of nonprofit organizations (see line 9 of Table 26 in the note at the end of this chapter). For the other estimated entries, "big" percentage errors would have only a slight effect on the gap. And our estimate of the dividend receipts of nonprofit organizations appears to be well above two others that have been made.[33] Thus on this score our estimates make for a smaller gap than would either of the two alternative figures just cited.

Income Class Distribution of Dividend Underreporting

Granted that taxpayers fail to report a slice of their dividend receipts and that the size and relative importance of this slice has apparently responded to variations in tax rates, it is also of interest to know, for example, where the underreporting is concentrated and how much of it might be uncovered by audit. An attempt to answer such questions is possible from the evidence uncovered for 1948 by the Internal Revenue Service (then the Bureau of Internal Revenue), and very recently for 1959.

[33] For 1952 we obtained a figure of $338 million. Selma Goldsmith puts it at $200 million for that year (see Selma F. Goldsmith, "The Relation of Census Income Distribution Statistics to Other Income Data," in *An Appraisal of the 1950 Census Income Data,* Studies in Income and Wealth 23; and the Federal Reserve Board's flow of funds estimate is $100 million for 1952 (data from Federal Reserve Board worksheets).

Dividends Under the Income Tax

The Bureau undertook a careful statistical investigation of the tax returns filed in 1948—the audit control program (hereinafter referred to as the ACP)—designed to "determine the size of the individual tax enforcement problem confronting the Bureau of Internal Revenue." [34] For a scientific sample of tax returns, errors (e.g., reporting less or more than should have been reported) and the amount of tax change associated with them were determined by audit, and from this information estimates for the whole taxpaying population were made.[35] These data on errors, including those made in reporting dividends, and the resulting tax change were tabulated in four broad income classes: under $7,000, $7,000 to $25,000, $25,000 to $100,000, and $100,- 000 and over. This makes it possible to analyze the income class distribution of underreporting as determined by dividing tax changes disclosed by audit by the appropriate marginal rates. Since a number of assumptions were necessary in obtaining these estimates, it is more appropriate to present them as ranges rather than to use a single figure that might spuriously suggest more precision than was possible.[36]

Table 21 shows our estimates for dividends uncovered by the ACP. In the aggregate we estimate that between $90 and $179 million of dividends would have been uncovered in 1948 had all returns been carefully audited, which comes to between 1.8 and 3.6 per cent of the amount of dividends actually reported by individuals. About one-third of dividend underreporting was found in the lowest income class, about half in the class $7,000 to $25,000, and the rest in the income groups of $25,000 and over. More significant, however, is the relative degree of underreporting among income classes. Reading from low to high income classes, a general tendency appears for the amount and relative importance of underreporting to vary inversely with income class. Dividends discovered by the ACP [37] fell in a range of something like 3 to 6 per cent of those voluntarily reported for the two lower income classes, and between 1 and 2 per cent for the $25,000-to-$100,000

[34] Bureau of Internal Revenue, *The Audit Control Program, A Summary of Preliminary Results,* p. 3. A generally similar survey was made for 1949, but no data relevant to our problem are currently available.

[35] The auditors and auditing procedures of the ACP were probably superior to those generally in use at that time.

[36] Details of the estimating procedures appear in the note to this chapter. The estimates are based on materials made available by the Internal Revenue Service in 1951.

[37] This, of course, is our estimate from the tax change data released by the ACP.

TABLE 21

ESTIMATES OF AMOUNT OF DIVIDEND UNDERREPORTING AND FREQUENCY OF SUCH ERRORS
IN 1948 DERIVED FROM AUDIT CONTROL PROGRAM DATA

Income Class (1)	Estimated Dividend Under- reporting (million dollars) (2)	Dividends Reported (3)	Col. 2 as Per Cent of Col. 3 (4)	Estimated Number of Under- reporting Errors [a] (thou- sands) (5)	Number of Returns Reporting Dividends (thou- sands) (6)	Col. 5 as Per Cent of Col. 6 (7)	Per Cent of Total Estimated Dividend Under- reporting (8)
Under $7,000	30.9–61.7	1,110.3	2.8–5.6	297.5	2,345.6	12.7	34.5
$7,000 to $25,000 [b]	42.2–84.3	1,351.2	3.1–6.2	159.5	794.9	20.1	47.1
$25,000 to $100,000	14.0–28.0	1,508.4	0.9–1.9	31.2	166.9	18.7	15.6
$100,000 and over	2.6–5.1	1,001.0	0.3–0.5	2.5	14.5	17.2	2.9
Total	89.6–179.1	4,970.9	1.8–3.6	490.7	3,321.9	14.8	100.0

[a] Includes both returns on which dividends were reported, but too low, and those that should have reported dividends, but did not. These latter, which should have been added to column 5, are not included there, because there is no way of estimating them.
[b] The estimate for this class also covers errors on business returns with adjusted gross income of less than $7,000 where gross receipts exceeded $25,000.

class, and between 0.25 and 0.5 per cent for the top income class. These results seem reasonable. In the upper income classes record-keeping is superior as a rule, the consequences of not reporting more serious, and audit is a more likely possibility. This ties in with some of our previous remarks and also with Crum's comment quoted in an earlier footnote.

The frequency of errors in dividend reporting was more prominent than the rather slight amount of unreported dividends as estimated from the ACP data. The estimated 490,700 returns with dividend underreporting errors represented close to 15 per cent of the total number of returns reporting dividends. For all but the lowest income class, however, the percentage was above this, ranging between 17 and 20 and varying but slightly with income class (see column 7 of Table 21). Thus the practice of underreporting was less prevalent (relatively) in terms of numbers in the lowest income class than any other, but otherwise about the same for the remainder of the income range. Together with the finding noted earlier on the relative importance of the amount underreported—the ratio of underreported to reported dividends tended to decline with income class—this suggests that individually underreporting errors were considerably more important in the

85

TABLE 22

ESTIMATED ABSOLUTE AND RELATIVE SIZE OF UNDERREPORTING AND OVERREPORTING ERRORS
FOR RETURNS WITH MAJOR AND MINOR ERRORS IN DIVIDENDS, 1948

| | | Returns with Major Errors in Dividends | | | Returns with Minor Errors in Dividends | | |
| | Average Amount of Dividends Reported (dollars) | Number of Returns (thous.) | Estimated Average Error (dollars) | Errors as Per Cent of Amount Reported Col. 4 ÷ Col. 2 | Number of Returns (thous.) | Estimated Average Error (dollars) | Errors as Per Cent of Amount Reported Col. 7 ÷ Col. 2 |
Income Class (1)	(2)	(3)	(4)	(5)	(6)	(7)	(8)
			UNDERREPORTING ERRORS				
Under $7,000 ª	265	129.2	110–220	41.5–90.0	128.5	126–251	47.5–95.0
$7,000 to $25,000 ᵇ	978	65.5	237–473	24.2–48.4	94.0	312–624	31.9–63.8
$25,000 to $100,000	7,939	12.2	426–852	5.4–10.8	19.0	542–1,084	6.8–13.6
$100,000 and over	66,732	1.0	1,000–2,000	1.5–3.0	1.5	1,334–2,667	2.0–4.0
			OVERREPORTING ERRORS				
Under $7,000 ª	265	7.6	39–78	14.7–29.8	13.8	77–154	29.0–58.0
$7,000 to $25,000	978	8.1	155–310	15.8–31.6	14.8	97–193	9.9–19.8
$25,000 to $100,000	7,939	1.8	231–461	2.9–5.8	3.3	341–682	4.3–8.6
$100,000 and over	66,732	0.2	700–1,400	1.0–2.0	0.4	688–1,375	1.0–2.0

ª Form 1040 returns only. Thus number of returns with underreporting error in this class differs from the number in Table 21.

ᵇ Includes business returns with adjusted gross income of less than $7,000, where gross receipts exceeded $25,000.

lower classes.[38] One way of gauging their importance is to compare the estimated average amount uncovered by the ACP with the average amount of dividends initially reported in each of the four broad income classes. Such a comparison is made in Table 22,[39] which is limited to 1040 returns.

On the average the underreporting error in the two lower income classes was serious. In the under-$7,000 class, its value probably ranged between approximately half to almost the whole average amount of

[38] "Lower" is defined with reference to the four income classes into which the ACP data are classified, rather than the usual income distributions for which the topmost classes would be close to the upper limits of our "lower" classes.

[39] Note that the classifications of major or minor error in dividend reporting is not related to the size of the dividend error, but to its importance relative to all errors made by the taxpayer. More specifically a major dividend error as defined by the ACP "means that (a) the error in dividends . . . was responsible for the largest portion of change in adjusted gross income and (b) the change in adjusted gross income was responsible for a larger portion of the tax change than either exemption change, or personal deduction change, or mathematical error." All other dividend errors were classified as minor. The fact that minor errors were at least as large as major errors means that the minor errors occurred on returns generally more error-prone and with a larger total tax change than returns with major errors.

dividends reported for returns with minor errors in dividends, somewhat below this for returns with major errors. In the income class $7,000 to $25,000, dividend errors averaged between one-quarter and two-thirds of the average amount reported. In the two upper income classes, judged this way, dividend underreporting errors were much less important—between 1 and 10 per cent. Note also the relatively large average overreporting error (lower half of Table 22), which also declines in importance relative to reported dividends moving up the income scale. This suggests that some of the underreporting of dividends, too, can be laid to carelessness and poor record-keeping rather than purposeful evasion. But this is not the whole story: overreporting errors averaged only half as much as or less than underreporting errors, not to mention the much greater frequency of underreporting errors.[40] The number of returns with dividend error and tax decrease was only about 11 per cent of the number of returns with dividend error and tax increase.

This section should not be concluded without some reference to the dividend gap discussed earlier. For 1948 we estimated the gap at about $260 million. (This is the variant 2 value which is much lower than the variant 1 or 3 values.) If we take account of the variance of the gap, it might better be described as falling in the interval of $190 to $330 million. By reasoning similar to that used earlier for 1958, about $100 million of this might be explained as dividend receipts of those not required to file. (This allows for the $40 million reported in classes below the filing requirement.) The rest presumably was pure underreporting. Thus somewhere between $90 and $230 million were not reported. And our estimate of the aggregate amount of unreported dividends based on the ACP data was between $90 and $179 million. Thus, the two measures of unreported dividends correspond quite closely. However, were we to use the variant 1 measure of the gap (since, as noted earlier, variant 2 tends for several reasons to understate it), there would be no such close congruence between the gap as we estimate it and aggregate underreporting as estimated from the ACP data. For this latter figure would fall far short of the $500 to $600 million of nonreported dividends provided for 1948 by variant 1 (adjusted for dividends of those not required to file). Variant 3 also yields a larger figure for the gap than is obtained from the ACP data.

[40] The data in Table 21 are net—i.e., the excess of estimated underreported dividends over estimated overreported dividends.

The ACP was designed to discover only the underreported dividends of those who filed tax returns. Some of the difference between our estimates and those derived from the ACP could be due to dividend receipts of persons who intentionally did not file.

THE DATA FOR 1959

The Internal Revenue Service's interest in dividend reporting (or nonreporting) errors did not, of course, stop with 1948. But no findings of any further investigations it may have undertaken were released until March 1961, when data for 1958 and 1959 were made public. In September 1961 a supplement to the March report based on audited data was released.

For each of these two years a survey of underreporting was made. A random sample of information returns (form 1099 returns which must be filed by corporations for any dividend payment of $10 or more) was chosen, and then matched against the recipients' income tax returns to see if the dividends were reported.[41] These two surveys are more pertinent than the 1948 data because they represent a more direct estimate of the amount of underreporting and they are more current. But since they are more direct estimates and since they have $25,000 and over as their highest income class, they are not strictly comparable with the 1948 data. Moreover, while the sample was randomly chosen from the body of 1099 returns, it is not known to what degree the distribution of 1040 returns determined by the sample of 1099 returns approximates the distribution of all dividend recipients. The 1948 ACP sample was chosen to represent the whole distribution of taxpayers. Therefore we report the 1959 data in their own terms. This does not mean that the findings cannot be compared at all; rather it suggests that only broad comparisons can be made.[42]

The data in Table 23 show the 1959 survey findings on the per-

[41] This is a rough statement of the procedure, sufficient for the present purpose, but it glosses over numerous details and technicalities.

[42] The description of the sample that follows is drawn from *Taxpayer Behavior in the Reporting of Dividends and Interest in Income Tax Returns for 1958 and 1959,* a report by Mortimer M. Caplin, Commissioner of Internal Revenue, March 10, 1961. But the data themselves, supplied by the Internal Revenue Service at a later date, are based on the audited survey results, some of which appear in "Supplement to Report on Taxpayer Behavior in the Reporting of Dividends and Interest in Income Tax Returns for 1958 and 1959," Mortimer M. Caplin, Commissioner of Internal Revenue, August 30, 1961. Because only the 1959 survey results were audited, our discussion here is limited to the 1959 data.

Dividend Underreporting on Tax Returns

TABLE 23

PERCENTAGE OF TAXPAYERS IN SAMPLE WHO FULLY REPORTED INFORMATION
DOCUMENT DIVIDENDS ON THEIR INCOME TAX RETURNS, 1959

(form 1040 returns only)

Adjusted Gross Income Class	Percentage of Taxpayers
Under $5,000	70
$5,000 to $10,000	69
$10,000 to $25,000	73
$25,000 and over	80
Total	71

SOURCE: Internal Revenue Service. These percentages are based on audited data and are, therefore, not the same as those in Caplin, *Taxpayer Behavior*.

centage of the total number of dividend recipients in each adjusted gross income class who reported all the dividends accounted for in the information documents. For the whole sample, 71 per cent were full reporters in 1959. Looking for income class differences, one finds that the highest class, $25,000 and over, had a higher percentage of full reporters than the others.[43] The 1959 results, therefore, seem different on this score from the results in column 7 of Table 21, which suggests, except for the lowest income class, substantially the same percentage of underreporters in all income classes.

For 1959, data are also available on the percentage in the sample who reported fully, arrayed by size of reportable dividends. The results, given in Table 24, present a somewhat different picture from that obtained from the income class percentages. For the lowest dividend class has a smaller percentage of full reporters than any other. But since such dividends, if reported, would be excluded from adjusted gross income anyway, it is understandable that there would not be as many full reporters relatively here as in the other dividend classes. The steady rise in the fully reported percentages reaching up the in-

[43] It should be remembered that these surveys' top income class is quite low, given the high concentration of dividends. More pronounced differences in the fully reporting percentage might show up at some point higher in the income scale. The fact that the total percentage was the same as all the low income class percentages does not necessarily preclude this possibility because the dividend recipients this high up would be few in number.

TABLE 24

PERCENTAGE OF TAXPAYERS WHO FULLY REPORTED INFORMATION DOCUMENT
DIVIDENDS, BY SIZE OF REPORTABLE DIVIDENDS, 1959

(form 1040 returns only)

Size of Report- able Dividends	Percentage of Taxpayers
Under $50	55
$50 to $100	69
$100 to $500	72
$500 to $1,000	74
$1,000 and over	75
Total	71

SOURCE: Internal Revenue Service. These percentages are based on audited data and are, therefore, not the same as those in Caplin, *Taxpayer Behavior*. Cases where reportable dividends totaled less than $50 were not audited since the amount involved was exceeded by the allowable dividend exclusion.

TABLE 25

PERCENTAGE OF INFORMATION DOCUMENT DIVIDENDS REPORTED
ON INCOME TAX RETURNS, 1959

(form 1040 returns only)

Adjusted Gross Income Class	Percentage of Dividends Reported
Under $5,000	92
$5,000 to $10,000	89
$10,000 to $25,000	93
$25,000 and over	98
Total	95

SOURCE: Internal Revenue Service. These percentages are based on audited data and are, therefore, not the same as those in Caplin, *Taxpayer Behavior*.

come scale is consistent enough to be accepted. In the light of the observation in footnote 44, which applies here also, however, the slight difference between the percentages in the $500-to-$1,000 and $1,000-and-over classes suggests that possibly, over some range in the over-$1,000 class, the percentage dips below 75 and then rises above it further up the dividend size scale.

More pertinent to the problem of this chapter than the *number* (or percentage) not fully reporting is the *amount* of dividends not reported that should have been. The surveys' findings on this subject are summarized in Table 25. With the exception of the lowest income class, the results follow a reasonable and familiar pattern, with the reporting percentage rising with income class.[44]

Effect of Voluntary Compliance Campaign on Dividend Gap

One general conclusion of this chapter has been that a dividend gap of some size which cannot be explained away by imputations to non-taxable institutional and individual stockholders has existed over long periods of time. Many would hold that some remedy is in order. At least three possibilities exist for dealing with the problem: (1) increased auditing of dividend returns, (2) specific reminders that dividend receipts are taxable and notification to the stockholder that information returns on dividend payments to him are in possession of the Internal Revenue Service,[45] or (3) instituting withholding of tax liability on dividend payments. Evaluation of the administrative feasibility and costs of these possibilities lies beyond the scope of our study. But, with reference to the data in the last section and information of a similar nature, a limited evaluation of the effectiveness of methods (1) and (2) can be made, for since the latter part of 1959, the Treasury Department has consciously sought to improve dividend reporting by these two devices—increased auditing and wider publicity—and has, in addition, on several occasions evaluated the efficacy of these attempts.

In 1959, motivated by a study of the gap for 1956 generally similar to the one described here for 1958, the U.S. Treasury Department in-

[44] There are good reasons to hold that the 95 per cent reporting for the whole sample does not permit us to conclude that the dividend gap is only 5 per cent. (See the next section of this chapter.)

[45] Currently any dividend payments in excess of $10 per annum must be reported to the Internal Revenue Service on form 1099. Many corporations, however, find it simpler to report all such payments no matter how small.

stituted a program to increase voluntary reporting of dividends and interest by taxpayers. The nature of the program and what it appears to have accomplished at an early date are best described by the Department itself.[46]

> Following the completion of the 1956 survey, it was determined to take action in two separate areas to improve the reporting of the amounts received by the recipients of dividends and interest. . . .

> All payers of $10 or more in dividends and $600 or more of interest must make reports of such payments to the Revenue Service on Form 1099 or other information documents. In every Revenue District a broadened and accelerated program of matching these forms with the returns of individual taxpayers is actively in progress. A vigorous follow-up audit will be made in cases where a return has not been filed or where additional assessments of tax and penalty are indicated by the information secured from the information documents.

> The second half of the program to insure proper reporting is the cooperative information program undertaken by the Revenue Service and by the payers of dividends and interest. Many of you participated in this program. More than 75 million special notices were mailed to recipients of dividends and interest. This distribution was supplemented by a coordinated information campaign using newspapers, magazines, radio and television. Excellent cooperation was given in this area by tens of thousands of corporations, banks and individuals active in the dividend and interest field.

> Written and oral communications have gone from the national associations to their state and local members urging full cooperation. Articles have been published in association journals, financial journals, monthly newsletters, and other trade publications. Posters have been prepared and distributed. In some areas in this state some of your members joined with other financial institutions in sponsoring newspaper ads on the subject.

> We know from the many comments we have received and from the many questions answered by our District Offices during the 1960 filing period, that the voluntary information program has been most successful. It is, of course, somewhat early to appraise fully

---

[46] The following paragraphs are taken from a speech delivered by Under Secretary of the Treasury Fred C. Scribner, Jr., at the Annual Convention of the Maine Bankers' Association, June 24, 1960.

the extent of the increased reporting of dividends and interest since only a little more than two months has elapsed since the filing date for the returns covering the year 1959.

However, some measure of the program's success has been obtained from checking some 8,000 individual cases selected as the result of a screening of approximately 100,000 cases.

In each of the 8,000 cases the information returns indicated that the taxpayer in the tax year 1958 had received $300 or more of dividends and interest. The documents indicated the possibility of a failure on the part of the taxpayer to report in full. We have now received audit reports on 1,340 of the 8,000 cases selected. The number of taxpayers in this group of 1,340 who failed to report dividend income or reported only in part dropped from 777 in 1958 to 407 in 1959, or a decrease of 48 per cent in the number of taxpayers underreporting dividends received. The amount of unreported dividends income from these 777 taxpayers decreased approximately 42 per cent from 1958 to 1959.

It is our belief that a substantial part of this increase has resulted from the voluntary program of cooperation in the dividend and interest field, coupled as it is with the stepped-up enforcement program. The Treasury Department greatly appreciates the many steps taken by payers of dividends and interest, steps in many instances involving substantial expenditures, to bring to the attention of recipients of dividends and interest income their obligation to report such income fully on their tax returns. . . .

More recent information on the success of the program was reported in *The New York Times* of October 9, 1960.

On the basis of the admittedly limited sample, Dana Latham, Tax Commissioner, says the educational program has been amazingly successful.

As of last Tuesday, the Treasury had audit reports on 1,801 of the selected cases. The Commissioner said that, based on the 1,801 cases, the number of persons failing to report dividends fully in 1958 decreased by 50 per cent in 1959. The unreported dividend income decreased by 45 per cent.

Following close on the heels of this evidence came some additional information that appeared to confirm that sizable inroads had been made on the dividend gap. The Treasury reported in a press release dated December 22, 1960, that analysis of the returns for the year 1959 filed during 1960 "show significant increases over the two prior years in the number of returns reporting interest and dividends. There were also sizable increases in the amount of dividends and interest reported." While these were preliminary estimates, the Treasury held that, on the basis of past experience, they were likely to stand at substantially their estimated level. Moreover, the contention was that this improvement indicated "a considerable degree of success for the first year of the Treasury's concerted drive to improve taxpayer reporting of dividend and interest income."

There is no basis for making as refined an estimate of the gap for 1959 as for earlier years since some of the basic data are not yet available. Nonetheless we can project the 1958 data with sufficient assurance to assert that, *if* the preliminary estimate released in December 1960 for dividends reported on tax returns was correct, then the gap had indeed declined. Making some rough projections and using the preliminary figure for dividends reported by individuals on tax returns of $10.3 billion for 1959, one gets a decline in the gap (very rough of course) on the order of one-half.

Thus, given what was known at the end of 1960, it did appear that the dimensions of the dividend gap were considerably smaller in 1959 than in 1958. We should not, of course, stop with a single value estimate, since, as emphasized above, the gap is most appropriately interpreted as falling within a specified range. But, for reasons that will become clear in the next several paragraphs, this refinement is not necessary.

In essence, what has happened since is that new and more accurate estimates have become available. One such set of data has been alluded to and discussed in the preceding section of this chapter—the random sample of dividend returns (form 1099) matched with personal income tax returns (form 1040) of the dividend recipients. Clearly this latter sample is drawn from a more appropriate universe for measuring underreporting and changes therein than a sample obtained by picking taxpayers for whom "the documents indicated the possibility of a failure on the part of the taxpayer to report in full" in 1958. And this was how the sample for the survey whose results were reported by Under Secretary Scribner in his speech of June 24, 1960, quoted above was obtained. This latter basis of choice partakes of the "regression fallacy." It chooses people who have a given attribute in one year and seeks to find to what extent they have that same attribute in the succeeding year. To the degree that the attribute is random, it will not show up as pronouncedly in the second year as in the first.

As pointed out by the present Commissioner of Internal Revenue, Mortimer Caplin, the earlier survey was subject to two limitations that restricted the inferences that could be drawn from it.[47] In the Commissioner's judgment there was no improvement in reporting between 1958 and 1959. He has concluded that "there was no material change in the degree of compliance of identical taxpayers between 1958 and 1959. The relatively small number of taxpayers who improved in their reporting in 1959, after the educational campaign, was roughly balanced or perhaps even over-balanced, in the case of dividends, by the number whose reporting deteriorated." [48]

As regards the aggregate amount of dividends reported by individuals on tax returns, the earlier and tentative estimate of $10.3 billion, admittedly less accurate than the estimates prepared for *Statistics of Income*, should be replaced by the *Statistics of Income* figure of $9.7 billion which has since been released.[49] In view of this evidence, it seems fairly certain that in 1959 at least, the voluntary compliance campaign had not resulted in a substantial reduction in the absolute amount of dividends not reported.

This may be why the Federal Government has recently turned its attention to another method of improving taxpayer compliance. President Kennedy, in his tax message of April 20, 1961, asked Congress to institute withholding on dividends (and some items of interest). At the time of writing, this is where the matter stands.[50]

On the face of it, the Internal Revenue Service sample survey for

[47] . . . "First, this tabulation was, in no sense, a survey of a representative sample of taxpayers, but was limited to taxpayers where a relatively large potential tax deficiency for 1958 was anticipated. Second, the methods of selection and audit introduced certain distinct biases into the results, so that we were much more apt to include in the program taxpayers who had improved in their reporting of dividends and interest than taxpayers whose reporting had declined. In short, the program was simply a by-product of our regular audit activity designed to check up on potentially flagrant cases of nonreporting, and to bring in revenue. The results were reported for information purposes, but the study was not designed to provide a measure of the improvement among taxpayers generally in the reporting of dividends and interest." (Commissioner Caplin in his report of March 10, 1961, to Senator Byrd as quoted in *President's Tax Message*, p. 165.)

[48] *Supplement to Report*, p. 1.

[49] *Statistics of Income, 1959*, Part 1 (preliminary), p. 2.

[50] A further discussion of these points and estimates of the dividend gap from 1955 through 1959 appears in *President's Tax Message*.

1959 appears to open our usual measure of the gap to suspicion, since the survey suggests a dividend gap of 5 per cent, while our estimate was 10 per cent for 1958 and should be about the same for 1959. But there are a number of features wherein the two procedures are not comparable. Rather than spell them out, we present Commissioner Caplin's conclusions on this point.[51]

Estimates of the overall nonreporting gap have been made by the Treasury Department, as well as by others, that show the total amounts of dividends and interest omitted from tax returns. Our sample surveys give specific evidence of nonreporting by taxpayers, but cannot be expected to provide overall gap estimates, especially when they are based on a rather small sample. Even though ours was a representative sample, it was based on only 3,000 taxpayers in each survey, in 9 Internal Revenue districts, and it was not a "probability sample" susceptible of being "blown" up to represent all taxpayers.

Summary of Findings on Dividend Underreporting

We end this chapter with a brief summary of the highlights of our survey of dividend coverage on tax returns, but the numerous qualification and caveats that attach to these findings and have been discussed above must be kept in mind in interpreting the results.

1. In the most recent year for which systematic estimates could be made—1958—a sizable gap existed between the dividends paid out to individuals and fiduciaries and the dividends they reported on tax returns. While the amount of such dividends is difficult to pinpoint, they appear to have run at about $1.0 billion in that year, or about 10 per cent of the reportable amount.

2. Not all the dividends that were not reported meant a loss of revenue to the Treasury because some dividends went to those who did not have to file or whose exemptions and deductions exceeded their income and would still have even if they had reported all their dividends. Adjusting as well as possible for these factors, we estimated the revenue loss due to unreported dividends at between $200 and $240 million in 1958. This may seem a small amount relative to total personal income tax collections. But the problem is not unimportant.

[51] *Supplement to Report*, p. 6. See note, p. 109, this chapter.

For unreported income may have repercussions more serious than the revenue loss that is directly traceable to it. Underreported income constitutes one piece of a broader problem. A general feeling that some types of income and some particular groups of taxpayers are not carrying their share of the tax load might undermine the zeal with which many taxpayers police themselves. We emphasize dividend underreporting here because that is what we are studying, but other sources of income are also underreported, some of them more so than dividends.

3. A review of the gap over the twenty-three-year period, 1936–1958, did not disclose a tendency for the underreporting of dividends to correct itself over time. During these years, which witnessed a revolutionary conversion of the personal income tax from a levy on very few citizens to one reaching almost every income recipient, the gap has tended to rise in absolute terms and to be relatively about as important near the end of the period as at its beginning.

4. An examination of the year-to-year changes in the dividend gap suggests that its relative size roughly reflects taxpayer response to variations in tax rates, especially tax rate increases. Thus during World War II, the dividend gap rose sharply, whereas it declined as tax rates were reduced in the several years following the war. But for the years since 1950, the evidence does not support the conjecture that higher rates discourage reporting and lower rates encourage it.

5. Estimates from a sample audit undertaken by the Bureau of Internal Revenue of the personal income tax returns for 1948 suggest that the most serious underreporting is found among dividend recipients with incomes of less than $25,000. Although, of course, particular individuals with higher incomes may underreport significantly, on the whole total underreporting at the higher incomes is not great, and, in any event, is more likely to be discovered. A more recent sample survey by the IRS for 1959 confirms this pattern.

6. Dividends, of course, do not stand alone as regards underreporting. Estimates made for other sources of income also show a gap. While subject to wide margins of error and not strictly comparable, evidence of other sources of income underreporting rounds out the discussion of dividend underreporting. For 1957, the following reporting percentages have been found (source reference appears earlier in this chapter):

Wages and salaries	97%
Dividends	91.5%
Business and professional proprietors' income	81%
Interest	63%
Farm operators' income	45%

The sharp differences in coverage percentages creates a presumption that this ranking, although not the estimated percentages, is very likely correct.

Technical Note

This note explains in detail some of the estimating procedures and tests used in developing the data of Chapter 2. It has four sections covering the following topics: (1) derivation of the dividend gap; (2) specifying the range of the gap and testing year-to-year changes for significance; (3) estimates of the amount of dividend underreporting as disclosed by the ACP, 1948 (Table 21); and (4) estimating the revenue gain from full correction of dividend underreporting.

DERIVATION OF DIVIDEND GAP

Table 26 presents the adjustments made in each year, while the accompanying notes explain how the entries were estimated.

RANGE OF DIVIDEND GAP AND TESTING YEAR-TO-YEAR CHANGES

A Confidence Interval for the Gap

R = Dividends of individuals and fiduciaries accounted for on tax returns (line 4 of Table 26).

M = Maximum estimate of dividends reportable by individuals and fiduciaries (line 14 of Table 26).

$G = M - R$ = Dividend gap (line 15 of Table 26).

Each of the components that make up R, lines 1, 2, and 3 of Table 26, are subject to sampling variability. That is to say, each of the components of R is a random variable as is, therefore, R itself. Likewise, most of the components of M are subject to sampling variability; hence M is a random variable. And since $G = M - R$, G too is a random variable. The observed (estimated) M and R are drawn from a universe of values. If numerous estimates of the lines of Table 26 were undertaken, every time the components of M and R were estimated we would obtain a different value for each one, a different value for M and R, and consequently a different value for G. Knowing the sampling variabilities of these components, we can state an interval which will cover G (i.e., within which G will fall) to any desired likelihood. For example, for the confidence interval associated with a .99 likelihood, one could assert that 99 times out of 100 this interval will cover the "true" gap. The "true" gap, of course, is not a random variable; our observed gap is.

The "model" neglecting nonrandom errors of measurement is this:

1. $M = M' + \epsilon$, where M is the observed value, M' is the "true" value, and ϵ is a sampling error with a mean of 0 and variance σ^2 to be determined from sampling variability of the components of M.

2. $R = R' + \nu$, again R is the observed (or estimated) value, R' is the "correct" value, and ν a sampling error with a mean 0 and variance σ^2.

3. $G = M - R = M' + \epsilon - R' - \nu$.

Let $E(\ )$ indicate the expected value.

4. $E(G) = E(M) - E(R) = E(M') + E(\epsilon) - E(R') - E(\nu)$. Since M' and R' are given numbers, their expected value is M' and R' respectively, while $E(\epsilon) = E(\nu) = 0$. Therefore $E(G) = M' - R'$.

Let σ^2 be the variance.

5. $\sigma_G^2 = \sigma_M^2 + \sigma_R^2 = \sigma_M^2 + \sigma_\epsilon^2 + \sigma_R^2 + \sigma_\nu^2$. Since M' and R' are given numbers, $\sigma_{M'}^2 = \sigma_{R'}^2 = 0$. Therefore, $\sigma_G^2 = \sigma_\epsilon^2 + \sigma_\nu^2$, if, as is the case, ϵ and ν are independent.

6. $\sigma_G = \sqrt{\sigma_\epsilon^2 + \sigma_\nu^2}$ and the confidence interval within which the true gap will lie 95 times out of 100 is equal to $G \pm 1.96\sigma_G$; while the confidence interval within which the true gap will lie 99 times out of 100 is equal to $G \pm 2.57\sigma_G$.

Estimates of the sampling variabilities of the components that are predominant in determining σ_G were made available by Ernest C. Engquist, Jr. of the Internal Revenue Service. Notice how σ_R^2, which is item 1 in the table dominates the results.

Testing for Significance of Year-to-Year Changes in the Gap

Define a new random variable, $G_2 - G_1$, which is the change in the gap between any two years, usually between one year and the next.

7. $\sigma_{G_2-G_1}^2 = \sigma_{G_2}^2 + \sigma_{G_1}^2$, and $\sigma_{G_2-G_1} = \sqrt{\sigma_{G_2}^2 + \sigma_{G_1}^2}$.

With this standard deviation, we can test for a significant change in the gap between year 1 and year 2. For we can set up the null hypo-

Dividends Under the Income Tax

		1936	1937	1938
	1. Dividends reported by individuals on personal income tax returns	3,174	3,188	2,212
Plus	2. Dividends included in "other income" on 1040A or W-2 returns	—	—	—
Plus	3. Dividends of fiduciaries (estates and trusts)			
	Variant 1	617	617	454
	Variant 2	860	860	626
	Variant 3	—	—	—
Equals	4. Dividends of individuals and fiduciaries accounted for on tax returns			
	Variant 1	3,791	3,805	2,666
	Variant 2	4,034	4,048	2,838
	Variant 3	—	—	—
	5. Dividends paid by domestic corporations	7,379	7,514	5,013
Minus	6. Intercorporate dividends	2,677	2,682	1,791
Plus	7. Dividends received by individuals from abroad	44	56	80
Minus	8. Dividends paid to foreigners	220	264	160
Minus	9. Dividends received by nonprofit organizations	97	103	71
Minus	10. Dividends received by noninsured pension funds	12	13	9
Minus	11. Capital gains dividends (paid out by investment trusts)	20	10	10
Minus	12. Dividends included in partnership income	24	25	17
Minus	13. Nontaxable dividends			
	Variant 1	63	64	44
	Variant 2	67	69	47
	Variant 3	—	—	—
Equals	14. Maximum estimate of dividends reportable by individuals and fiduciaries (estates and trusts)			
	Variant 1	4,310	4,409	2,991
	Variant 2	4,306	4,404	2,988
	Variant 3	—	—	—
	15. Dividend gap (line 14 minus line 4)			
	Variant 1	519	604	325
	Variant 2	272	356	150
	Variant 3	—	—	—
	16. Relative dividend gap (line 15 ÷ line 14) times 100			
	Variant 1	12.0	13.7	10.9
	Variant 2	6.3	8.1	5.0
	Variant 3	—	—	—

Dividend Underreporting on Tax Returns

26

REPORTED ON TAX RETURNS, 1936–1958

dollars)

1939	1940	1941	1942	1943	1944	1945	1946	1947
2,544	2,999	3,299	2,833	2,780	2,986	3,010	3,674	4,295
—	—	109	151	97	15	16	18	15
555	629	643	558	579	623	674	766	912
747	791	821	824	848	888	889	1,100	1,229
—	781	901	669	750	716	895	1,071	1,140
3,099	3,628	4,051	3,542	3,456	3,624	3,700	4,458	5,222
3,291	3,790	4,229	3,808	3,725	3,889	3,915	4,792	5,539
—	3,780	4,309	3,653	3,627	3,717	3,921	4,763	5,450
5,747	6,089	6,701	5,607	5,728	6,057	6,081	7,497	8,365
1,906	2,021	2,235	1,344	1,334	1,429	1,418	1,713	1,882
68	70	58	51	57	50	47	64	72
193	187	185	160	154	161	163	200	211
87	92	101	97	100	106	106	159	196
11	11	13	12	13	13	14	24	33
8	8	9	6	8	20	46	73	58
20	22	24	24	25	27	27	41	55
51	60	67	61	57	57	58	57	59
55	62	70	66	63	62	62	61	63
—	62	71	63	60	59	62	61	62
3,539	3,758	4,125	3,954	4,094	4,294	4,296	5,294	5,943
3,535	3,756	4,122	3,949	4,088	4,289	4,292	5,290	5,939
—	3,756	4,121	3,952	4,091	4,292	4,292	5,290	5,940
440	130	74	412	638	670	596	836	721
244	−34	−107	141	363	400	377	498	400
—	−24	−188	299	464	575	371	527	490
12.4	3.5	1.8	10.4	15.6	15.6	13.9	15.8	12.1
6.9	−0.9	−2.6	3.6	8.9	9.3	8.8	9.4	6.7
—	−0.6	−4.6	7.6	11.3	13.4	8.6	10.1	8.2

(continued)

101

TABLE 26

		1948	1949	1950
	1. Dividends reported by individuals on personal income tax returns	4,971	5,246	6,158
Plus	2. Dividends included in "other income" on 1040A or W-2 returns	12	10	9
Plus	3. Dividends of fiduciaries (estates and trusts)			
	Variant 1	993	915	1,330
	Variant 2	1,357	1,391	1,701
	Variant 3	1,185	1,209	1,583
Equals	4. Dividends of individuals and fiduciaries accounted for on tax returns			
	Variant 1	5,976	6,171	7,497
	Variant 2	6,340	6,647	7,868
	Variant 3	6,168	6,465	7,750
	5. Dividends paid by domestic corporations	9,386	9,569	11,553
Minus	6. Intercorporate dividends	2,194	2,162	2,460
Plus	7. Dividends received by individuals from abroad	77	85	91
Minus	8. Dividends paid to foreigners	233	248	285
Minus	9. Dividends received by nonprofit organizations	234	232	302
Minus	10. Dividends received by noninsured pension funds	44	47	65
Minus	11. Capital gains dividends (paid out by investment trusts)	35	30	45
Minus	12. Dividends included in partnership income	58	57	67
Minus	13. Nontaxable dividends			
	Variant 1	61	61	60
	Variant 2	65	66	63
	Variant 3	63	64	63
Equals	14. Maximum estimate of dividends reportable by individuals and fiduciaries (estates and trusts)			
	Variant 1	6,604	6,817	8,360
	Variant 2	6,600	6,812	8,357
	Variant 3	6,602	6,814	8,357
	15. Dividend gap (line 14 minus line 4)			
	Variant 1	628	646	863
	Variant 2	260	165	489
	Variant 3	434	349	607
	16. Relative dividend gap (line 15 ÷ line 14) times 100			
	Variant 1	9.5	9.5	10.3
	Variant 2	3.9	2.4	5.9
	Variant 3	6.6	5.1	7.3

(concluded)

1951	1952	1953	1954	1955	1956	1957	1958
6,056	5,860	5,828	7,269	8,100	8,892	9,432	9,058
8	6	5	6	3	3	3	3
1,331	1,393	1,377	331	320	309	313	317
1,660	1,650	1,721	368	362	356	366	375
1,516	—	—	—	—	—	—	—
7,395	7,259	7,210	7,606	8,423	9,204	9,748	9,378
7,724	7,516	7,554	7,643	8,465	9,251	9,801	9,436
7,580	—	—	—	—	—	—	—
11,299	11,263	11,601	11,913	13,592	14,498	14,914	14,952
2,377	2,350	2,389	2,332	2,572	2,688	2,681	2,829
92	85	108	115	140	165	176	179
286	299	320	305	357	378	401	413
320	338	330	390	455	488	505	501
69	99	131	192	210	262	338	402
87	102	83	162	276	365	346	327
62	56	55	—	—	—	—	—
60	63	65	70	71	76	110	230
62	65	68	70	71	77	112	230
62	—	—	—	—	—	—	—
8,130	8,041	8,336	8,577	9,791	10,406	10,709	10,429
8,128	8,039	8,333	8,577	9,791	10,405	10,707	10,429
8,128	—	—	—	—	—	—	—
735	782	1,126	971	1,368	1,202	961	1,051
404	523	779	934	1,326	1,154	906	993
548	—	—	—	—	—	—	—
9.0	9.7	13.5	11.3	14.0	11.6	9.0	10.0
5.0	6.5	9.3	10.9	13.5	11.1	8.5	9.5
6.7	—	—	—	—	—	—	—

Dividends Under the Income Tax

Line 1: As tabulated annually in *Statistics of Income*, Part 1. For 1944 and 1945, when a combined dividend and interest figure was reported, dividends were estimated on the basis of the 1946 ratio of dividends to dividends and interest combined.

Line 2: Estimated for 1944–1956 by taking dividends and interest to be half of wages and salaries not withheld on and dividends and interest of under $100 on form W-2 or 1040A returns as given in a footnote to table 2 of *Statistics of Income*, Part 1 (cf. Selma Goldsmith, "Appraisal of Basic Data Available for Constructing Income Size Distribution," in *Studies in Income and Wealth*, 13, pp. 360–361), and then applying to this figure the fraction that dividends constituted of dividends plus interest for all returns under $5,000 as tabulated in *Statistics of Income*. For 1957 and 1958, arbitrarily put at $3 million.

Estimated for 1941–1943 by applying the ratio of dividends to total property income (of specified types) on 1040 returns to the property income component of 1040A returns.

Line 3: Variant 1, 1936–1953: Sum of (a) dividend component of individual income from estates and trusts and (b) dividends retained by fiduciaries. Value for (a) is estimated annually by applying ratio of dividends to total income of taxable fiduciaries to income from estates and trusts reported by individuals. Value for (b) is estimated by applying the same ratio used for (a) to the retained income of fiduciaries. For 1944 and 1945, dividends are estimated from combined dividend and interest totals on basis of 1946 percentages.

1954–1958: Starting in 1954, dividend component of individual income from estates and trusts is reported under dividends and shows up in line 1 total. Value for (b) is estimated from tabulations for fiduciaries in 1954 and 1956 as sum of excluded dividends, fiduciaries share of dividend tax credit blown up to its dividend equivalent, and an adjustment to take account of dividends not eligible for exclusion and credit. For 1954, two additional adjustments are needed: (1) Because only 92 per cent of returns were filed on new basis of IRC of 1954 (this being a transitional year), the tabulated dividend total was assumed to be only 92 per cent of correct figure and was adjusted accordingly; (2) credit was applied to dividends received after July 1, 1954, and tabulated credit was raised on this basis to a full year's equivalent. 1955 and 1957 values were obtained by interpolating between 1954 and 1956 and 1956 and 1958, respectively.

Variant 2: Dividends of taxable and nontaxable fiduciaries as tabulated in *Statistics of Income*, 1937, 1938, 1939, and 1952. Assumed same in 1936 as 1937. Estimated for 1940–1951 on the basis of interpolation between 1939 and 1952 percentage that dividends of fiduciaries represented of NID personal dividend receipts. 1953 estimated by interpolation between similar percentages for 1952 and 1954. From 1954 on, same as variant 1 above with addition of dividend component of fiduciary charitable contributions estimated by applying fraction dividends comprised of total fiduciary income to charitable contributions of fiduciaries. For 1944 and 1955, dividend figure was broken out of combined dividend and interest total by applying 1946 ratio.

Variant 3: Applies only for 1940–1951. Derived by applying values obtained by interpolating between the 1939 and 1952 ratios of dividends of taxable fiduciaries to total fiduciary dividends to the dividends of taxable fiduciaries as tabulated in *Statistics of Income*. 1944 and 1945 dividends were separated out from combined dividend and interest tabulation by using ratio for 1946.

Line 5: From *Statistics of Income*, Part 2, for each year.

Line 6: Same as line 5.

Line 7: Data that served as basic estimates were supplied by Samuel Pizer, U.S. Department of Commerce. For 1946–1958, equals dividend receipts on other investments plus 5 per cent of dividend receipts on direct investments (total investments

Dividend Underreporting on Tax Returns

abroad equal direct plus other) blown up by division by .85 to get amount before withholding. In getting the estimate for 1945–1936, the 1946 estimate was computed as a percentage of total dividend receipts on foreign investment and again blown up by dividing by .85.

Line 8: As in line 7, basic data were supplied by Samuel Pizer. To his estimates of dividend payments to foreigners (which were net of tax), we added estimated tax withheld as supplied again by National Income Division, Department of Commerce, up through 1954, applying the 1954 percentage of tax withheld to get the remaining years.

9. Estimated by applying to net dividends (line 5 minus line 6) the ratio of non-profit organization stockholdings to total stockholdings (net of corporate holdings). For 1936–1944 total stockholdings were estimated by Raymond Goldsmith (Table F-4 of Appendix F of *Financial Intermediaries in the American Economy since 1900*, Princeton for NBER, 1958) for benchmark dates 1933, 1939, and 1945, and interpolated for the other years in the period; for 1945–1955, estimates were provided by Morris Mendelson from the National Bureau Postwar Capital Markets study. For 1936–1949, nonprofit organization stockholdings were estimated by Raymond Goldsmith (*A Study of Saving in the United States*, Vol. III, Princeton, 1956, pp. 450, 452) for benchmark dates 1933, 1939, 1945, and 1949 and interpolated for the other years in the period; for 1950 and 1951, similarly estimated on basis of Goldsmith's 1949 figure and estimate for 1952 in Morris Mendelson, *The Flow-of-Funds Through the Financial Markets, 1953-1955*, Working Memorandum, New York, NBER, 1959; for 1953–1955, from this same source. For 1956–1958, the 1956 percentage of total stockholdings was used.

Line 10: For 1936–1951, estimated in essentially the same manner as line 9. Stock-holdings of pension funds for 1939, 1945, and 1949, from Goldsmith's *Financial Intermediaries* Table A-10, and for 1952 from Mendelson's *Flow-of-Funds*; for the remaining years, estimated by interpolation using the values for these four years and 1933. For 1952–1958, estimated as follows from data in SEC, "Corporate Pension Funds," annual releases: yield figures were applied to the pension fund bondholdings and the esti-mated interest receipts were subtracted from the total of interest and dividends re-ceived by pension funds. The dividend figure thus obtained was raised by 5 per cent to take account of omissions in the coverage of the SEC survey.

Line 11: Estimates for 1953–1958 were derived by taking the data of the National Association of Investment Companies (as published in *Investment Companies, A Statis-tical Summary, 1940-1959*) as 96 per cent of the total according to New York Stock Exchange estimates by Stan West and Milton Leontiades, who explain: "The NAIC membership represents about 96% of the assets of open-end investment companies and about one-third of closed-end investment companies' and holding companies' assets. However, the remaining two-thirds of closed-end investment and holding com-panies are principally represented by the holdings of Christiana Securities and Dela-ware Realty Company, both of which maintain stable security portfolios and thus do not distribute capital gains."

Estimates for 1952–1939 were obtained by computing percentage that 1953 estimate above comprised of the average of 1953 and 1952 realized net long-term gains of holding and other investment companies as published in *Statistics of Income*, Part 2; applying this percentage to average of each year and the year before it, i.e., year $x + 1$ and year x; and attributing estimate thus obtained to year $x + 1$.

Estimates for years 1936–1938 are guesses based on a "reasonable" relation to 1939.

Line 12: Values for 1939, 1945, 1947, and 1953 are from special supplements to *Statistics of Income*. For all other years between 1936 and 1953, estimates were obtained by interpolation using dividends of partnerships as a percentage of the sum of lines 5, 6, 7, and 8.

105

Line 13: Estimates for 1956–1958 were obtained from all reported nontaxable dividends in the Commerce Clearing House's *Capital Changes Reporter* (tabulations therefrom generously made available by Stan West and Milton Leontiades) increased by 10 per cent for small companies not reported on. The 1958 figure includes the dividend of "tax-option" corporations which elected to be taxed as partnerships as tabulated in *Statistics of Income.*

Similarly, tabulations were made from the *Capital Changes Reporter*, with $100,000 added for each company noted for which no dividend data were available, and increased by 10 per cent for 1941, 1946, and 1951.

Estimates for 1952–1955 were obtained by interpolation between 1951 and 1956 values. Estimates for 1941–1950 were taken to be the figure for each year that seemed the most reasonable on the basis of the tabulated 1941, 1946, and 1951 totals.

Estimates for 1940–1936 were derived by applying the 1941 percentage for nontaxable dividends to total net dividends (line 5 minus line 6). This procedure gives about the same figures as applying the 1941 percentage of nontaxable dividends to dividends of investment, etc., companies which in this period were the main payers of nontaxable dividends.

Three variant measures for nontaxable dividends represent the triumph of principle over pragmatism. For, in principle, such dividends go to all stockholding entities, and to individuals and fiduciaries one should impute only a fraction of all nontaxable dividends. We carried out this principle, in relation to net domestic dividends (the sum of lines 5, 6, 7, and 8) for the three variant measures of dividends of individuals and fiduciaries even though it turned out, in practice, to constitute a numerically unimportant refinement.

thesis, i.e., assert that the difference in the gap between these two years is equal to zero; and depending on the level of significance deemed relevant, we can accept or reject the hypothesis.

Let H_0 designate the null hypothesis.

8. H_0: $G_2 - G_1 = 0$ or $G_2 = G_1$.

To test this hypothesis, we measure the normal deviate Z where,

$$Z = \frac{G_2 - G_1}{\sqrt{\sigma_{G_2}^2 + \sigma_{G_1}^2}}.$$

If we choose a .05 level of significance, Z must be equal to or greater than $|1.96|$ for the null hypothesis to be rejected, i.e., for the change in the gap between these two years to be considered statistically significant. If a .01 level of significance is chosen, the null hypothesis will be rejected only if $Z \geq |2.57|$.

This test was applied to every year-by-year change in the gap for variants 1 and 2. Almost all such changes were significant except as noted in Table 17. We also tested by the same method the difference between the average gap for 1937–1939 and for 1956 and 1958. The

TABLE 27

VALUES OF Z_1 AND Z_2 FOR YEAR-TO-YEAR CHANGES IN THE GAP, 1936–1958

Change Between	Z_1	Z_2	Change Between	Z_1	Z_2
1936–1937	3.18	3.15	1947–1948	−2.38	−3.59
1937–1938	−12.08	−8.92	1948–1949	0.42	−2.21
1938–1939	5.72	4.68	1949–1950	4.52	6.75
1939–1940	−13.25	−11.88	1950–1951	−2.46	−1.63
1940–1941	−2.08	−2.71	1951–1952	0.81	2.05
1941–1942	12.61	9.25	1952–1953	6.23	4.86
1942–1943	9.19	9.02	1953–1954	−3.23	1.54
1943–1944	1.30	1.50	1954–1955	5.75	5.68
1944–1945	−2.92	−0.91	1955–1956	−2.18	−2.26
1945–1946	8.48	4.28	1956–1957	−3.44	−3.54
1946–1947	−3.38	−2.88	1957–1958	1.54	1.49

difference, of course, was significant. Table 27 shows the values of Z, where Z_1 applies to variant 1 and Z_2 to variant 2.

In making these tests, as already noted, the variance associated with dividends reported by individuals was by far the most important component of the total variance.

ESTIMATES OF DIVIDEND UNDERREPORTING BASED ON ACP DATA

The estimates of dividend underreporting in Tables 21 and 22 are based on tabulations of the ACP data made available by the Internal Revenue Service in 1951. We describe the estimates incorporated in Table 21.

The estimate of underreporting must be made as a range rather than a single value because, with only the total tax change reported for returns with dividend errors, it was necessary arbitrarily to assign fractions of that total to the dividend error alone. In the ACP tabulations dividend errors were classified as major or minor errors. All returns that met the following conditions were placed in the major error category.

1. The error in dividends accounted for the largest portion of the change in adjusted gross income, i.e., the addition (or subtraction) due to audit.

2. The change in adjusted gross income was responsible for a bigger fraction of the total tax change than exemption or deduction changes, or mathematical error.

All other returns with dividend errors were placed in the minor error category.

Following this classification, we set up three possibilities for major error returns: 100, 75, and 50 per cent of the total tax change due to the dividend error; and three percentage assumptions for minor error returns: 40, 30, and 20 per cent. In every case we estimated the dividends not covered by the ACP by dividing the tax change assumed due to the errors in dividend reporting by the marginal rate that applied on the average to all taxpayers (taken from *Statistics of Income*) in each of the broad income classes by which the ACP data were tabulated and for joint and separate returns.

The lower value of the estimates in Table 21 is the sum of the 50 per cent for major errors and 25 per cent for minor error assumptions; the upper values of the range come from adding the results of the 100 and 40 per cent assumptions. The upper value of the range is almost surely above the actual figure, but it cannot be stated as positively that the lower limit of our range is below the real value.

Table 22 is derived from 21 and data from *Statistics of Income*.

ESTIMATING REVENUE GAIN FROM FULL CORRECTION OF DIVIDEND UNDERREPORTING IN 1958

From Table 21 we derived the income class distribution of dividend underreporting, applied these percentages to our estimated increment to the tax base of $900 million that would follow elimination of underreporting, and multiplied the amounts thus obtained by the marginal rates (weighted by the proportion of joint and separate returns) that applied to the taxable income in each of the broad adjusted gross income classes. Having the data conveniently at hand, we assumed that the 1956 marginal rates applied in 1958, hardly a drastic assumption.

A numerical summary of our procedure follows in Table 28.

Note on Difference Between Aggregate Gap and Survey Gap

Earlier it was asserted that our 10 per cent gap and the 1959 Survey's 5 per cent were not necessarily inconsistent. More correctly, using a .99 confidence interval, our gap of 9 to 11 per cent (8.5 to 10.5 under variant 2) is not necessarily in conflict with the Survey's 2.5 to 7.5 per cent gap. For the two sets of estimates are not comparable in many ways.

Rather than elaborate on all these differences, we note here the Survey features that might tend to understate the gap. For one thing,

TABLE 28

ESTIMATED REVENUE LOSS DUE TO DIVIDEND UNDERREPORTING IN 1958

Adjusted Gross Income Class (1)	Percentage of Total Under-reporting in Each Class (2)	$650 Million Allocated by % in Col. 2 (3)	$850 Million Allocated by % in Col. 2 (4)	Weighted-Average Marginal Rate (per cent) (5)	Revenue Gain	
					Low Estimate (6)	High Estimate (7)
Under $7,000	34.5	$224	$293	20.0	$ 45	$ 59
$7,000 to $25,000	47.1	306	400	22.3	68	89
$25,000 to $100,000	15.6	101	133	51.7	52	69
$100,000 and over	2.9	19	25	82.5	16	21
Total	100.0	650	850	—	201	238

1040A and 1040W returns, on which underreporting could very well be more pronounced, were excluded. For another, some 1099 returns may not have been filed, and hence no indication of underreporting would be uncovered. This could be a danger, particularly in small, closely held corporations. Moreover, the Survey did not cover foreign dividends on which underreporting might be greater because no information returns are filed. Finally, for about 16 per cent of the sample it was impossible to match 1040 returns and information returns. To the extent that this represented a failure to file, the Survey overstates the degree of reporting. There are, then, reasons for thinking that the Survey may have understated the gap, but there is no way of determining if it actually did and how much.

On the other hand, the unaudited Survey showed a 9 per cent gap; the audited Survey only a 5 per cent gap. Three points of this four-percentage-point decline can be explained by dividends reported under other headings on form 1040. We made no adjustment for this possibility; on this score, our measure of the gap tends to be too large. Against this should be put an item not taken account of by our method—other income reported as dividends, for instance, saving and loan "dividends" which are not in our aggregate dividend totals, but which might be reported as dividends on tax returns.

What follows from all this is not clear. In general, the Survey results do suggest that our measure overstates the gap, but not by as much as the difference between our 10 per cent and the Survey's 5 per cent. We have, then, this additional caution which, unavoidably, could not be worked into the text, because the Survey results came too late.

It is hoped the future surveys, focused more directly on under-reporting, will permit a more precise statement on the size of the gap.

CHAPTER 3

Dividend Receipts and Income Tax Liability

Variations in Tax Liability Attributable to Dividend Receipts

FOR every year from 1918 through 1957, the total tax liability has been apportioned among the various components of taxpayers' adjusted gross income. The method, while quite elaborate, essentially involved prorating the tax liability of each income class proportionately among the sources of income reported in that class with due allowance for a number of special features of the tax law including the earned income credit, the special treatment of capital gains, the exemption of dividends from normal tax up to 1936, etc.[1]

The total tax liability attributable to dividend receipts is the resultant of a complex set of relations—the absolute amount of corporate dividend payments, their distribution among taxpayers, the height and progressivity of the personal income tax schedule, and the specific provisions, if any, relating to the taxation of dividends contained in the revenue law.[2] The following illustrates the varied range of results: The amount of dividends reported on taxable returns was about the same in 1926, 1940, and 1942—$3.5 billion. In 1926, the tax liability attributable to dividend receipts came to $208 million, in 1940 to $557 million, and in 1942 to just under $1 billion.

During the 1920's, the tax liability traceable to taxpayers' dividend

---

[1] Only one feature of the method needs particular mention here. Because of changes introduced in the tax revision of 1954 and in the tabulations of tax return data, the dividend tax liability from 1954 on relates only to persons, whereas prior to that date fiduciaries were also included. Thus the estimates for 1954–1957 are not strictly comparable with the other years covered by our study.

[2] In this chapter and the following one no adjustment is made in the tax liability measurements for dividend underreporting.

110

receipts ran between $150 and $300 million. In the early thirties, a smaller amount was raised from dividends (as from the other sources of income)—something between $125 and $200 million. In the later thirties about $300 to $500 million of tax liability was due to the dividend income of taxpayers. The sharp increases in tax rates in the forties and the increase in dividend payments in the years following World War II show up in the sharply increased tax liability on taxpayers' dividend receipts in this period which ranged between $1 and over $2 billion (see Table 29 and Chart 4).

These data are more significant when related to total personal income tax liability. The distribution of dividends is highly concentrated and the personal income tax has always been progressive; on these grounds, then, tax liability on dividends would be expected to constitute a higher percentage of total tax liability than dividends comprise of adjusted gross income. Tending to offset this, up to 1936, was the exemption of dividends from normal tax. But even before 1936, and certainly thereafter, the proportionate share of dividend tax liability in total tax liability ranged between one and a half and over two and a half times higher than the proportionate share of dividends in adjusted gross income (see Table 29).

Through 1941 the tax liability traceable to dividend receipts constituted a very sizable proportion of the annual total personal income tax levy. During the twenties the proportion ranged between 22 and 29 per cent. In the early thirties, while the amount of the dividend tax liability was considerably lower than in the previous decade (as was the total personal income tax assessment), it comprised from 30 to over 50 per cent of total tax liability (the latter proportion being found in 1931 during the period when dividend receipts were exempt from normal tax). Over the rest of the thirties too, a very high proportion of the personal income tax assessment was attributable to dividend receipts—about 40 per cent. Starting in 1941, however, it fell rapidly until it reached 7 or 8 per cent (although its absolute level continued to increase) because of the more rapid rise in the wages and salaries and entrepreneurial income components of the adjusted gross income of taxpayers.

These figures, in conjunction with the data presented in an earlier chapter, indicate that throughout the period under analysis, 1918–1957, there was a magnification effect in moving from (1) the dividend fraction of personal income to (2) the dividend proportion of adjusted gross income of taxable returns to (3) the share of dividend tax liability

111

TABLE 29

Selected Data on Dividends and Dividend Tax Liability, 1918–1957

Year (1)	Tax Liability on Dividends (million dollars) (2)	Effective Rate of Tax on Dividends (per cent) (3)	Tax Liability on Dividends as a Per Cent of Total Personal Tax Liability (per cent) (4)	Dividends as a Per Cent of Adjusted Gross Income (Taxable Returns) (per cent) (5)	Col. 4 ÷ Col. 5 (6)	Dividends on Taxable Returns as a Per Cent of Personal Dividend Receipts (per cent) (7)
1918	290	12.5	25.7	14.8	1.7	66
1919	279	12.1	21.9	11.4	1.9	79
1920	240	9.4	22.3	10.9	2.0	78
1921	177	8.6	24.6	13.4	1.8	70
1922	206	9.0	23.9	13.3	1.8	77
1923	164	6.1	24.8	13.3	1.9	71
1924	207	7.3	29.3	12.6	2.3	74
1925	170	5.5	23.2	15.5	1.5	70
1926	208	5.9	28.5	17.7	1.6	74
1927	229	6.0	27.5	18.7	1.5	76
1928	261	6.4	22.4	17.3	1.3	75
1929	262	6.1	26.2	18.6	1.4	74
1930	203	5.3	42.6	24.4	1.7	71
1931	126	4.8	51.2	24.8	2.1	63
1932	140	8.5	42.4	18.4	2.3	62
1933	120	9.3	32.1	16.0	2.0	62
1934	202	12.1	39.5	17.7	2.2	65
1935	245	12.9	37.3	16.7	2.2	66
1936	536	15.4	44.2	21.9	2.0	78
1937	543	14.3	47.6	21.8	2.2	81
1938	280	11.3	36.6	17.2	2.1	78
1939	384	12.8	41.3	16.8	2.5	79
1940	557	16.0	37.2	13.4	2.8	88
1941	847	21.4	21.7	8.0	2.7	89
1942	999	28.3	11.2	4.8	2.3	81
1943	1,133	32.0	7.8	3.3	2.3	78
1944	1,167	31.8	7.2	3.2	2.3	79
1945	1,182	31.7	6.9	3.1	2.2	79
1946	1,333	29.2	8.2	3.9	2.2	79
1947	1,594	30.1	8.7	3.9	2.2	81
1948	1,339	21.2	9.1	4.1	2.2	82
1949	1,510	24.0	10.3	4.5	2.3	84
1950	2,031	27.1	10.9	4.7	2.3	81
1951	2,120	28.6	8.7	4.0	2.2	82
1952	2,109	28.9	7.5	3.7	2.1	82
1953	1,995	27.7	6.7	3.4	2.0	78
EXCLUDING FIDUCIARIES						
1954	1,672	24.2	6.2	3.3	1.9	71
1955	1,765	23.0	5.9	3.3	1.8	69
1956	1,937	22.9	5.8	3.4	1.7	70
1957	1,992	22.4	5.8	3.4	1.7	71

Note: The exclusion of fiduciaries from 1954 on explains the difference for these years between the values in column 7 of this table and column 8 of Table 1.

CHART 4

Tax Liability Attributable to Dividends as a Percentage of Total Personal
Income Tax Liability, 1918–1957

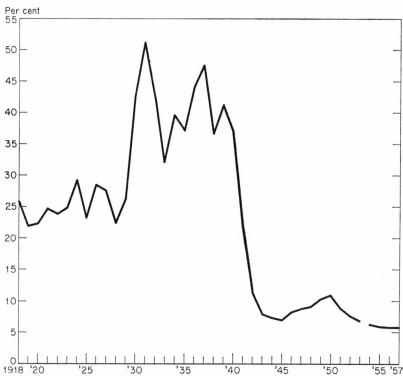

NOTE: From 1954 on, tax liability is for individuals only; in prior years it is
for individuals and fiduciaries.

in total tax liability. Dividends constituted a higher percentage of the
adjusted gross income of taxable returns than of personal income
receipts, while the share of dividends in total tax liability was higher
than their share in adjusted gross income (see column 6 of Table 29).
We note parenthetically here that the decline in the effective rate of
tax on dividends (column 3 of Table 29) from 1954 on is due to the
dividend exclusion and credit.

Effect of Dividends on Revenue Flexibility of Tax Structure

If dividend tax liability fluctuated relatively more than the share of
dividends in the tax base (measured by the adjusted gross income

of taxable returns), the relations noted under 2 and 3 in the preceding paragraph suggest that dividends have added to the revenue flexibility of the personal income tax. More particularly, revenue flexibility is defined as the ratio of proportionate change in tax liability to that in tax base. This discussion, of course, deals with changes in tax liability and tax base associated with changes in dividends. Revenue flexibility —designated Φ—so conceived is an elasticity measure, and values of Φ measure the degree of revenue flexibility. Throughout this discussion, tax liability and tax revenue mean the same thing, although in practice, of course, the liability on tax returns and the tax revenue of the Treasury Department are not identical.

Let:

D = dividends

B = tax base (adjusted gross income of taxable returns)

T_d = tax liability attributable to dividend receipts

T = total income tax liability

Φ = revenue flexibility.

Then we define:

$$\Phi = \frac{\Delta T_d/T}{\Delta D/B}.$$

Both the ratios entering into Φ may be expressed as themselves the product of ratios. Examining these component relationships will permit some a priori judgments of the value of Φ.

Thus,

$$\frac{\Delta T_d}{T} = \frac{\Delta T_d}{T_d} \cdot \frac{T_d}{T},$$

and

$$\frac{\Delta D}{B} = \frac{\Delta D}{D} \cdot \frac{D}{B}.$$

If these terms are rearranged, Φ can now be defined as

$$\Phi = \left(\frac{\Delta T_d/T_d}{\Delta D/D}\right)\left(\frac{T_d}{T} \cdot \frac{B}{D}\right).$$

114

Dividend Receipts and Income Tax Liability

We know that dividends have accounted for a higher fraction of tax liability than of tax base. (See Table 24, columns 4 and 5.) In terms of the symbols used here, $T_d/T > D/B$. So we also know [3] that

$$\frac{T_d}{T} \cdot \frac{B}{D} > 1.$$

Thus Φ will certainly exceed 1; i.e., dividends will have imparted revenue flexibility to the personal income tax structure, if [4]

$$\frac{\Delta T_d/T_d}{\Delta D/D} > 1.$$

The next step, then, is to measure the ratio

$$\frac{\Delta T_d/T_d}{\Delta D/D}.$$

But more than arithmetic is involved here. For the revenue laws—specifically the exemption and rate structure of the personal income tax—changed frequently over the period of our study. So year-to-year changes in the tax liability attributable to dividends and in the amount of dividends in the adjusted gross income of taxable returns could be the net resultant of a number of factors, most of them extraneous to the "stable" relationship we are seeking to measure; that is, it would be impossible under these conditions to isolate the revenue flexibility effect of the particular relation under discussion—the differential importance of dividends in the tax base and tax liability. However, this difficulty can be circumvented by restricting examination of the ratio of proportionate changes in dividend tax liability and dividends to those two-year periods over which the provisions of the revenue law remained unchanged.

Table 30 contains the values of

$$\frac{T_d/T_d}{\Delta D/D}$$

[3] By dividing both sides of the inequality by D/B.

[4] Φ could, of course, be greater than 1 even if this ratio fell below 1, if the excess of $(T_d/T)(B/D)$ over 1 is large enough. But this depends on particular values for each expression and cannot, therefore, be asserted as a general result a priori.

TABLE 30

<small>COMPARISON OF PERCENTAGE CHANGES IN DIVIDENDS REPORTED ON TAXABLE
RETURNS AND DIVIDEND TAX LIABILITY</small>

(per cent)

Years of Similar Tax Treatment (1)	Percentage Change in Dividends Reported on Taxable Returns (2)	Percentage Change in Tax Liability Attributable to Dividends (3)	Ratio of Col. 3 to Col. 2 (4)
1919–1920	+10.6	−13.8	−1.30
1925–1926	+13.8	+21.8	+1.58
1926–1927	+8.9	+10.1	+1.13
1930–1931	−32.6	−38.0	+1.17
1932–1933	−21.6	−14.8	+0.69
1934–1935	−14.1	+21.3	+1.51
1936–1937	+9.0	+1.3	+0.14
1938–1939	+21.1	+37.2	+1.76
1944–1945	+1.5	+1.3	+0.87
1946–1947	+16.1	+19.6	+1.22
1948–1949	+6.7	+11.2	+1.67
1952–1953	−0.99	−5.4	+5.45
1955–1956 [a]	+10.2	+9.7	+0.95
1956–1957	+5.3	+2.8	+0.53

[a] Tax rates applying to dividends were not invariant between 1954 and 1955, because the exclusion and credit applied for the whole of 1955, but only the latter half of 1954. Hence we do not include 1954–1955.

computed on this basis; they are listed in column 4. Of the fourteen two-year periods of invariant tax provisions, eight show a value greater than 1, and hence a Φ greater than 1. In one case, dividends moved one way, and dividend tax liability the other (hence, a negative value in column 4); this result is nonsense in the context of revenue flexibility, since the measure is based on "reasonable" conditions, i.e., those instances where a larger amount of an income type in the tax base leads to a higher tax liability on it. In the remaining five instances, the sign is right, but more investigation is needed to determine whether Φ is greater than 1 or not. Φ must be calculated.

The computed values of Φ for the thirteen (of the total of fourteen) periods in which the response of tax liability to dividend change was "correct," i.e., in the same direction, are given in Table 31. For all

Dividend Receipts and Income Tax Liability

TABLE 31

DERIVATION OF MEASURE OF REVENUE FLEXIBILITY

Year (1)	$\dfrac{\Delta T_d/T_d}{\Delta D/D}$ (2)	$\dfrac{T_d}{T}$ (3) [a]	$\dfrac{B}{D}$ (4) [a]	$\Phi =$ (2) $\times$ (3) $\times$ (4) (5)
1925–1926	1.58	0.29	5.65	2.59
1926–1927	1.13	0.27	5.35	1.63
1930–1931	1.17	0.51	4.03	2.40
1932–1933	0.69	0.32	6.25	1.38
1934–1935	1.51	0.37	5.99	3.35
1936–1937	0.14	0.48	4.59	0.31
1938–1939	1.76	0.41	5.95	4.29
1944–1945	0.87	0.07	32.26	1.96
1946–1947	1.22	0.09	25.64	2.82
1948–1949	1.67	0.10	22.22	3.71
1952–1953	5.45	0.07	29.41	11.22
1955–1956	0.95	0.06	29.51	1.68
1956–1957	0.53	0.06	29.46	0.78

[a] In second year of period.

but two of these periods, Φ had a value greater than 1. Thus we may conclude that, in a majority (eleven out of fourteen) of the periods for which it is legitimate to make such a comparison, the proportionate change in tax liability due to dividends was a multiple of the relative change in the tax base due to the change in dividend receipts. As a general rule dividends have imparted revenue flexibility to the personal income tax structure. To take a specific example or two: In 1926 when Φ was 2.6, a small change in the tax base due to dividends, say a 1 per cent change in tax base, would have meant a change in tax liability of over 2.6 per cent; in 1953 something like an 11 per cent change in tax liability would have been associated with a 1 per cent change in tax base due to dividends.

But to give some sense of the relative importance of dividend change and associated tax liability change in the revenue structure, we must go beyond the simple measure of Φ and relations of the kind discussed above. For Φ, a pure measure of elasticity, is divorced from the absolute size of the magnitudes involved. To revert to the numbers just cited, a 1 per cent change in tax base in 1926 attributable to dividends would have required an increase of about $200 million (less than 6 per cent)

TABLE 32

PERSONAL DIVIDEND RECEIPTS BEFORE AND AFTER TAXES, 1918–1957

Year (1)	Personal Dividend Receipts (million dollars) (2)	Dividend Tax Liability (3)	Personal Dividend Receipts After Taxes on Dividends (col. 2 − col. 3) (4)	After-Tax Personal Dividend Receipts as a Percentage of Before-Tax Personal Dividend Receipts (col. 4 ÷ col. 2) (5)
1918	3,518	290	3,228	92
1919	2,882	278	2,604	90
1920	3,211	240	2,971	93
1921	2,959	177	2,782	94
1922	3,044	206	2,838	93
1923	3,837	164	3,673	96
1924	3,811	207	3,604	95
1925	4,421	170	4,251	96
1926	4,721	210	4,511	96
1927	5,046	228	4,818	95
1928	5,485	261	5,224	95
1929	5,823	262	5,561	95
1930	5,500	203	5,297	96
1931	4,098	126	3,972	97
1932	2,574	140	2,434	95
1933	2,066	120	1,946	94
1934	2,592	202	2,390	92
1935	2,872	245	2,627	91
1936	4,557	536	4,021	88
1937	4,693	543	4,150	88
1938	3,195	280	2,915	91
1939	3,796	384	3,412	90
1940	4,049	557	3,492	86
1941	4,465	847	3,618	81
1942	4,297	999	3,298	77
1943	4,493	1,133	3,360	75
1944	4,680	1,167	3,513	75
1945	4,699	1,182	3,517	75
1946	5,808	1,333	4,475	77
1947	6,561	1,594	4,967	76
1948	7,248	1,339	5,909	82
1949	7,458	1,510	5,948	80
1950	9,208	2,031	7,177	78
1951	9,029	2,120	6,909	77
1952	8,954	2,109	6,845	76
1953	9,225	1,995	7,230	78
EXCLUDING FIDUCIARIES				
1953	9,225	1,832	7,393	81
1954	9,839	1,672	8,167	83
1955	11,215	1,765	9,450	84
1956	12,132	1,937	10,195	84
1957	12,588	1,992	10,596	84

in dividends on taxable returns. To produce a 1 per cent change in tax base in 1953, however, an increase of over $2 billion (about 30 per cent) in dividends would have been necessary. Clearly the one case illustrates a variation that could very well happen between one year and the next; the other represents a highly unusual event.

That the value of Φ alone is insufficient for assessing the importance of the revenue flexibility imparted by dividends can be seen in another way. Consider a given absolute amount of increase in dividends, say $100 million, to have taken place in 1927 or 1945. (Dividends reported on taxable returns came to about the same figure in both these years; thus the $100 million increase would have meant the same percentage change—less than 3 per cent—in dividends in both years.) In 1927 this increase in dividends would have increased the tax base by 0.5 per cent, and, with Φ at 1.63, personal income tax liability by about 0.8 per cent. But in 1945, the tax base would have increased by less than 0.1 per cent, and tax liability by less than 0.2 per cent. A given dividend change would have been much less powerful in its relative effect on tax revenue in 1945 than in 1927 despite the higher Φ in 1945. This result, of course, reflects the fact that in 1945 the income tax base covered most persons and their income, while in 1927 it did not. With over three-quarters of personal dividends showing up in both years, dividends comprised a much more important component of the tax base in 1927.

Dividend Receipts After Taxes

How much of the net outflow of dividends from the corporate system was left to the recipients can be estimated by subtracting the tax liability due to dividends from the aggregate of personal dividend receipts. This calculation (see Table 32) shows more than 95 per cent of total personal dividend receipts left after taxes in the twenties and early thirties, around 90 per cent in the middle thirties, about 75 per cent from 1942 to 1954, and an increase to around 84 per cent from 1954 on, due to the tax relief provided for dividends in the Internal Revenue Code of 1954. A specific contrast will point up these sharp changes. In both 1929 and 1946, personal dividend receipts came to $5.8 billion. In the peak year of the "golden" twenties all but a quarter of a billion of this was available for reinvestment or for consumption after the government had made its reckoning with tax-

119

payers.[5] In 1946, however, over a billion dollars less was available after taxes. But in all years, a much lower percentage of any "small" increase in dividends would have remained with taxpayers.

This, of course, is saying nothing more than that under a progressive tax structure the rate that applies to the highest bracket of taxable income exceeds the weighted average of the rates that apply to each of the brackets into which taxable income falls. Yet for dividends it is worth noting because the divergence between the marginal rate and the effective rate has been so large, and because the marginal rate is the more appropriate evidence in connection with a number of problems.

That there has been a wide divergence between effective and marginal rates stands out clearly from the data of Table 33. The rates in column 2 of that table—average rate applying to all dividend receipts —are taken from column 3 of Table 29. They are to be interpreted this way: In the aggregate for all taxpayers in 1929, the federal personal income tax liability that can be traced to their dividend receipts amounted to 6.1 per cent of such receipts. Or, after taxes attributable to them, about 94 per cent of the dividends received by taxpayers were left. This is familiar ground. (But note that the paragraph above considers what is left over from all dividend receipts, not merely those of taxpayers.)

TABLE 33

WEIGHTED-AVERAGE MARGINAL AND AGGREGATE AVERAGE RATES OF TAX ON DIVIDENDS, SELECTED YEARS, 1929–1952

(per cent)

Year	Weighted-Average Marginal Rate (1)	Aggregate Average Rate (2)
1929	13.2	6.1
1936	28.0	15.4
1941	35.1	21.4
1947	49.6	30.1
1952	55.6	28.9

[5] Throughout this chapter we discuss only the personal income tax on dividends received, taking no account of the corporate income tax on earnings out of which these dividends are paid. This latter matter is covered in Chapter 4.

The values in column 1—weighted-average marginal rate—are a measure of the tax liability that would be associated with a small increase in aggregate dividend payments distributed among taxpayers in the same proportions as the actual total of dividends. In computing it, the marginal rate in each stockholder income class was multiplied by the amount of dividends in that class (using for this purpose the income classes of Table 7). The fact that the values in column 1 exceed considerably those of column 2 follows from the progressive personal income tax rate schedule. The entries of column 1 should be read this way. In 1929, for example, had all dividend recipients experienced a 0.1 per cent increase in dividends, in the aggregate 13.2 per cent of this would have gone for taxes; by 1952 the tax liability would have been almost 56 per cent of the small proportionate increase in aggregate dividend payments. And between these dates there was a steady upward movement in the marginal rate that applied to the aggregate of all taxpayers.

The marginal rate on dividends increased more than the average rate in absolute amount; the latter between 1929 and 1952 rose by 23 percentage points, the marginal rate by 42.[6] (But the average rate increased *relatively* more than the marginal rate.)

In broad terms the marginal rate can be considered as applying to the aggregate of dividend-receiving taxpayers, a factor that should enter into the decision surrounding corporate dividend payments. In this context it is interesting to know that "small" step-ups in dividends would have led on average to about half as large an increase in stockholders' income after tax in 1952 as in 1929. It would be unwarranted within this study's scope to go any further than to note that this suggests that personal income taxes represented a stronger deterrent to dividend payments in the last twenty years or so than they did in an earlier period. To conclude that corporations have, as a general rule, responded to this incentive with lower dividend pay-outs would not necessarily follow: first, because many factors—tax and otherwise—other than those we have cited enter into the determination of the

---

[6] The disparity between 1947 and 1952—average rate lower in 1952 and marginal rate higher—can be explained this way: The income-splitting which permitted married persons to file jointly (instituted in 1948) makes for lower effective rates, but dividends have moved up with incomes to a point where the marginal rate is weighted more heavily by higher income class dividends. (Thus Table 2 shows a slight fall between 1947 and 1952 in the absolute amount of dividends in the under-$5,000 class, but a rise of $1.2 billion in the $5,000-to-$50,000 class, and a rise of $900 million in the over-$50,000 class.)

level of dividends; second, because, in fact, it seems that no real down-ward revision of pay-out rates can be said to have occurred in the last generation, taking due account of the war and its aftermath; and third, because it appears that the dividend pay-out ratio for the cor-porate system as a whole can be substantially explained by a model that gives no explicit weight to stockholders' marginal rates.[7]

Comparison of Tax Liability Attributable to Dividends and Other Sources of Income

With reference to dividends, the effect of personal income taxes on the distribution of income can be examined from at least two points of view: comparison of the effects of taxation on dividends and on all personal income or specific components thereof, and analysis of the change in the distribution of dividends among taxpayers.

Reflecting the concentration of dividends in the hands of taxpayers in the upper income brackets, the tax system led to a change in their relative importance in personal income. Dividends, after the deduc-tion of the tax liability traceable to them, comprised a smaller propor-tion of after-tax than of before-tax personal income (see Table 34). This effect was most pronounced between 1942 and 1953. In 1929, for instance, the respective before- and after-income tax percentages that dividends comprised of personal income were 7.1 and 6.8—their share of total income was reduced 4 per cent by taxation; in 1937 the re-duction was 10 per cent; in 1941, 14 per cent; in 1947 the after-tax share was 17 per cent lower than the pre-tax proportion; in 1953, the difference was 13 per cent. The dividend tax relief provided in 1954, of course, shows up in the smaller change in the before- and after-tax proportion of dividends in the years 1954–1956.

This matter can be probed further by examining the redistribution effect for several components of personal income and comparing the results for dividends with what happened in the case of the other im-

[7] John Lintner, "Distribution of Incomes of Corporations among Dividends, Re-tained Earnings, and Taxes," *American Economic Review*, May 1956, pp. 97–113. This is not to deny the possibility that for particular enterprises the controlling or predominant stockholders' marginal rate of personal income tax may not be an important consideration in determining the amount of dividend payments. Moreover, since Lintner's published work on this subject to date has dealt with aggregate data, one cannot rule out the possibility that sharp differences in pay-out rates and dividend behavior might characterize different subgroups of cor-porations.

portant sources of income. In general, the income tax made wages and salaries a slightly more important component of personal income, left interest and rents and royalties about as important (relatively) as they were before taxes up to 1940 and raised their share thereafter, and led to a slight fall in the relative importance of entrepreneurial income (Table 34). By far the most pronounced change caused by taxation in the relative proportion of each component in personal income took place in dividends.

Equalizing Effect of Taxes on Dividends

To how great an extent was the distribution of dividends among the recipients thereof equalized by the personal income tax? The equalizing effect (defined in terms of the movement of a Lorenz curve closer to the line of complete "equality") exercised by the personal income tax is a function of two variables: (1) the degree of concentration of dividends and (2) the progressivity of the income tax rate schedule. For a given tax schedule, the more concentrated the distribution of dividend receipts, the greater the push toward "equality." Similarly, for a given distribution of dividends, the more progressive the tax system, the more powerful its equalizing effect.

For five years—1934, 1937, 1941, 1947, and 1952—we computed the coefficient of inequality of the distribution of dividends among dividend recipients arrayed by income classes both before and after the personal income tax liability on dividends.[8] A comparison of these coefficients will indicate the strength of the equalization effect. For any given distribution of dividends, under a progressive tax system dividends will be more evenly distributed after taxes. But the degree of equalization accomplished, i.e., the proportionate "push" toward equality will vary with rate structures and their progressivity.

The entries in Table 35 summarize the results of these calculations. In every year for which this particular point was investigated, the income class distribution of dividends approached equality more closely after taxes than before. Worth noting is the tendency for the pre-tax distribution to become more uniform over time (column 2), and the more pronounced equalization effects from 1941 on (column 4).

---

[8] The reader is reminded that the Gini coefficient of inequality is measured by the ratio between the area under the outer boundary of the Lorenz curve and the diagonal line, and the area between the diagonal and the X and Y axes. Its value ranges between 1 (complete "inequality") and 0 (complete "equality").

COMPARISON OF PERCENTAGE SHARES OF SELECTED COMPONENTS

(per

	Wages and Salaries, etc.			Entrepreneurial Income		
Year	Before Tax	After Tax	After-Tax Share as Per Cent of Before-Tax Share	Before Tax	After Tax	After-Tax Share as Per Cent of Before-Tax Share
1918	54.5	55.0	100.7	27.4	27.4	100.0
1919 a	52.3	52.8	101.0	30.8	30.8	100.0
1919	56.6	57.2	101.1	28.0	28.0	100.0
1920	63.4	63.9	100.8	20.4	20.3	99.5
1921	63.6	64.0	100.6	15.9	15.9	100.0
1922	61.7	62.1	100.6	18.5	18.5	100.0
1923	62.5	62.8	100.5	18.3	18.3	100.0
1924	61.8	62.2	100.6	18.5	18.5	100.0
1925	60.8	61.2	100.7	19.6	19.6	100.0
1926	62.6	63.0	100.6	18.4	18.4	100.0
1927	62.8	63.3	100.8	17.6	17.7	100.6
1928	62.6	63.3	101.1	17.6	17.7	100.6
1929 a	62.6	63.2	101.0	17.3	17.3	100.0
1929	62.5	63.1	101.0	17.6	17.6	100.0
1930	64.1	64.3	100.3	15.4	15.4	100.0
1931	65.9	66.0	100.2	13.7	13.7	100.0
1932	68.1	68.3	100.3	11.1	11.1	100.0
1933	68.6	68.9	100.4	12.5	12.4	99.2
1934	69.9	70.3	100.6	13.7	13.7	100.0
1935	67.5	67.9	100.6	18.0	18.0	100.0
1936	69.0	69.9	101.3	16.0	16.0	100.0
1937	67.8	68.5	101.0	17.7	17.8	100.6
1938	69.3	69.7	100.6	16.7	16.8	100.6
1939	69.5	70.0	100.7	16.5	16.5	100.0
1940	69.6	70.3	101.0	17.0	17.0	100.0
1941	69.6	70.5	101.3	18.5	18.4	99.5
1942	70.5	71.5	101.4	19.7	19.4	98.5
1943	72.8	74.0	101.6	18.8	18.2	96.8
1944	73.9	75.1	101.6	18.0	17.5	97.2
1945	73.6	75.1	102.0	18.2	17.5	96.2
1946	70.2	71.1	101.3	20.5	20.0	97.6
1947	71.8	72.6	101.1	18.7	18.2	97.3
1948	71.3	72.0	101.0	19.3	18.8	97.4
1949	72.4	73.1	101.0	17.4	17.0	97.7
1950	72.9	73.3	100.5	16.5	16.6	100.6
1951	73.6	73.7	100.1	16.6	16.8	101.2
1952	74.8	75.0	100.3	15.6	15.6	100.0
1953	76.2	76.3	100.1	14.3	14.2	99.3
						EXCLUDING
1953	76.2	76.2	100.0	14.3	14.2	99.3
1954	75.9	75.9	100.0	14.1	13.9	98.6
1955	76.3	76.4	100.1	13.7	13.6	99.3
1956	77.2	77.3	100.1	13.0	12.8	98.5

IN PERSONAL INCOME, BEFORE AND AFTER TAXES, 1918–1956

cent)

Dividends			Interest			Rents		
Before Tax	After Tax	After-Tax Share as Per Cent of Before-Tax Share	Before Tax	After Tax	After-Tax Share as Per Cent of Before-Tax Share	Before Tax	After Tax	After-Tax Share as Per Cent of Before-Tax Share
6.0	5.6	93.3	3.4	3.3	97.1	8.6	8.7	101.2
4.8	4.5	93.8	3.9	3.8	97.4	8.2	8.2	100.0
4.4	4.1	93.2	4.9	4.8	98.0	6.1	6.1	100.0
4.6	4.3	93.5	5.4	5.3	98.1	6.2	6.2	100.0
5.4	5.1	94.4	7.0	6.9	98.6	8.1	8.1	100.0
5.0	4.7	94.0	6.7	6.6	98.5	8.2	8.2	100.0
5.5	5.3	96.4	6.1	6.0	98.4	7.5	7.5	100.0
5.4	5.2	96.3	6.3	6.2	98.4	8.0	8.0	100.0
5.9	5.8	98.3	6.2	6.2	100.0	7.4	7.5	101.4
6.1	5.9	96.7	6.1	6.1	100.0	6.7	6.7	100.0
6.6	6.4	97.0	6.4	6.3	98.4	6.6	6.7	101.5
7.0	6.7	95.7	6.7	6.7	100.0	6.2	6.3	101.6
7.6	7.3	96.1	6.7	6.7	100.0	5.9	5.9	100.0
7.0	6.8	97.1	6.4	6.4	100.0	6.5	6.6	101.5
7.4	7.1	95.9	6.7	6.7	100.0	6.4	6.5	101.6
6.5	6.3	96.9	7.9	7.9	100.0	6.0	6.0	100.0
5.5	5.2	94.5	9.6	9.6	100.0	5.7	5.7	100.0
4.7	4.4	93.6	9.8	9.8	100.0	4.4	4.5	102.3
5.1	4.7	92.2	8.0	8.0	100.0	3.3	3.3	100.0
5.0	4.6	92.0	6.6	6.6	100.0	2.9	3.0	103.4
6.8	6.1	89.7	5.5	5.5	100.0	2.7	2.8	103.7
6.6	5.9	89.4	5.0	5.0	100.0	2.9	2.9	100.0
4.8	4.4	91.7	5.3	5.3	100.0	3.9	3.9	100.0
5.4	4.9	90.7	4.8	4.8	100.0	3.8	3.8	100.0
5.2	4.6	88.5	4.3	4.3	100.0	3.8	3.8	100.0
4.8	4.1	85.4	3.4	3.4	100.0	3.7	3.8	102.7
3.5	2.9	82.9	2.6	2.6	100.0	3.7	3.8	102.7
2.9	2.5	86.2	2.1	2.1	100.0	3.4	3.6	105.9
2.9	2.4	82.8	1.9	2.0	105.3	3.3	3.5	106.1
2.8	2.3	82.1	2.2	2.3	104.5	3.3	3.5	106.1
3.3	2.8	84.8	2.5	2.5	100.0	3.5	3.6	102.9
3.6	2.9	85.3	2.6	2.7	103.8	3.5	3.6	102.9
3.5	3.1	88.6	2.4	2.5	104.2	3.5	3.6	102.9
3.6	3.1	86.1	2.5	2.6	104.0	4.1	4.2	102.4
4.0	3.4	85.0	2.6	2.7	103.8	4.0	4.1	102.5
3.5	3.0	85.7	2.5	2.6	104.0	3.8	3.9	102.6
3.3	2.8	84.8	2.5	2.6	104.0	3.8	4.0	105.3
3.2	2.8	87.5	2.6	2.8	107.7	3.7	3.9	105.4
FIDUCIARIES								
3.2	2.9	90.6	2.6	2.8	107.7	3.7	3.9	105.4
3.4	3.2	94.1	2.8	3.0	107.2	3.8	4.0	105.3
3.7	3.4	91.9	2.8	3.3	117.9	3.5	3.7	105.7
3.7	3.5	94.6	2.8	2.9	103.6	3.3	3.5	106.1

Dividends Under the Income Tax

NOTES TO TABLE 34

SOURCE: Personal income data: 1918–1929, Daniel Creamer, *Personal Income During Business Cycles*, Princeton for NBER, 1956, pp. 116–117; 1929–1951, *National Income, 1954*; 1952–1956, *Survey of Current Business*, July 1957, both adjusted as follows:

(a) Labor income = Sum of Table 3, lines 2, 3, and 7 minus Table 4, line 19.

(b) Entrepreneurial income = Table 1, line 10.

(c) Dividends = Table 1, line 20.

(d) Interest = Table 37, personal interest income less imputed interest (line 12 plus line 6 minus line 4).

(e) Rent = Table 1, line 15.

Tax liability: as computed for Personal Income Tax Study.

ᵃ Two values for 1919 and 1929 are presented by Creamer to provide overlapping data for years in which he started using a new series.

Although a comparison of the before-tax distributions is somewhat inconclusive, since they relate to a particular category—taxable returns—whose composition changed from year to year not only as a result of "economic" forces but also because of changes in exemptions and tax law, the degree of equalization effected by the tax system can be compared. That this fell off in 1952 compared with 1941 or 1947 can be explained largely by the softer "bite" of the tax system that followed the introduction of general income-splitting in 1948.

TABLE 35

DIVIDEND DISTRIBUTION EQUALIZATION EFFECT OF THE PERSONAL INCOME TAX,
1934, 1937, 1941, 1947, AND 1952

| | Coefficient of Inequality | | |
Year (1)	Before-Tax Distribution of Dividends (2)	After-Tax Distributions of Dividends (3)	Degree of Equalization (4)
1934	0.7255	0.6926	4.5%
1937	0.6710	0.6248	6.9
1941	0.6030	0.5162	14.4
1947	0.6374	0.5456	14.4
1952	0.5950	0.5250	11.8

NOTE: Column 4 (derived by subtracting col. 3 from col. 2 and dividing the result by col. 2) is a measure of the "push toward equality" exercised by the tax system on the distribution of dividends. Column 2 shows how much equalization was possible; the difference between it and column 3 shows how much the distribution was equalized in absolute terms; column 4 shows what proportion of the total possible equalization was effected by the tax system.

Dividend Receipts and Income Tax Liability

Distribution of Dividend Tax Liability and of Dividends

Because of the progressive nature of the personal income tax, the distribution of the dividend tax liability has always been more concentrated than the income class distribution of dividends. Another factor making for this result, through 1935, was the exemption of dividend receipts from normal tax. The data are summarized by broad income ranges in Table 36 and plotted on Chart 5.

Through 1935 taxpayers with net incomes of under $5,000 who received, depending on the year, anywhere from 2 to 10 per cent of the dividends reported by all taxpayers (see Table 2), accounted for none of the dividend tax liability. Because of the exemption of dividends from normal tax and the relatively high level of income at which surtax started, dividends received by this income group were not subject to personal income tax. After 1935, coincident with the rise in this group's share of dividends, their share of the dividend tax liability increased. But only from 1941 on was the latter over 2 per cent, and in all these years it was less than half their share of taxable dividends.

For taxpayers in the income class $5,000 to $50,000 the story is quite different. Over the period covered by this study the proportion of taxable dividends flowing to this segment of the taxpaying population was notably stable—fluctuating between about 40 and 50 per cent, and being about the same at the end of the period as at the beginning. No such stability was shown by this income group's share of the dividend tax liability, however. This percentage had a wide range—from under 11 (in 1928) to over 47 (in 1945). It remained fairly low through 1933 (except for 1920 and 1921), jumped suddenly in 1934 to 20 per cent, and then grew slowly up to 1940 where it reached 31. In 1941 another sudden jump occurred up to 40 per cent, then a regular rise to a maximum of 47 per cent in 1945 followed by a falling tendency over the remaining years. Over the latter half of the period 1918–1957, there was a substantial increase in the proportion of the total dividend tax liability that came from taxpayers in this income class; at the same time, however, their share of taxable dividends remained about the same.

Just the reverse pattern appears in the class $50,000 and over. Through 1933, this group's share of the dividend tax liability was very high and fairly stable—characteristically between 85 and 90 per cent. Starting with 1934 a noticeable and continuous decline in this per-

Dividends Under the Income Tax

TABLE 36

SHARE OF DIVIDEND TAX LIABILITY BY INCOME CLASSES, 1918–1957

(per cent)

Year	Under $5,000	$5,000 to $50,000	$50,000 and over
1918	0.0	13.3	86.8
1919	0.0	13.9	86.2
1920	0 0	18.6	81.4
1921	0.0	20.4	79.6
1922	0.0	14.8	85.2
1923	0.0	16.1	83.9
1924	0.0	11.4	88.7
1925	0.0	14.0	86.0
1926	0.0	12.5	87.6
1927	0.0	11.8	88.2
1928	0.0	10.5	89.5
1929	0.0	11.2	88.8
1930	0.0	13.1	86.8
1931	0.0	13.5	86.5
1932	0.0	13.3	86.7
1933	0.0	12.8	87.2
1934	0.0	20.2	79.8
1935	0.0	18.9	81.1
1936	1.1	24.2	74.9
1937	1.2	25.3	73.6
1938	2.0	30.5	67.5
1939	1.8	27.4	70.9
1940	1.9	30.8	67.3
1941	5.1	39.9	55.0
1942	8.3	44.1	47.6
1943	7.7	45.9	46.4
1944	7.4	45.6	47.0
1945	6.7	47.2	46.3
1946	5.7	44.6	49.7
1947	5.0	43.3	51.7
1948	3.2	35.2	61.7
1949	4.1	36.4	59.4
1950	2.9	34.0	63.2
1951	3.1	37.2	59.6
1952	3.4	40.9	55.8
1953	3.7	43.5	52.7
EXCLUDING FIDUCIARIES			
1954	2.1	38.5	59.4
1955	1.6	35.5	62.9
1956	1.5	36.1	62.4
1957	1.6	36.6	61.8

CHART 5

Percentage Breakdown of Dividend Tax Liability by Income Classes, 1918–1957

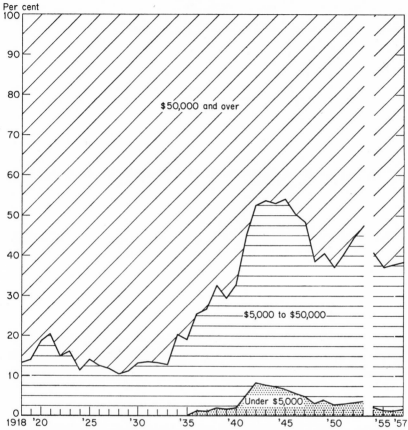

NOTE: From 1954 on, tax liability is for individuals only; in prior years it is for individuals and fiduciaries.

centage set in. It reached a low of 46 per cent in 1945, but has tended to rise since.

In analyzing the proportion of total taxable dividends reported in the various income classes earlier in this study, we concluded that there had been long swings in the distribution—the share of the uppermost classes rose up to 1929, fell up through 1943, and then rose thereafter; the share of the middle groups remained substantially the

129

same, and the proportion going to the lowest income classes moved opposite to the uppermost class share. In the case of the dividend tax liability, too, we find a pattern of long swings. And, as one would expect in going from income to tax liability, the swings in the income class shares of total dividend tax liability were more pronounced. Again we remind the reader of our earlier warning that the evidence for money income classes over periods of sharply varying price and income levels is ambiguous.

Share of Dividend Tax Liability in Total Tax Liability

The importance of the dividend tax liability in relation to total tax liability is different for each income class. The results depend on the relative importance of dividends in adjusted gross income qualified by: (1) the fact that up to 1936 dividend receipts were exempt from normal tax and (2) the exclusion and credit introduced in 1954. The data assembled under a few broad income groupings are presented in Table 37 and are plotted on Chart 6.

The point of most obvious interest in connection with taxpayers in the under-$5,000 group is that, through 1935, their dividend receipts were responsible for none of the personal income tax liability levied on them. From 1936 through 1940 dividend tax comprised a more substantial percentage of total tax liability for this group, but afterward fell to an insignificant level. Through 1935, because dividends were excluded from normal tax income, in the other two broad income classes the ratio of dividend tax liability to total tax liability was lower than the proportionate share of dividends in adjusted gross income. Since 1936, however, for all income classes, the dividend tax liability has been a higher percentage of total personal income tax liability than dividends have been of adjusted gross income. This represents the result of a conceptual decision on our part. In our method the presumed tax saving due to certain income types, e.g., partnership losses, is offset against the tax liability due to the positive income from this source—the tax liability is taken as a net amount for these income types, which means that for those income shares that have no negative counterpart, such as dividends, for instance, the effective tax rate is computed as higher than that on the total adjusted gross income in this class.

TABLE 37

Dividend Tax Liability as a Percentage of Total Personal Income Tax Liability, 1918–1957

		Income Class	
Year	Under $5,000	$5,000 to $50,000	$50,000 and over
1918	0.0	10.5	40.8
1919	0.0	9.3	32.9
1920	0.0	10.5	40.3
1921	0.0	11.7	44.3
1922	0.0	9.5	39.4
1923	0.0	10.1	43.0
1924	0.0	10.9	41.6
1925	0.0	11.2	28.9
1926	0.0	12.7	35.8
1927	0.0	12.6	33.3
1928	0.0	11.3	25.7
1929	0.0	16.0	28.6
1930	0.0	19.0	53.9
1931	0.0	20.1	70.4
1932	0.0	14.5	77.2
1933	0.0	10.7	53.5
1934	0.0	19.3	61.0
1935	0.0	17.9	55.6
1936	9.2	29.0	56.7
1937	9.2	31.3	63.3
1938	8.9	26.2	50.4
1939	7.5	27.1	60.8
1940	5.4	26.6	56.5
1941	3.6	20.3	44.2
1942	2.0	14.3	29.6
1943	1.1	11.3	25.4
1944	1.0	9.7	26.4
1945	0.9	8.9	23.9
1946	1.1	9.0	26.5
1947	0.9	9.7	33.3
1948	0.7	7.0	28.7
1949	1.1	8.4	37.1
1950	0.9	8.1	34.9
1951	0.8	6.4	32.0
1952	0.8	5.6	31.9
1953	0.9	5.0	32.0
EXCLUDING FIDUCIARIES			
1953	0.8	4.6	30.3
1954	0.5	4.1	29.1
1955	0.4	3.4	28.8
1956	0.4	3.3	28.8
1957	0.4	3.2	29.6

Dividends Under the Income Tax

CHART 6

Tax Liability Attributable to Dividends as a Percentage of Total Personal Income Tax Liability, by Income Classes, 1918–1957

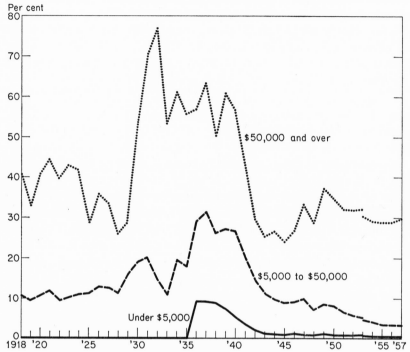

NOTE: From 1954 on, tax liability is for individuals only; in prior years it is for individuals and fiduciaries.

Effective Tax Rates on Dividends Compared with Other Sources of Property Income

Starting in 1936 and continuing through 1953, dividends were subject to the same tax provisions and rates as the other sources of property income (except for tax-exempt interest and capital gains).[9] Earlier, however, the exemption of dividends from normal tax meant a substantially lower rate on this income source as compared with, say, fully taxable interest. How great a difference it was can be seen from Table 38, which also shows in the 1956 panel the effect of the exclusion and

[9] This statement neglects, of course, any consideration of the corporate tax load on earnings made for dividend payments.

credit introduced in 1954. For dividends per se, the relief provided in these periods of special tax treatment was relatively more powerful the lower the taxpayer's income class. For the more recent set of special tax provisions for dividends, the degree of relief does not vary among income classes as much as it did in the pre-1936 tax treatment. On the other hand, the absolute amount (number of percentage points of effective rate) of relief increased with taxpayer's income in the earlier period, but appears to be fairly constant from class to class for the Internal Revenue Code of 1954 provisions. Reverting to the relative lightening of the tax liability on dividends, it is interesting to note that in the three highest income classes, the relative difference between dividends and regular income, here summarized by fully taxable interest, is about the same for 1935 and 1956.

Comparisons of the type embodied in Table 38 are inexact at best, for the income classes, particularly the higher ones, are so broad that some of the difference in dividend taxation will be obscured by the effective rate variations between dividends and interest attributable to the different distribution within a given income class of the two types of income. But a more serious criticism is that these data do not focus on the real issue. What would have happened to stockholders' income and taxes had there not been a corporation income tax, i.e., had there been only one tax on corporate earnings? Comparisons of this sort barely scratch the surface of that thorny problem—the "double taxation of dividends" and related matters. It is to this subject that the next chapter is devoted. Before turning to this, however, it is convenient to take up here the corporate income tax liability which, together with the personal income tax liability attributable to dividends, makes up the total tax liability on corporate earnings. But these data as presented directly below are not the most germane to the problem of "double taxation."

Tax Liability on Corporate Earnings

For the federal tax structure, the theme pursued in this chapter can be extended: on the income side we can go from dividends to total corporate earnings (before any taxes); and on the tax side we can obtain the total income tax liability on corporate earnings by adding annually the corporation income tax to the personal income tax liability attributable to dividend receipts. In a general sense, then, we

Dividends Under the Income Tax

TABLE 38

COMPARISON OF EFFECTIVE RATES ON FULLY TAXABLE INTEREST AND DIVIDENDS,
1924, 1929, 1935, AND 1956

(per cent)

Income Class (thousand dollars)	1924			1929		
	Fully Taxable Interest	Divi-dends	Dividend Rate as a Percent of Rate on Fully Taxable Interest	Fully Taxable Interest	Divi-dends	Dividend Rate as a Percent of Rate on Fully Taxable Interest
Under 2	0.4	0.0	. . .	0.1	0.0	. . .
2 to 3	0.5	0.0	. . .	0.1	0.0	. . .
3 to 5	0.4	0.0	. . .	0.1	0.0	. . .
5 to 10	1.0	0.0	. . .	0.3	0.0	. . .
10 to 25	2.9	0.6	21	1.7	0.6	35
25 to 50	6.9	3.5	51	5.3	3.2	60
50 to 100	12.5	8.9	71	9.1	6.7	74
100 to 500	23.1	19.5	84	14.6	11.8	81
500 and over	30.9	27.9	90	18.7	15.6	83

Income Class (thousand dollars)	1935			1956		
	Fully Taxable Interest	Divi-dends	Dividend Rate as a Percent-age of Rate on Fully Taxable Interest	Fully Taxable Interest	Divi-dends	Dividend Rate as a Percent-age of Rate on Fully Taxable Interest
Under 2	0.9	0.0	. . .	7.3	5.0	68
2 to 3	1.2	0.0	. . .	7.5	4.8	64
3 to 5	1.0	. . . [a]	. . .	7.7	4.5	58
5 to 10	2.1	0.5	24	10.7	6.9	64
10 to 25 [b]	5.4	3.2	59	15.8	11.9	75
25 to 50 [c]	11.1	8.6	77	25.1	20.7	82
50 to 100	19.0	16.4	86	35.9	32.1	89
100 to 500	33.9	32.3	95	44.9	42.1	94
500 and over	46.2	44.1	95	55.4	52.9	95

[a] Less than 0.5 per cent.
[b] 10 to 20.
[c] 20 to 50.

would be talking about corporate earnings and the tax liability attributable to them. This latter, of course, can also be considered the taxes "paid out of" corporate earnings. On the assumption that the incidence of corporate taxes is on profits, and the incidence of personal income tax on the taxpayer, this section will compare the amount of income generated for stockholders with the amount of income accruing to stockholders after taxes on this income source. And by considering the corporate tax and the relevant portion of the personal income tax as a combined income tax on corporate earnings, we can also address ourselves to this question: What proportion of total federal income tax revenue has come from corporate earnings, and how does this compare with the proportion that corporate earnings represent of income generated in the course of production? (We neglect, however, the capital gains tax liability on capital gains due to retained earnings.)

The intent here is merely to assess the importance of this income component as a revenue source, *not* to suggest that corporate earnings are inequitably or unequally taxed. Before a judgment could be reached on this latter matter, a standard of equity or "appropriate" taxation would have to be established. Corporate earnings would have to be related to the taxpaying capacity ("ability to pay") of the beneficial owners or corporate enterprise, and the actual tax load at selected stockholder income levels under the combined corporate-personal income tax could then be compared with what the tax liability would then have been had corporate earnings fully and promptly been subject to the personal income tax alone.[10]

But here our procedure simply is to sum up corporate tax liability and that portion of the personal income tax liability attributable to dividend receipts and relate this to the total income tax liability—corporate plus personal.[11] (In other words, the latter total differs from

[10] In Chapter 4 such comparisons are made for the distributed component of corporate earnings, and there is a relatively brief consideration of all corporate earnings, both distributed and retained. The whole question is discussed at length and relevant measurements are provided in the author's study, *The Income-Tax Burden on Stockholders.*

[11] The reader will appreciate that this is a rough and ready method, the results of which are only indicative. There is no need to list its shortcomings in detail. Briefly, however, no adjustment is made in the annual figures because of dividends from earnings of prior years (although such a correction would probably not change the figures much); nor is any account taken in the tax liability on corporate earnings figure for the capital gains tax that would be due in later years should a stockholder realize gains on corporate shares that have risen in value because of the reinvestment of earnings of earlier years. As another qualification, we talk about

the former by inclusion of all personal income tax liability rather than merely that incurred on dividends.) Viewed in this framework, it appears that over the whole of our period, corporate earnings have constituted a very important source of income tax revenue (Table 39). Anywhere from 81 per cent of total income tax revenue in 1931 to 40 per cent in 1946 came from corporate earnings. The broad swing has been downward. Taking the whole of our period, it can be described this way: The fraction that corporate earnings tax liability represented of total tax liability ran at between one-half and two-thirds in the twenties, at between two-thirds and three-quarters in the thirties, and from two-fifths to one-half in the forties and fifties. The results since 1940, of course, follow from the great expansion that has occurred in the personal income tax. But although they have constituted a small fraction of national income, corporate earnings are still the major revenue producer among the sources of income. In recent years, with corporate earnings running at from 10 to 15 per cent of national income, personal and corporate income taxes on corporate earnings were responsible, as noted, for between one-half and two-fifths of total income tax liabilities.

Thus we can say that currently corporate earnings contribute between three and four times as much to tax liability as to income, and that in earlier years the ratio was considerably higher (Table 39, column 3).

We end on the note on which we began. This is presented simply as a statistic, nothing more. For given the progressive personal income tax as the benchmark and the very concentrated distribution of corporate earnings, there is nothing outlandish or necessarily inequitable in these disparate proportions of tax liability and income. That is to say, if we define equity or "appropriate" taxation of income in terms of the scale of progressive rates Congress establishes, then the tax liabilities of Table 39 are not necessarily inequitable. Aggregates, at best, cast little light on this question. The next chapter of this book will venture a little into this area. The reader who desires to go still further might look at the book cited in footnote 10 above.

tax liabilities incurred on the income of a given year, not the taxes actually collected in that year. Finally, the results given in Table 39 mirror not only corporate and personal tax rates (and hence, of course, the concentration of the dividend distribution), but also the fact that, even though in the aggregate corporate earnings are negative in some years, income corporations paid a tax.

TABLE 39

COMPARISON OF CONTRIBUTIONS OF CORPORATE EARNINGS TO TAX LIABILITY
AND TO NATIONAL INCOME, 1918–1957

Year	Combined Personal-Corporate Tax on Corporate Earnings as a Per Cent of Total Income Tax Liability (1)	Corporate Earnings as a Per Cent of National Income (2)	Ratio of Col. 1 to Col. 2 (3)
1918	53.0	a	—
1919	50.8	a	—
1920	51.2	a	—
1921	50.0	a	—
1922	60.0	a	—
1923	68.9	a	—
1924	68.6	a	—
1925	70.4	a	—
1926	73.3	a	—
1927	69.3	a	—
1928	61.5	a	—
1929	66.3	11.0	6.0
1930	77.0	4.6	16.7
1931	81.3	−1.4	b
1932	69.2	−7.3	b
1933	68.1	0.4	170.2
1934	72.1	3.5	20.6
1935	70.4	5.5	12.8
1936	71.8	8.9	8.1
1937	75.2	8.5	8.8
1938	70.1	5.0	14.0
1939	74.8	8.7	8.6
1940	76.8	11.4	6.7
1941	72.4	15.8	4.6
1942	62.6	15.0	4.2
1943	55.9	14.4	3.9
1944	51.4	12.7	4.0
1945	42.6	10.4	4.1
1946	40.2	12.2	3.3
1947	42.6	14.5	3.0
1948	48.8	14.6	3.3
1949	46.8	12.2	3.8
1950	53.8	16.4	3.3
1951	52.0	15.0	3.5
1952	45.0	12.6	3.6
1953	44.1	12.5	3.5
1954	42.6	11.3	3.6
1955	45.8	14.0	3.8
1956	43.0	12.9	3.3
1957	40.3	11.7	3.4

SOURCE: Tax liability: *Statistics of Income*, Parts 1 and 2, and National Bureau of Economic Research Personal Income Tax Study. Corporate earnings and national income: *U.S. Income and Output*, p. 127, Table I-8. Corporate earnings line 19, national income line 1 minus line 24 (i.e., national income is adjusted by adding back the inventory valuation adjustment); for 1956 and 1957, *Survey of Current Business*, July 1960.

a Not available.
b Minus figure.

CHAPTER 4

"Double Taxation" of Dividends, Differential Taxation of Stockholders, and Income Tax Relief

Taxation of Corporate Earnings

To discuss the personal income tax on dividends and neglect the fact that the corporate earnings out of which dividends are paid have been taxed at the corporate level, as in the first part of Chapter 3, does not get at the heart of stockholder taxation. To proceed, as in the latter part of Chapter 3, to take account of corporate earnings and the corporation income tax without relating them to the individual's "capacity to pay" and combined income tax burden fails to remedy this deficiency.

This chapter is addressed directly to the problem of the differential income tax burden on stockholders. First, the "double taxation" of dividends is examined, and then the broader question of the taxation of corporate earnings whether distributed or retained is taken up. Finally there is a discussion of the income tax relief for stockholders introduced in 1954 which Congress was asked by President Kennedy (April 1961) to repeal. All that follows, unless otherwise specified, is based on the tax incidence assumption implicit in the charge of "double taxation" of dividends (or corporate earnings), viz., that the incidence of the corporate income tax is on stockholders via a direct and commensurate reduction in the corporate earnings available to them. Thus we steer clear of two unsettled issues: (1) who in fact bears the corporate tax, and (2) to what degree the tax has been capitalized, i.e., to what degree present holders have purchased their stock at a price lower, by the discounted value of all expected future tax payments, than that which would have prevailed. With the tax so capitalized, those who are burdened by it would be those who held stock at the time the tax was imposed; those who hold stock presently would in many cases have purchased their shares "free of tax."

As to incidence, I claim no special knowledge, accept it as a matter requiring further investigation, and adopt the nonshifting assumption first because it is the assumption implicit in the much-used phrase "double taxation," and secondly because it has not, in my judgment, been disproved. If the corporate tax is shifted it resembles a sales tax and/or tax on productive services and the analysis that follows is inappropriate.

Concerning capitalization of the tax, I am unable to go any further than other tax burden studies have gone with this problem, but suggest that this may not be as severe a handicap as has sometimes been assumed.

To the question whether, in fact, the corporate income tax is capitalized and to what degree, it is impossible to find a quantitative answer or even some general consensus on broad ranges of magnitudes. Thus, while Dan T. Smith has pointed out that an "increase in the corporation income tax, assuming a constant price-earnings ratio for the stock, will depress the price of the stock commensurately,"[1] one cannot (and he does not) stop there. Crucial to the argument in this precise form is the assumption of a constant price-earnings ratio, i.e., a constant capitalization rate. But it is unlikely that this will actually be the case. For the corporate tax cuts such a wide swath that its repercussions will affect the rate by which the capital value of assets is reckoned; in other words, it is of the nature of a general tax whereas the capitalization argument strictly applies to a partial tax—a tax that affects one industry or type of asset.

Smith[2] has noted a number of qualifications to the simple capitalization argument:

> The exact relationship between changes in corporate income tax rates and stock prices is vastly involved. Though prospective earnings per share are probably the most important single factor influencing the market value of most securities, they are certainly not the only, or even at all times the dominant, one. Present dividends,

[1] Dan Throop Smith, *Effects of Taxation: Corporate Financial Policy,* Boston, 1952, p. 87.
[2] *Ibid.,* pp. 86–87.

book value, estimated liquidating value, and prospective changes in all of these are among the other interrelated factors which make impossible any assurance about the precise effects of changes in tax rates on market values.

Also, any general readjustment of stock prices arising from a change in corporate income tax rates would lead to significant but quantitatively indeterminate changes in the yields of other forms of investments, with inevitable readjustment in investors' portfolios and a new pattern of yield differentials. Even more fundamentally, a full analysis of the effects of corporate taxation is complicated by such important but very elusive problems as the effects of the government expenditures financed by the tax on the general level and direction of economic activity and the comparative effects of alternative revenue sources. These more involved analytical problems can only be noted here as important qualifications to any simple conclusions on the extent of influence of corporate income taxation on stock prices.

His comments on capitalization point up how complicated the problem is. However, they permit these conclusions: First, for any degree of capitalization to occur the initial incidence of the corporation income tax must be on stockholders; secondly, whether the corporation income tax is capitalized and, if so, to what extent remains a problem fraught with uncertainty.

Moreover, is capitalization all important? Even if it had occurred, it would have been uneven for various persons and would have been, in general, a transitional phenomenon. If one is concerned with equality of tax treatment for different sources of income and not necessarily with specific persons, then capitalization appears in a somewhat different light. For, to the extent that it has occurred, alleviation of the extra burden on distributed earnings would call for an accompanying capital gains tax to recapture the windfall gains of those who had purchased their stocks free of tax.

On this point Professor Carl S. Shoup says: [3]

Have present owners of common stock, by and large, purchased their holdings, either from former holders, or from issuing corporations, with no expectation whatsoever of diminution in extra taxation? This is surely one of the most difficult factual questions ever

[3] "The Dividend Exclusion and Credit in the Revenue Code of 1954," *National Tax Journal*, March 1955, p. 144.

posed in contemporary public finance. But if the answer were strongly in the affirmative, the case for reducing extra taxation on already outstanding issues of common stocks would be weak, from the viewpoint of tax equity. Those whom the extra taxation had truly harmed—the former holders of common stocks and those who were deterred from buying new issues—can no longer be identified and recompensed for the tax injustice.

This point does not, of course, weigh against reducing the extra taxation with respect to new stock issues if there are any practicable means of making such a distinction. And I am inclined to think that the era of high tax rates and high extra taxation has not yet lasted so long that more bonus would be given than injustice remedied by granting the privilege to outstanding issues. Here we are on highly subjective grounds. In any case, the problem would be mitigated if approximately full taxation of capital gains could be achieved before a truly substantial (dividend tax) credit was put into effect.

Now, back to the problem at hand. Taking into account both the distributed and retained components of the corporate earnings of a given year, and relating them proportionately to stockholder claimants thereof, we may say that at no time since 1913 has our income tax structure (corporate and personal combined) led to complete equivalence of tax liability for corporate earnings and other categories of income. But, for the distributed component alone which is our prime concern in this section, equivalence was initially sought.

The personal income tax act of 1913 exempted dividends from normal tax. Both the tax rate on corporate income and the normal tax rate on personal income were set at 1 per cent; thus for distributed earnings the corporate tax operated as a withholding feature of the personal levy. In effect there was a legislative admission (or assumption) that the corporation income tax was a tax on the stockholder. This treatment continued through 1918, as increases in the personal normal rate were matched by increases in the corporate rate.[4] But after 1919 the corporate rate exceeded the personal normal rate and thus the corporate tax became, in part, a separate and distinct levy on distributed corporate earnings. The rate gap widened gradually until 1936, when the bridge between the two taxes was removed completely

---

[4] With these exceptions: a corporate rate greater than the personal normal rate in 1917, and greater than the rate applicable to the first $4,000 of normal tax income in 1918.

by the abolition of the dividend exemption. A return to legislation that gave some recognition to the idea of "double taxation" appears in the Internal Revenue Code of 1954 in the form of a tax credit based on dividends received. But here, too, a substantial gap exists between the personal income tax credit and the rate of corporate tax. Therefore, since 1919 the distributed earnings of corporate enterprises have been treated differently from the other sources of income for federal income tax purposes: from 1919 through 1935, because the corporate rate was higher than the personal normal rate; from 1936 through 1953, because corporate earnings were taxed at the corporate level when earned with no allowance at the personal level when distributed; and from 1954 on, because the personal income tax relief accorded distributed earnings falls short of the corporate tax rate.

Of course, especially in the earlier years of the income tax, because both personal and corporate rates were "low," the failure to achieve a tax treatment for distributed earnings equivalent to that for other income shares might have had "slight" consequences. And, naturally, much more severe disparities could be expected with the rapid rise of tax rates in the last twenty years. The magnitudes associated with this lack of uniformity in tax treatment will be explored shortly. First, however, it is necessary to explain some conceptual procedures. This can most conveniently be done by referring to the situation that existed from 1936 through 1953. Then qualifications relevant to the earlier period and the more recent modifications can be examined separately.

Conceptual Framework [5]

1936–1953

We are interested in developing a measure of the degree to which distributed corporate earnings have been differentially taxed. For simplicity, we start with the relation that characterized the period 1936 through 1953. Over these years dividends upon receipt by the stockholder were subject in full to personal income tax rates, while the

[5] The main outlines of this conceptual framework are not novel. In setting it up, I have drawn on the work of previous investigators, in particular: Richard B. Goode, *The Corporation Income Tax,* New York, 1951; *The Postwar Corporation Tax Structure,* Washington, 1946; and W. L. Crum, "The Taxation of Stockholders," *Quarterly Journal of Economics,* February 1950.

The considerations set out here are discussed at greater length in Holland, *Income-Tax Burden,* Chapter 1.

earnings out of which dividends were paid had already been taxed at the corporate level. This differs from other corporate payments such as wages or interest which were free of corporate tax. Hence the charge of "double taxation of dividends." But literally interpreted this charge is wrong, since it is not dividends but the earnings permitting their payment which were taxed twice. And the charge is not very informative since it seems to suggest an equally onerous extra burden on all stockholders regardless of their level of income.

For our problem, dividends are not the relevant component of stockholders' income. Rather, in estimating the reduction caused, in potentially disposable income, by this tax, we must work with the pre-tax equivalent of distributed earnings, to which we give the title of earnings for distribution. Assuming for simplicity a corporate tax rate of 50 per cent, then for every dollar of dividends paid out, corporations must earn two dollars. If a given stockholder, therefore, has $100 of dividends, the earnings-for-distribution component of his income will be $200. The difference between earnings for distribution and dividends measures the corporate tax on the distributed segment of net corporate earnings. To this is added the personal income tax on dividends (considered an increment to the stockholder's taxable income from other sources) in order to obtain the total income tax actually levied on earnings for distribution.

But this does not measure the differential tax load. For the personal income taxpayer is not deprived of an amount of potential income equal to the corporate tax payment on earnings for distribution. Had this sum been paid to him instead of to the government, it would have been taxable as personal income. So it is only the difference between the corporate tax and the product of the corporate tax multiplied by the marginal rate of personal income tax that represents the extra burden on stockholders' earnings for distribution. For example, with the corporate rate at 50 per cent, every dollar of earnings for distribution bears a 50-cent corporate tax, but had this 50 cents been paid to stockholders it would have represented something less than a 50-cent addition to their personal income after tax. If the relevant marginal rate is 20 per cent, the deprivation due to the corporate tax will be 40 cents; if the potential marginal rate is 90 per cent, the corporate tax causes a loss of potential disposable income of only 5 cents. Thus in our measure of the extra burden on dividend recipients the potential personal income tax on earnings for distribution is computed and subtracted from the actual combined corporate-personal income tax

143

on that component of stockholder income to find the net extra burden on the distributed portion of net corporate earnings. For comparisons among income levels and between years, which will be undertaken later in this chapter, the absolute extra burden was converted to an incremental effective rate by taking it as a percentage of the earnings for the distribution component of stockholders' income. We call this measure the differential against earnings for distribution.

The derivation of the measure may be summarized symbolically as follows (for simplicity, all tax rates and differentials are expressed as ratios):

C_e = effective rate of corporate tax on earnings for distribution

D = dividends received

E = earnings for distribution; $E - C_e E = D$

P = applicable marginal rate of personal income tax [6]

N_e = absolute extra burden on earnings for distribution

$\dfrac{N_e}{E}$ = differential against earnings for distribution.

Then

$$N_e = PD + C_e E - PE$$
$$= PD + C_e E - (PD + PC_e E)$$
$$= C_e E(1 - P)$$
$$\frac{N_e}{E} = C_e(1 - P).$$

Since P rises as stockholder income rises but never reaches 100 per cent, the differential against earnings for distribution is a declining function of stockholders' income, but is always positive. In relation to the distributed segment of net corporate earnings, then, the corporate tax constitutes a burden that is always smaller than its face amount and that varies inversely with the level of stockholders' income.

[6] The relevant P here varies with stockholder taxable income level. Better notation, therefore, would be P_i with i running from zero to the top tax rate. However, for reasons that will become clearer when we consider other years as well as the extra burden (or benefit) on earnings for retention, precision would require quite complicated notation.

Double Taxation, Differential Taxation, and Tax Relief

1913–1935

The remarks above apply strictly to the years 1936–1953. They need some modifications for earlier years when dividends were exempt from personal normal tax (and from 1954 on because of the exclusion and credit). Specifically, prior to 1954 the extra burden on earnings for distribution was not always positive. In other words, stockholders sometimes paid a smaller tax on their share of earnings for distribution then would have been due had these earnings been singly taxed in full as part of their personal income.

To apply the formula developed above to this earlier period, we need explicitly to take account of personal normal and surtax rates. Therefore, let:

P_n = normal rate of personal income tax

P_s = applicable surtax rate of personal income tax;

rewrite the formula above as

$$N_e = P_n D + P_s D + C_e E - (P_n E + P_s E).$$

Now consider the situation as it existed in the first few years of the income tax—i.e., when the corporate rate and the personal normal rate were the same, and start with a "low" income stockholder not subject to the surtax. The equivalence of the two rates means that $C_e E$ equals $P_n E$, the nonapplicability of the surtax eliminates the P_s terms, and the exemption of dividends from normal tax gets rid of $P_n D$, leaving no "extra" burden; N_e is equal to zero. But a different result applies for the stockholder whose income was high enough to get him into a surtax bracket.[7] Then, $C_e E$ and $P_n E$ would wash out of the formula as before (with corporate and personal normal rates equal) and $P_n D$ would drop out as explained, leaving $N_e = P_s D - P_s E$. But clearly E is always greater than D. Note that the difference between D and E is precisely the corporate tax. It is the failure to include the corporate tax payment in taxable personal income that leads to this tax benefit. Under these conditions, therefore, the "extra" burden would always be negative. Compare, for example, for 1916 the zero differential at the $1,000 income level (not subject to surtax) with the tax benefit (negative differential) of 0.2 per cent at the $500,000 income level in Table 41.

[7] Up through 1916, the surtax was applicable to net incomes of $20,000 and over.

We have failed so far to take account of those years—a large majority of the years between 1913 and 1936—in which the corporate tax rate and the personal normal rate were different. For formal completeness we might examine both $P_n > C$ and $P_n < C$, but since during this period when they were not equal the corporate rate always exceeded the personal normal rate, the latter is the only case that will be considered. As before, we start with the no surtax situation first. Then, in the formulae above, everything falls out except $C_e E - P_n E$. With C_e greater than P_n, N_e will always be positive, i.e., stockholders would always be "overtaxed" on their earnings for distribution. This conclusion, however, would not necessarily apply to those dividend recipients who were subject to surtax as well as normal tax. For we now must add to the value of N_e a term $P_s D - P_s E$ which, since E exceeds D, is always negative. With this as an offset to $C_e E - P_n E$, which is always positive, then in the case where personal surtax applies with corporate tax higher than personal normal tax, there may be "overtaxation," "undertaxation," or equal taxation, depending on the relative size of the positive and negative terms.

We can, of course, say this much more: Since $P_s E$ equals $P_s D + P_s(C_e E)$, then $P_s D$ drops out and, after division by E, the negative term becomes $P_s(C_e)$. Also, dividing by E, $C_e E - P_n E$ becomes merely $C_e - P_n$. Therefore: As between years, the greater the excess of C_e over P_n, the more likely overtaxation at any given income level, while in any particular year, the higher the applicable P_s, the greater $P_s(C_e)$, and the more probable undertaxation (i.e., a negative N_e). Since P_s is a function of stockholders' income, we can rephrase this conclusion to the effect that the higher the stockholders' income, the more likely is a negative differential against his earnings for distribution.

Again, to illustrate with data from Table 41: Note the 1.5 per cent negative differential at $100,000 in 1922, and the 8.5 percentage points of "overtaxation" at $1,000 of taxable income.

SINCE 1954

The tax burden on dividend recipients was lowered in two ways in 1954. President Eisenhower originally proposed relief of this order of magnitude: "Specifically, I recommend that the credit be allowed on an increasing scale over the next three years. For this year, I recommend that a credit of 5 per cent be allowed; for 1955, a credit of 10 per cent; and, in 1956 and later years, 15 per cent. To avoid shifts in the payment dates of corporation dividends, these credits should apply to dividends received after July 31, of each year. To give the full benefit immediately to small stockholders, I recommend that the first $50 of dividends be completely exempted from tax in 1954 and that the first $100 be exempted in 1955 and later years." [8]

This proposal proved to be one of the thorniest and most controversial considered in writing the revenue bill. After hearings and debate, Congress followed the outlines of the President's suggestion but set the amounts at a lower level. Marion B. Folsom, then Under Secretary of the Treasury, noted, "Under the new Code each stockholder will be permitted to exclude from his gross income up to $50 of dividends and will be allowed a credit against tax equal to 4 per cent of the dividends in excess of the exclusion. The amount of the credit is limited to 2 per cent of the stockholders' total taxable income in 1954 and to 4 per cent in later years." [9]

The formula at the start of this section that summarized the "extra" burden, viz., $N_e/E = C_e(1 - P)$, now must be adjusted because of the relief provisions. First, we take up the credit. Recall that $D = E - C_eE$. Therefore the credit which is equal to 0.04D, also equals as a rate (i.e., after division by E) $0.04 - 0.04(C_e)$, and with C_e equal to 52 per cent,[10] this comes to 0.0192. So at all income levels, the "extra" burden is lowered by 1.92 percentage points.[11] (It is worth noting that had President Eisenhower's original proposal been adopted, currently the credit would amount to 15 per cent of dividends or 7.2 cents per dollar of earnings for distribution; this would provide a net tax benefit at higher income levels.) Because of the credit, we adjust downward our

[8] *The Budget of the United States Government for the Fiscal Year Ending June 30, 1955*, Washington, 1954, p. M 18.

[9] Remarks by Marion B. Folsom, Under Secretary of the Treasury, before the American Management Association, New York City, August 19, 1954. The $50 exclusion applies to separate returns. Stockholders filing jointly are permitted an exclusion of $100, if each has at least $50 of dividends. See *Internal Revenue Code of 1954*, Public Law 591, Chapter 736, Sections 34 and 116.

[10] The use of a 52 per cent rate, of course, is a gross simplification. Only in the limit is this 52 per cent approached, although for large corporations it is approached closely enough to be a realistic figure. Many corporations pay only 30 per cent. The average rate on all corporations was less than 43 per cent in 1956. But some corporations, those filing consolidated returns, may pay close to 54 per cent. Moreover, there are numerous special provisions and tax rates. In sum, the average rate (effective rate) on corporations in the aggregate is well below 52 per cent; the marginal rate in the aggregate is probably quite close to 52 per cent.

[11] This is the same as saying that since, with a corporate tax of 52 per cent, $D = 0.48$ of E, the credit of 0.04D equals 0.0192 or 1.92 percentage points.

measure of the differential (the "extra" burden as a rate) against earnings for distribution; i.e., it now reads

$$\frac{N_e}{E} = C_e(1 - P) - 0.04(1 - C_e).$$

The credit, of course, will lower the differential by a flat amount (as noted above, under existing law, assuming the full corporate rate of 52 per cent to apply, the differential will be cut by 1.92 percentage points). But the differential itself varies inversely with P, i.e., with the stockholder's taxable income. Thus near the bottom of the income scale the credit would be responsible for a very slight relative reduction in the differential; near the top of the income scale, however, we should expect to find the "extra" burden reduced by a substantial percentage. This feature of the credit is somewhat obscured in comparing the *Statistics of Income* data from tax returns for 1953 and 1955 (the first year in which the full credit was operative) because tax rate changes between these two years, particularly the decline in personal income tax rates, tended, *ceteris paribus*, to make for higher differentials in 1955 than 1953.

The credit, as we have just observed, gives a flat amount of relief at all stockholder income levels, and thus is not directly geared to the condition for which it is designed to provide relief. But the exclusion is even less focused on the problem. For, like any deduction, it is the more valuable the higher the applicable marginal rates of tax, while the differential declines in severity the higher the stockholder's marginal rate of tax.[12] But limited to a specific amount of dividends, the exclusion has a strong effect only on those who receive a small amount of dividends. In our tabular comparisons for 1954–60, those related to marginal dollars (Table 41) neglect the exclusion completely (assuming the marginal dollar to come in above the exclusion), while those that are based on assuming all income to be corporate earnings (Table 40) tend to swamp out the exclusion's effect since it is limited to $100 of dividends at most.

For a more general statement, the exclusion and credit can be combined as follows: with the corporate tax at 52 per cent, earnings for

[12] For example, not paying tax on $1 of dividends saves 20 cents in the 20 per cent rate bracket and 90 cents in the 90 per cent rate bracket. Yet at the former level, the differential is 40 per cent (assuming, for simplicity, a corporate rate of 50 per cent) and only 5 per cent at the latter level.

TABLE 40

DIFFERENTIAL AS A PERCENTAGE OF EARNINGS FOR DISTRIBUTION, COMPUTED AT AVERAGE
RATES AT SELECTED TAXABLE INCOME LEVELS, 1913–1961 [a]

(per cent)

Year	\$1,000	\$3,000	\$5,000	\$10,000	\$25,000	\$50,000	\$100,000	\$500,000	\$1,000,000
				Taxable Income Level					
1913–1915	0.0	0.0	0.0	0.0	0.0	[c]	[e]	[g]	[h]
1916	0.0	0.0	0.0	0.0	[b]	[d]	[f]	−1.8	−2.0
1917	2.0	1.3	0.8	0.3	−0.2	−0.4	−0.8	−1.8	−2.2
1918	6.0	6.0	4.8	2.0	−0.3	−2.2	−5.2	−7.5	−7.7
1919–1921	6.0	6.0	5.2	3.3	1.6	0.1	−2.4	−4.3	−4.5
1922	8.5	8.5	7.7	6.0	4.0	2.2	−0.9	−1.7	−1.7
1923	9.5	9.5	8.9	7.6	6.7	4.8	2.5	1.8	1.8
1924	11.0	11.0	10.7	9.0	7.0	5.0	2.6	1.9	1.5
1925	11.8	11.9	11.6	10.4	8.2	6.9	5.8	5.4	5.4
1926–1927	12.3	12.4	12.2	10.9	8.6	7.4	6.2	5.8	5.4
1928	10.8	10.9	10.6	9.4	7.2	6.0	5.0	4.6	4.6
1929	10.6	10.6	10.4	9.3	6.4	5.7	5.1	4.8	4.8
1930–1931	10.8	10.9	10.6	9.4	7.2	6.0	5.0	4.6	4.6
1932–1933	9.8	9.7	9.9	7.2	5.2	3.2	−0.2	−1.4	−1.6
1934–1935	10.2	10.1	9.2	8.9	7.4	6.1	4.1	2.0	1.8
1936–1937	14.4	14.5	13.8	13.5	11.9	10.4	7.4	4.2	3.6
1938–1939	18.3	18.3	17.4	17.2	15.2	13.3	8.1	5.2	4.6
1940	23.4	23.1	22.1	20.9	16.3	12.9	9.1	5.1	3.9
1941	28.3	28.5	26.8	26.4	20.0	13.3	10.4	7.6	6.9
1942–1943	32.5	32.6	31.1	27.6	18.9	15.6	8.3	4.8	4.8
1944–1945	30.8	30.1	29.0	26.0	17.0	11.6	5.8	2.4	3.9
1946–1947	30.6	30.1	29.3	26.0	18.0	15.0	8.0	5.1	5.3
				SEPARATE RETURNS					
1948–1949	31.6	30.8	29.9	27.1	19.4	15.2	10.3	6.8	8.7 [i]
1950	34.6	33.8	32.8	29.9	21.4	16.1	10.6	6.6	8.4 [i]
1951	38.6	39.7	38.5	34.8	23.8	16.6	9.6	4.6	5.9 [i]
1952–1953	40.4	39.7	38.3	34.1	21.8	15.5	9.2	4.2	5.8 [i]
1954	40.9	40.2	38.7	35.1	24.0	16.5	9.1	3.7	5.2 [i]
1955–1961	38.9	38.7	37.7	34.1	23.0	15.5	8.1	2.6	4.2 [i]
				JOINT RETURNS					
1948–1949	31.6	31.7	31.7	29.4	25.3	16.7	15.2	9.2	6.8
1950	34.6	34.7	34.7	32.4	28.2	21.4	16.1	6.7	6.4
1951	38.6	39.7	40.2	38.5	34.6	23.8	16.6	4.9	4.6
1952–1953	40.4	40.5	39.8	38.3	32.8	21.0	15.5	4.6	4.0
1954	39.7	40.3	40.1	38.7	32.8	24.0	16.5	4.2	3.7
1955–1961	38.1	39.1	39.0	37.7	31.8	23.0	13.3	3.2	2.8

[a] Assumes all taxable income from earnings for distribution.
[b] −0.02.
[c] −0.01.
[d] −0.04.
[e] −0.03.
[f] −0.08.
[g] −0.05.
[h] −0.06.
[i] Effective rate limit in effect.

Dividends Under the Income Tax

Corporate taxes are taken at the highest rate, excluding excess profits tax. Dividends exempt from individuals' normal tax until 1936.

From 1924 through 1943 (excluding 1932, 1933) there was an earned income credit. In 1924 credit was against tax, while in other years against income.

Dividends and interest are treated the same way with respect to the credit.

From 1944 on, limitation on effective rate of tax comes into effect.

For 1954 $25 is deducted ($50 for joint) from taxable income and 2 per cent of dividends credited against tax.

For 1955–1961 $50 (and $100) exclusion and 4 per cent tax credit used.

distribution would be slightly more than twice as great as dividends, and the exclusion limits would then be $104 (i.e., the pre-tax equivalent of $50) for separate and $208 (i.e., the pre-tax equivalent of $100) for joint returns. For brevity, only joint returns (the majority) will be considered. The maximum relief afforded by the exclusion varies from $20 to $91, or from 20 to 91 per cent of the excluded amount. With the corporate tax at 52 per cent and dividends equal to 48 per cent of earnings for distribution (designated as E), the relief provided by the tax credit equals 0.04 $(0.48E - \$100)$ for all stockholders. Hence the combined relief, i.e., the sum of the credit and exclusion, covers a span from $0.02E + \$16$ for stockholders in the 20 per cent rate bracket to $0.02E + \$87$ for those subject to a marginal rate of 91 per cent; or, measured as a differential relative to E, from $0.02 + \$16/E$ to $0.02 + \$87/E$.

When E is small, say $250 (i.e., when dividends are $120), the fractions $\$16/E$ and $\$87/E$ will be considerably larger than 0.02 and noticeably different from each other. The exclusion feature will outweigh the credit. When E is large, say $100,000, the two fractions and the differences between them become insignificant. The credit predominates; the relief is very close to 2 per cent of earnings for distribution. We cannot, therefore, simply conclude that the patterns of relief described for the credit and exclusion separately will characterize their combination. The degree of relief will vary with the amount of what we have defined as earnings for distribution. This, of course, has reference only to comparisons of average (effective) rates and differentials based thereon (as in Table 40) but not to those comparisons concerned with marginal (incremental) dollars of earnings for distribution (as in Table 41).

TABLE 41

DIFFERENTIAL AS A PERCENTAGE OF EARNINGS FOR DISTRIBUTION, COMPUTED FOR MARGINAL
INCREMENTS AT SELECTED TAXABLE INCOME LEVELS, 1913–1961

(per cent)

Year	\$1,000	\$3,000	\$5,000	\$10,000	\$25,000	\$50,000	\$100,000	\$500,000	\$1,000,000
					Taxable Income Level				
1913–1915	0.0	0.0	0.0	0.0	a	c	b	d	d
1916	0.0	0.0	0.0	0.0	c	b	−0.1	−0.2	−0.2
1917	2.0	0.0	b	−0.1	−0.3	−0.5	−1.1	−2.0	−2.4
1918	6.0	6.0	−0.1	−0.5	−1.3	−2.9	−6.2	−7.7	−7.8
1919–1921	6.0	6.0	1.9	1.6	0.9	−0.4	−3.2	−4.4	−4.5
1922	8.5	8.5	4.5	4.3	3.3	1.6	−1.5	−1.8	−1.8
1923	9.5	9.5	6.5	6.3	5.6	4.3	2.0	1.8	1.8
1924	10.5	10.5	8.5	6.4	5.6	3.6	0.5	0.3	0.3
1925	11.5	11.5	10.0	7.9	7.1	6.3	5.4	5.4	5.4
1926–1927	12.0	12.0	10.5	8.4	7.6	6.7	5.8	5.8	5.8
1928	10.5	10.5	9.0	6.9	6.2	5.4	4.6	4.6	4.6
1929	10.5	10.5	9.0	6.9	6.2	5.8	4.8	4.8	4.8
1930–1931	10.5	10.5	9.0	6.9	6.2	5.4	4.6	4.6	4.6
1932–1933	9.8	9.8	5.8	5.5	4.4	2.6	−0.9	−1.5	−1.8
1934–1935	9.8	9.8	9.2	8.8	7.4	5.6	2.6	1.9	1.6
1936–1937	14.4	14.4	13.8	13.4	11.9	9.8	5.7	3.9	3.5
1938–1939	18.2	18.2	17.5	16.9	15.0	12.4	7.2	4.9	4.4
1940	22.9	22.9	21.9	20.3	15.8	11.3	7.6	4.5	3.7
1941	27.9	27.0	25.7	22.0	16.1	12.1	9.6	7.1	6.5
1942–1943	32.4	31.2	29.6	24.8	16.8	11.2	6.0	4.8	4.8
1944–1945	30.8	30.2	28.4	23.6	15.2	8.8	4.0	2.4	4.0
1946–1947	30.8	30.1	28.6	24.3	16.7	10.9	5.9	5.2	5.2
				SEPARATE RETURNS					
1948–1949	31.7	30.6	29.3	25.3	18.3	12.9	8.2	6.8	9.7
1950	34.7	33.6	32.1	27.5	21.5	13.3	8.0	6.6	8.4 e
1951	40.4	39.4	37.1	31.0	20.3	12.7	5.6	4.6	6.5 e
1952–1953	40.5	39.2	36.9	30.2	17.7	12.0	5.2	4.2	6.2 e
1954	40.7	39.6	37.5	31.3	20.4	12.0	4.8	3.7	5.3 e
1955–1961	39.7	38.6	36.6	30.3	19.4	11.1	3.8	2.8	2.8 e
				JOINT RETURNS					
1948–1949	31.7	31.7	30.6	29.3	23.6	18.3	12.9	6.8	6.8
1950	34.7	33.6	32.1	27.5	25.6	21.5	13.3	6.6	6.6
1951	40.4	40.4	39.4	37.1	28.9	20.3	12.7	4.6	4.6
1952–1953	40.5	40.5	39.2	36.9	27.0	17.7	12.0	4.2	4.2
1954	40.6	40.6	39.6	37.5	28.7	20.4	12.0	3.7	3.7
1955–1961	39.7	39.7	38.6	36.6	27.7	19.4	11.1	2.8	2.8

a 0.01.
b 0.04.
c 0.02.
d 0.06.
e Effective rate limit in effect.

151

Dividends Under the Income Tax

Highest corporate rate is applied each year excluding excess profits tax.

All reductions or increases in personal rates are included in rates. (E.g., for 1923 the 25 per cent refund is taken into account in computing the rates.)

Dividends excluded from normal tax until 1936.

Earned income credits are ignored.

In years where there is a limit to the effective rate, figures apply to limit rather than marginal rate. (E.g., in 1944–1945, 90 per cent limit applies to upper bracket.)

For 1954–1961 dividend exclusion provision is ignored since marginal rates on dividends assumed in excess of exclusions are being applied. In 1954, a 2 per cent credit is used, for 1955–1961 the credit is 4 per cent.

An Alternative Measure

There is, of course, nothing unique about the measure chosen. In my judgment it is simple, direct, and meaningful. Moreover, it can be easily and conveniently extended to the retained component of corporate earnings, as will be seen later in this chapter.

In particular, our measure of the differential relates the extra tax to the base on which it is levied—corporate earnings. There is nothing wrong with such a measure; indeed, it seems a natural thing to do. But it could be argued that to stop at this point is to leave part of the story untold. For another interesting and valid base is income *after* tax. At the very least it would be an incomplete presentation of the facts if we failed to consider the "extra" burden on stockholders in relation to income after tax; and it could be downright misleading to fail to do so.[13]

This is a convenient place to examine the "extra" burden in relation to income after tax. As a start, we restate the particular measure used so far and the effect of the dividend tax credit in more general terms. Then some comparisons using income after tax are made. The symbols are as defined earlier unless otherwise stated with these exceptions:

To avoid too much notation, what was C_e will be written more simply as C. Also, N_B will designate the extra burden before the credit; N_A will denote the extra burden after the relief provided by the credit.

1. "The" differential, i.e., our measure of the "extra" tax on earnings for distribution is:

[13] For a recent statement that stresses the necessity of analyzing tax liabilities and changes therein in relation to income both before and after tax, see Dan Throop Smith, *Federal Tax Reform*, New York, 1961, particularly page 37.

$$N_B = CE(1 - P)$$

and

$$\frac{N_B}{E} = C(1 - P)$$

also

$$N_A = CE(1 - P) - \alpha(E - CE)$$

$$\frac{N_A}{E} = C(1 - P) - \alpha(1 - C)$$

where α is the fraction of dividends allowed as a tax credit.

The conclusion from this formulation is familiar by now. The extra burden, $C(1 - P)$, declines as P increases; the relief, $\alpha(1 - C)$, is constant for all doubly taxed stockholders. The amount of relief is the same for all stockholders, but the degree of relief varies directly with their income level.

To take some illustrative figures: with $C = 50$ per cent, $\alpha = 4$ per cent, and P's of 20 and 90 per cent (all personal income taxpayers in effect fall in rate brackets bounded by these two), then the 20 per cent rate stockholder's differential is reduced from 40 to 38 per cent; for the 90 per cent rate stockholder, the reduction is from 5 to 3 per cent. The proportionate relief, i.e., the relative degree of relief, can be obtained by relating the credit to the extra burden.

$$\beta = \frac{\alpha(1 - C)}{C(1 - P)}$$

where β can be considered to be the degree of relief.

With the numerator constant and the denominator declining with increasing P, then the higher P, the larger β.

2. Now consider $N_B/(E - PE)$, that is to say, consider the extra burden in relation to earnings for distribution after tax, the tax in this case being the personal income tax that would have applied to earnings for distribution in the absence of the corporate tax.

$$\frac{N_B}{E - PE} = \frac{CE(1 - P)}{E(1 - P)} = C.$$

This appears to be quite a different result from our usual formulation, for here we find the extra burden to be invariant with stockholder income level; it is simply the corporate tax rate. Yet the conclusion

153

previously reached that the credit provides proportionately greater relief for higher income stockholders still holds. Because:

$$\frac{N_A}{E - PE} = \frac{CE(1 - P) - \alpha(E - EC)}{E(1 - P)}$$

$$= C - \frac{\alpha E(1 - C)}{E(1 - P)}$$

$$= C - \frac{\alpha(1 - C)}{1 - P}.$$

C is a constant for all doubly taxed stockholders, as is the term $\alpha(1 - C)$. As P gets larger, $\alpha(1 - C)/(1 - P)$ gets larger. Therefore $C - \alpha(1 - C)/(1 - P)$ gets smaller. To insert some illustrative numbers, as before let:

$$C = 0.5, \quad \alpha = 0.04, \quad P_1 = 0.2 \quad \text{and} \quad P_2 = 0.9.$$

Then for the 20 per cent bracket stockholder we have:

$$\frac{N_A}{E - PE} = C - \frac{\alpha(1 - C)}{1 - P_1} = 0.5 - \frac{0.04(1 - 0.5)}{1 - 0.2} = 0.475.$$

While for the 90 per cent bracket stockholder we have:

$$\frac{N_A}{E - PE} = C - \frac{\alpha(1 - C)}{1 - P_2} = 0.5 - \frac{0.04(1 - 0.5)}{1 - 0.9} = 0.300.$$

The extra burden is reduced from 50 to 47.5 per cent in the one case, and from 50 to 30 per cent in the other. That is to say, before taking account of the dividend tax credit on $1,000 of earnings for distribution, the 20 per cent tax bracket stockholder would have $400 left after corporate-personal tax, while he would have $800 left under the personal tax alone. Similarly, again on $1,000, the 90 per cent bracket stockholder would have $50 and $100, respectively. In both cases, the reduction in after-tax income would be one half, i.e., $400/$800 = $50/$100 = ½. After relief, however, the reduction would be $380/$800 and $30/$100. Both have been given $20 of relief, but clearly, the high rate stockholder has been given a proportionately higher degree of relief, relative to the after-tax income he would have in the absence of the corporate income tax.

It should be observed that this measure of "overtaxation" implies that a given percentage reduction in after-tax income has the same significance regardless of the extent to which the before-tax income has been reduced by the personal income tax. That is, although the 50 per cent reduction in the $800 after-tax income of the low income stockholder is arithmetically the same as the 50 per cent reduction in the $100 after-tax income of the high income stockholder, these equal percentage reductions may not necessarily be regarded as equivalent by the taxpayers concerned, or by legislators. Although the additional $1,000 of before-tax earnings for distribution have been brought 50 per cent closer to zero dollars in both instances, that belonging to the high income taxpayer was nearer that point to begin with. The reason for this, of course, lies basically with the progressivity of the personal income tax schedule, but this does not necessarily justify an assumption that equal percentage reductions in income after the personal tax are, from the point of view of tax equity, really equal.

To revert to the main theme of this section, it appears that the deprivation due to the corporate tax amounts to the same fraction for all stockholders. If the corporate rate were 20 per cent, for example, then after the corporate and personal tax on their earnings for distribution, all stockholders, *regardless* of income level, would have left after taxes 20 per cent less than they would have had were there no corporate tax and were their earnings for distribution (equal to dividends in this case) taxed under the personal income tax. With the corporate rate at 50 per cent, then the reduction in income after tax due to "double taxation" amounts to 50 per cent of what they would have had under the personal income tax alone.

But it would not be correct to argue from this proportionality that because stockholders are deprived of a similar fraction of after-tax income, an equal amount of relief per dollar of dividends, such as is provided by the credit, is the appropriate remedy for their overtaxation. For one thing, as already noted, equal amounts of relief mean varying degrees of relief, a fact which the reader is free to qualify in accordance with his attitudes toward the considerations pointed out two paragraphs above. But, in addition, there is a simple arithmetic fact that does not depend on attitudes for interpretation. At present the credit leaves all stockholders overtaxed to some degree, but a larger credit would change this. Whatever credit is chosen, however,[14]

[14] Sometimes 10 per cent is suggested; Canada's 20 per cent has been cited as appropriate; a 15 per cent credit was initially proposed in 1954.

it will achieve equal taxation of earnings for distribution and other income in only one particular marginal rate bracket. In rate brackets higher than this, undertaxation will prevail, while overtaxation will still be the case in rate brackets lower than the particular one.

That is to say, for equal tax treatment of earnings for distribution and other income, it must be:

$$E - \hat{P}E = E - CE - \hat{P}(E - CE) + \hat{\alpha}(E - CE)$$

or
$$C(1 - \hat{P}) = \hat{\alpha}(1 - C)$$

and
$$\hat{\alpha} = \frac{C(1 - \hat{P})}{1 - C}$$

where $\hat{\alpha}$ is the credit that equalizes the tax liabilities for a stockholder in a given tax bracket denoted by $\hat{P}$. Therefore, α is a function of P, and from the expression $C(1 - \hat{P}) = \hat{\alpha}(1 - C)$, it can be seen that, given $\hat{\alpha}$, then for any P higher than $\hat{P}$, $C(1 - P) < \hat{\alpha}(1 - C)$, while for any P lower than $\hat{P}$, $C(1 - P) > \hat{\alpha}(1 - C)$.[15]

If the extra burden due to the corporate tax is to be reduced proportionately for each stockholder, the credit should be a constant fraction of the extra burden. If this fraction were r then

$$N_A = CE(1 - P) - rCE(1 - P) = CE(1 - P)(1 - r)$$

and
$$\frac{N_A}{E - PE} = C(1 - r).$$

The effect on after-tax income of such a credit would be equivalent to that provided by a straight reduction in the corporate tax rate. Also, of course,

$$\frac{N_A}{E} = C(1 - P)(1 - r)$$

$$= [C(1 - r)](1 - P),$$

where the term in brackets is, in effect, a lower corporate rate. Thus a simple way of providing the equivalent of a proportional cut in the extra burden is to lower the corporate rate. This might be done for

[15] A discussion of this point with particular reference to the 15 per cent credit originally proposed in 1954 appears later in this chapter.

all corporate earnings, or, directed to earnings for distribution only via a credit against corporate tax for dividends paid. An alternative procedure but with equivalent results would be to assume some fraction of dividends received, say w, represented the amount of tax withheld at source. From this would be subtracted the personal tax due on this withheld amount, and the difference would be the net credit allowed.[16] This procedure would provide proportionate relief since the extra burden would be:

$$CE(1 - P) - [w(E - CE) - Pw(E - CE)]$$

which simplifies to

$$(1 - P)[C - w(1 - C)].$$

Finally the two procedures can be precisely related since for any given r, the equivalent (in terms of relief provided) w would be given by

$$w = \frac{Cr}{1 - C}.\text{[17]}$$

In summary, every statement about the credit and the type of relief it provides based on our preferred formulation could be phrased in terms of relationships based on income after tax. Indeed, it would be surprising if it could not be since nothing new has been introduced; terms have merely been rearranged. Yet a purpose is served by this relatively lengthy aside. First, the similarity of the conclusions based on after-tax measures and pre-tax measures is not immediately obvious. Secondly, this similarity relates to conclusions concerning the dividend credit and its appropriateness. In other connections, the two sets of bases for measuring the extra burden may give different results. In particular, we will remark on this once again when the trend in overtaxation is discussed.

Variation of "Extra" Burden Among Income Levels and over Time

In addition to what we have noted about the special provisions in particular periods, it is worth reminding the reader that a "push-pull"

[16] For a recent discussion of these two procedures and a demonstration of their equivalence by numerical examples, see *Growth and Taxes*, Committee for Economic Development, Washington, 1961, pp. A-1 through A-G.

[17] Set $C(1 - r)(1 - P) = (1 - P)[C - w(1 - C)]$ and simplify to get this expression for w.

relationship between the corporate and personal tax rates determines the differential. Other things equal, a rise in the corporate rate will send it up, a rise in the personal rate will send it down.

The relevant data, the "extra" burden as a percentage of earnings for distribution, i.e., the differential, are summarized for stockholders with selected amounts of taxable income in Tables 40 and 41. Table 40 presents the differentials calculated on the assumption that all of the stockholder's taxable income was in the form of earnings for distribution, while in Table 41 the differentials are calculated on marginal increments (strictly one dollar, but more generally the amount that falls in the highest applicable bracket) of earnings for distribution at the chosen taxable income levels. Both tables cover the period 1913–1961, and in both, starting with 1948, there are two sets of entries—one for joint returns, the other for separate returns. This distinction was, of course, not necessary before 1948.

Basically, they tell the same story. The discussion will center on the data of Table 41, and, wherever it is necessary to choose, joint returns will be considered since they represent the more usual situation.[18] This will obscure no matters of principle and make it easier to focus on the broad sweep of the differentials. It also makes for simplicity to take four typical taxable income levels—$1,000 to symbolize low, $5,000 and $50,000 to stand for lower middle and upper middle respectively, and $500,000 to represent the top of the income range.

One of the most important conclusions that emerges from Table 41 is the simple one that as a general rule over the whole of our income tax history earnings for distribution have been "overtaxed," that is to say the tax load on them was heavier than if the pre-corporate-tax counterpart of dividends had been included in personal taxable income and so taxed.[19] But it is equally important to point out that the degree of overtaxation was uneven, particularly among income classes. This is what our earlier discussion would lead us to expect. In every year, the greatest degree of "overtaxation" occurred at the lowest income level, the least at the top of the income range.[20] Thus, to cite

18 In 1956, for example, joint returns accounted for two-thirds of dividend recipients and 65 per cent of total dividends on taxable returns. (See *Statistics of Income, Individual Income Tax Returns—1956*, pp. 23 and 27.)

19 With the corporate tax paid thereon taken as a credit against personal income tax liability so computed.

20 Outside the purview of our tables fall those most heavily "overtaxed"—stockholders with income too low to be taxable. Their earnings for distribution paid the corporate tax, while the personal tax that would have been due was zero.

the evidence for only a sprinkling of years: In 1929, the differential against earnings for distribution ranged from a high of 10.5 per cent at the $1,000 stockholder taxable income level to a low of 4.8 per cent at $1,000,000; or take 1939, where the span was from 18.2 to 4.4 per cent, again being higher the lower the stockholder's income; or 1949 where the range was 31.7 to 6.8 per cent; or the 1955–1960 gamut from 39.7 to 2.8 per cent; and going back to an early period, in 1919 it was 6 per cent at the lowest income and −7.8 per cent at the highest. Even in the earliest years of our period 1913–1917, when the lower taxable income range suffered no "extra" burden at all, i.e., the differential was zero, it is still true that the higher incomes were taxed less heavily, for in these years (and some later ones as well) their differential was negative; i.e., they enjoyed a tax benefit. (The reasons for this have been developed above.)

Now let us look at variations over time for the four chosen income levels (see Chart 7). But before undertaking a discussion of the trend in the differential, it is important to pick up the thread of the note on alternative measures that appeared several pages earlier. When movements in overtaxation over time are analyzed on the basis of $C_e(1 - P)$ as summarized in Table 41 and Chart 7, we are talking about the "extra" tax as a decimal fraction (or percentage) of a given amount of earnings for distribution. Everything that is said relates to this particular way of measuring overtaxation, which varies among income classes markedly. The alternative measure, which relates the "extra tax" to income after tax, shows for the period 1936–1953 a degree of overtaxation invariant with stockholder income level (i.e., marginal personal rate), and generally for the other years of our study, when personal income tax relief was provided for dividend receipts, it exhibits a less pronounced difference among income levels than does $C_e(1 - P)$. The relevant data, which appear in Table 42 and are plotted on Chart 8, will be taken up after we examine the trend in $C_e(1 - P)$. Reading from the beginning to the end of our period, at the $1,000 level there is virtually continuous growth in the "extra" burden. Thus we can summarize what happened very quickly by citing the zero differential of 1913, the sizable 39.7 per cent differential in 1955–1960, and the additional information that from 1923 on it was 10 per cent or more. At $5,000 of stockholder's taxable income, much the same pattern is found. At $50,000, too, a general tendency for the weight of the extra "burden" to grow over time is apparent, yet there are some noteworthy exceptions. Thus, until 1922, it was either zero

159

CHART 7

Differential on Marginal Increments of Earnings for Distribution
at Four Selected Taxable Income Levels, 1913–1961
(joint returns)

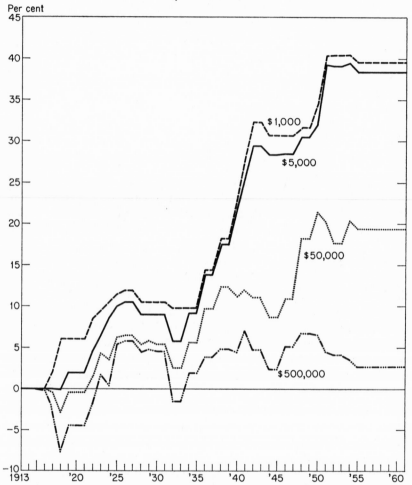

or negative, and from 1922 through 1935, it was at a moderate level, generally 6 per cent or less. From that date to the present, the differential, of course, increased, but still remained well below those at the lower income levels. At the $500,000 level, we find a result quite different from those noted heretofore. Definite undertaxation existed

160

from 1913 through 1922, reaching almost an 8 per cent tax benefit in 1918. This, by the way, was greater than any positive differential experienced at this income level since that date. With negative differentials in 1932 and 1933 also, this gives "undertaxation" for twelve years, "overtaxation" of under 3 per cent for eleven years, "overtaxation" of between 3 and 6 per cent for twenty-one years, and a differential of over 6 per cent for only four years. Thus at this very high income level, "overtaxation" was not a severe problem. Comparing merely the terminal years of the period, we get a rise from −0.06 per cent to 2.8 per cent—certainly a moderate experience when judged against that of most stockholders.

The explanation of this moderate "overtaxation" and its failure to vary much [21] over time lies in the "push-pull" relation between corporate and personal rates. Given the personal rate, the higher the corporate rate, the higher the differential. Given the corporate rate, the higher the personal rate, the lower the differential. The same relation applies, of course, when both rates rise or fall together, as long as they change differentially.[22] Thus in 1938 stockholders at the top of the income scale were more heavily "overtaxed" than in 1951, despite a corporate rate of 50.75 per cent in this latter year compared with 19 per cent in 1938, and a rise in personal marginal rates from 74 in 1938 to 91 in 1951. For while C_e rose by 31.75 points, $1 - P$ fell from 26 to 9, i.e., proportionately more than the increase in the corporate rate. This is the explanation also that lies behind one of the summary observations in the introduction where it was noted that using the differential as the measure of overtaxation, for low and moderate income stockholders the trend in overtaxation was sharply upward, while for stockholders with very high incomes there was a very modest rise. Indeed, for them overtaxation has been less severe since 1952 than it was in 1925–1931.[23] More generally than is brought

[21] Compared with that of other income levels.

[22] Or more precisely, to revert to our earlier symbols, as long as the change in C_e and the change in $1 - P$ are proportionately different. When C_e increases and P falls, the differential will always increase; when C_e falls and P rises, the differential will always decline.

[23] To emphasize that it is overtaxation as measured by the differential against earnings for distribution that is under discussion here, and to clarify further why it is not incongruous to find a decline in overtaxation so measured coincident with a rise in tax rates, the relevant data for two taxable income levels for the years 1926–1927 and 1955 to date are set forth.

In 1926 and 1927 the corporate rate was 13.5 per cent; the normal tax from which out in these numerical examples, what is involved in the *change* in overtaxation when both the corporate rate and the personal rate rise can be expressed as follows. (For convenience we use simpler notation than heretofore.)

Let ρ_1 and ρ_2 = the amount of overtaxation per incremental dollar of earnings for distribution where 1 and 2 denote two different years.

C_1 and C_2 = the corporate rate in each of these years; $C_2 > C$.

P_1 and P_2 = the relevant marginal personal rate in each of these years; $P_2 > P_1$.

To avoid undue complications, without really losing sight of principle, let us restrict the comparison to periods when neither the exemption of dividends from normal tax nor the dividend tax credit prevailed, i.e., 1936–1953.

1. If $\rho_2 = \rho_1$, i.e., both corporate and personal rates rise, but overtaxation remains unchanged, then:

$$\rho_2 = \rho_1, \quad \text{or} \quad \frac{C_2(1 - P_2)}{C_1(1 - P_1)} = 1, \quad \text{hence} \quad \frac{C_2}{C_1} = \frac{1 - P_1}{1 - P_2}.$$

dividends were exempt was 1.5 per cent at the $1,000 taxable income level and 5 per cent for those with incomes of more than $8,000; no surtax applied if taxable income was less than $10,000; the surtax on income over $100,000 was 20 per cent. For the years 1955 to date, the corporate rate is taken to be 52 per cent; the marginal rate applicable to $1,000 of taxable income is 20 per cent; while the marginal rate for married persons with taxable incomes in excess of $400,000 income is 91 per cent. Against personal income tax there is a credit equal to 4 per cent of dividends received.

Let a = corporate tax on additional $1,000 of earnings for distribution; b = personal tax on $1,000 minus a; $c = a + b$ = total tax on additional $1,000 of earnings for distribution; d = personal tax on additional $1,000 of income from other sources; and $e = c - d$ = extra burden on an additional $1,000 of earnings for distribution = overtaxation.

Note: $1,000 is chosen as a value that will give convenient numbers with no decimal points. The additional amount could equally well be $1, $10, etc.

	Stockholder with $1,000 of Taxable Income		Stockholder with $500,000 of Taxable Income	
	1926 and 1927	1955 to date	1926 and 1927	1955 to date
a	$135	$520	$135	$520
b	0	77	173	418
c	135	597	308	938
d	15	200	250	910
e	120	397	58	28

As a reminder that there are other ways of measuring the degree of overtaxation, from these same figures we compute the percentage reduction in after-tax income

162

2. If overtaxation increased following a rise in both corporate and personal rates, then:

$$\rho_2 > \rho_1, \quad \text{or} \quad \frac{C_2(1 - P_2)}{C_1(1 - P_1)} > 1, \quad \text{hence} \quad \frac{C_2}{C_1} > \frac{1 - P_1}{1 - P_2}.$$

3. If overtaxation decreased following a rise in both corporate and personal rates, then:

$$\rho_2 < \rho_1 \quad \text{or} \quad \frac{C_2(1 - P_2)}{C_1(1 - P_1)} < 1, \quad \text{hence} \quad \frac{C_2}{C_1} < \frac{1 - P_1}{1 - P_2}.$$

Thus

$$\rho_2 \gtreqless \rho_1, \quad \text{as} \quad \frac{C_2}{C_1} \gtreqless \frac{1 - P_1}{1 - P_2}.$$

Since C_2/C_1 is the same no matter what the stockholders income level, while $(1 - P_1)/(1 - P_2)$ generally varies with income, it is perfectly consistent to find overtaxation between two years increasing for some taxpayers and declining for others. Now, by rearranging terms, attention can be turned more directly to those cases where overtaxation declines as rates rise. By rewriting (3), we note that this requires that:

---

occasioned by the corporate tax, i.e., the measure considered in the note several pages earlier. For the stockholder with $1,000 of taxable income, we get:

1926 and 1927: $\dfrac{\$120}{\$1,000 - \$15} = \dfrac{\$120}{\$985} = 0.12$

1955 to date: $\dfrac{\$397}{\$1,000 - \$200} = \dfrac{\$397}{\$800} = 0.50$

For the stockholder with $500,000 of taxable income we have:

1926 and 1927: $\dfrac{\$58}{\$1,000 - \$250} = \dfrac{\$58}{\$750} = 0.08$

1955 to date: $\dfrac{\$28}{\$1,000 - \$910} = \dfrac{\$28}{\$90} = 0.31.$

The results here may seem to contradict the conclusions in the note that explained this measure, because the $500,000 taxable income stockholder is less heavily overtaxed than the $1,000 taxable income stockholder. But this is because both in 1926 and 1927 and 1955 to date special provisions related to the taxation of dividends: in the earlier years they were exempt from normal tax, and in the later period the tax credit was in effect.

4. $\dfrac{1 - P_1}{1 - P_2} > \dfrac{C_2}{C_1}$ which by further manipulation can be expressed as:

5. $P_2 > \dfrac{C_1}{C_2}(P_1 - 1) + 1.$

If we let $C_1/C_2 = k$, the general expression for the P_2 required for overtaxation to increase, given P_1 and the proportionate increase in corporate rates (measured not directly but by k which is its inverse) is:

6. $P_2 > k(P_1 - 1) + 1$ and

7. $P_2 - P_1 > k(P_1 - 1) + 1 - P_1.$

Thus, using fractions to represent percentages,

If $P_{1i} =$ ⠀⠀0.10, ⠀⠀⠀⠀0.20, ⠀⠀$\cdots$, ⠀⠀⠀0.90.

$P_{2i} - P_{1i} > 0.9 - 0.9k,\ > 0.8 - 0.8k,\ \cdots,\ > 0.1 - 0.1k,$ or

$P_{2i} - P_{1i} > 0.9(1 - k),\ 70.8(1 - k)\ \cdots,\ 70.1(1 - k).$

Thus it is clear that for any $k < 1$ (which is the case we are considering), the required rise in P, i.e., $P_{2i} - P_{1i}$, is absolutely (and also, of course, relative to P_{1i}) smaller, the larger P_{1i}. For $0.9(1 - k) > 0.8(1 - k) > \cdots > 0.1(1 - k).$

One further observation is in order here. Going back to inequality (2), we note that as P_2 approaches 1 (i.e., confiscatory taxation of 100 per cent), $(1 - P_1)/(1 - P_2)$ grows larger without limit, and therefore, if, as is the case, $C_1 > 0$, then no conceivable increase in C_2 (limited to tax rates no greater than 100 per cent) could make $(C_2)/(C_1) > (1 - P_1)/(1 - P_2)$. In this case the situation in (3) would apply automatically. Is it not a strange result to find overtaxation inevitably declining as personal rates approach 100 per cent? The answer, of course, is that the result is strange only if one fails to distinguish between *level of taxation* and *overtaxation*. If personal rates were 100 per cent, then overtaxation would not exist, because payment of a tax on corporate earnings would deprive stockholders of nothing, since had that money come to them instead of going to the government, they would have kept none of it.

This is not to argue that the way to cure overtaxation, if indeed it does exist (remember the incidence and capitalization assumptions behind our analysis), is to raise the personal rate to 100 per cent. Rather, the purpose of this explanation is to remind the reader that we measure overtaxation relative to a standard—that schedule of rates which applies to personal income other than corporate earnings.

Earlier, in the section on alternative measures, it was pointed out that the degree of overtaxation could be measured in different ways, namely, in terms of the percentage reduction in income after the personal tax that is attributable to the corporate tax on earnings for distribution. This measure was invariant with stockholder income level from 1936 through 1953. But from 1913 through 1935, because of the exemption of dividends from personal normal tax, and from 1954 on, because of the credit (for simplicity the exclusion is neglected), the upper income stockholders experienced a smaller percentage reduction in after-tax income (or in a number of the earlier years a positive increase) than the low marginal rate stockholders. The main interest here is in the trend of overtaxation, and the relevant information appears in Table 42 and Chart 8. At all income levels overtaxation existed from 1925 on, and at the lowest income level from 1917 on. Thus overtaxation set in earlier and in a slightly more pronounced form at the lower income levels, and this difference persisted until 1936 when the complete divorce between the corporate and personal tax that lasted through 1953 brought all income levels together; and over this period overtaxation became increasingly severe. It bottomed out in 1954 with the introduction of the dividend tax credit, but only at the high income levels has there been any really sizable reversal of trend.

Effect of a More Liberal Dividend Credit

The relativity of answers according to what base is chosen that has just been observed in discussing the variation in overtaxation over time is not, as has been noted earlier, relevant to judgment on the effect of the dividend tax credit. Therefore, without ambiguity, we can point up a basic limitation of the credit by exploring more fully what would have happened had the 15 per cent credit proposed by President Eisenhower been in effect in, say, 1960. Table 43 lists the differential tax rates on an added dollar of earnings for distribution:

1. As it would have been without any credit (column 2).
2. As it stood with the 4 per cent of dividends tax credit (column 3).
3. As it would have been with a 15 per cent credit (column 4).

Dividends Under the Income Tax

TABLE 42

PERCENTAGE REDUCTION IN EARNINGS FOR DISTRIBUTION AFTER PERSONAL TAX [a]
BECAUSE OF CORPORATE TAX, 1913–1961

(marginal increments at selected taxable income levels, joint returns)

	Taxable Income Level			
Period	$1,000	$5,000	$50,000	$500,000
1913–1915	0	0	−1 [b]	0 −
1916	0	0	−1 [b]	0 −
1917	2	0	−1 [b]	−4 [b]
1918	6	0	−4 [b]	−32 [b]
1919–1921	6	1	−1 [b]	−14 [b]
1922	9	5	2	−4 [b]
1923	10	7	5	0+
1924	11	9	6	−1 [b]
1925	12	10	8	7
1926–1927	12	11	8	8
1928	11	9	7	6
1929	11	9	8	6
1930–1931	11	9	7	6
1932–1933	10	6	4	−4 [b]
1934–1935	10	10	6	5
1936–1937	15	15	15	15
1938–1939	19	19	19	19
1940	24	24	24	24
1941	31	31	31	31
1942–1943	40	40	40	40
1944–1945	40	40	40	40
1946–1947	38	38	38	38
1948–1949	38	38	38	38
1950	42	42	42	42
1951	51	51	51	51
1952–1953	52	52	52	52
1954	51	51	50	41
1955–1961	50	50	48	31

NOTE: In computing the degree of overtaxation for the table only corporate normal and surtax rates were used, and the corporate rate was taken to be the maximum rate of normal tax and surtax combined. But no account was taken of the excess profits tax. Had there been some adjustment on this score (it is difficult to think of what it could have been because of the uneven impact of the EPT), overtaxation would have shown up as more severe than the table indicates.

[a] This is the personal tax on the full amount of earnings for distribution, i.e., assuming no corporate tax or, alternatively, the personal tax on an equivalent amount of other income.

[b] Percentage increase indicated by a minus sign.

CHART 8

Percentage Reduction in Earnings for Distribution After Personal Tax
Because of Corporate Tax, 1913–1961

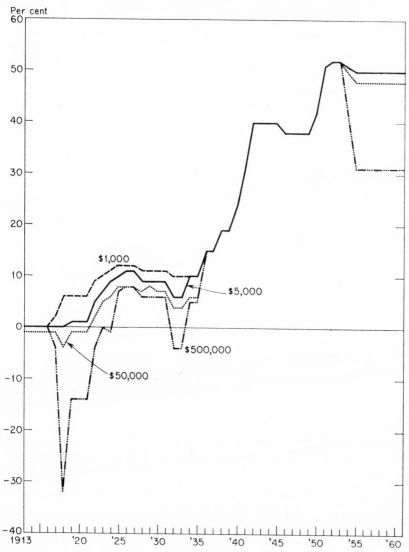

TABLE 43

"Extra" Burden Computed on Marginal Rates and Relief Provided by
Dividend Tax Credits of 4 and 15 Per Cent, at Selected Levels of
Stockholders' Taxable Income, 1961 [a]

Taxable Income Level (1)	"Extra" Burden in the Absence of Any Relief (2)	"Extra" Burden After Dividend Tax Credit of 4% (Present Law) (3)	"Extra" Burden After Dividend Tax Credit 15% [b] (4)	Percentage Reduction in "Extra" Burden Due to 4% Credit (5)	Percentage Reduction in "Extra" Burden Due to 15% Credit (6)
$ 1,000	$0.4160	$0.3968	$0.3440	4.6%	17.3%
3,000	.4160	.3968	.3440	4.6	17.3
5,000	.4056	.3864	.3336	4.7	17.8
10,000	.3848	.3656	.3128	5.0	18.7
25,000	.2964	.2772	.2244	6.5	24.3
50,000	.2132	.1940	.1412	9.0	33.8
100,000	.1300	.1108	.0580	14.8	55.4
500,000	.0468	.0276	−.0252	41.0	[c]
1,000,000	.0468	.0276	−.0252	41.0	[c]

Note: Col. 3 = col. 2 − $0.0192; col. 4 = col. 2 − $0.072.

[a] Computed on the basis of a corporate tax rate of 52 per cent and personal marginal rates applicable to joint returns in 1957.

[b] As originally proposed by President Eisenhower, see the *Budget of the United States Government for the Fiscal Year Ending June 30, 1955*, Washington, 1954, p. 1718.

[c] "Extra" burden converted to a tax saving.

Because P is always positive, in the absence of any credit a positive (albeit declining) differential would exist at all income levels. The relief presently afforded by the credit is not sufficient to change this, involving at all income levels a cut of slightly under 2 points in the differential. Had the 15 per cent tax credit been effective, however, the relief would have been enough to cause a negative "extra" burden on earnings for distribution at the top two of the taxable incomes listed in our table.[24] Any higher credit would mean a shift from "burden" to "benefit" at a lower level.[25]

[24] More precisely, with a 52 per cent corporate rate assumed, the "break-even" point would have been $180,000 of taxable income. This is for joint returns. For separate returns, subject to higher marginal rates and, hence, lower differentials, the "break-even" point would have come at $90,000 of taxable income. (For a neat and precise formulation of the relationships involved here, see Carl S. Shoup, "The Dividend Exclusion and Credit in the Revenue Code of 1954," *National Tax Journal*,

Double Taxation, Differential Taxation, and Tax Relief

The last three columns of Table 43 are designed to illustrate a feature of the credit already noted. With a flat amount of credit per dollar of earnings for distribution [26] and an "extra" burden that falls with rising stockholder income, the degree of relief, i.e., the percentage by which the "extra" burden is cut by the credit, increases with stockholder income. Thus, the credit ameliorates less than 5 per cent of the "extra" burden at the lower income levels (per marginal dollar of earnings for distribution), but relieves those at the top of the income range of over 40 per cent of their differentially heavier tax load. If the 15 per cent credit had been enacted, then, with tax rates assumed unchanged, less than 20 per cent of the "extra" burden would have been removed, for the lower stockholder incomes, while substantial relief would have occurred higher up—well over half at $100,000, and relief so great as to result in a tax saving for the very highest incomes.[27]

The relief actually obtained is, of course, determined by total amount of dividends, not marginal dollars thereof. An estimate of what it comes to for stockholders at different income levels appears in the latter part of this chapter.[28]

Differential Taxation of Stockholders

The tax liability on distributed earnings by no means exhausts the stockholder's tax burden. For while we have been able to identify an inequality in the tax burden on stockholders' dividend receipts (or, more precisely, on earnings for distribution), we have not yet evaluated the extent to which the rest of the income generated by corporations

---

March 1955, p. 147.) In terms of our symbols we must find a P so that $C_e(1 - P) = 0.15(1 - C_e)$. With C_e at 0.52, the relevant P is about 0.86, the closest bracket rate to which is 0.87, applicable at the taxable incomes cited.

[25] Canada's dividend tax credit, instituted in 1949 at 10 per cent, currently is 20 per cent.

[26] Assuming a corporate rate of 52 per cent, the credit is 0.04 ($0.48) or $.0192 per dollar of earnings for distribution.

[27] Remember that this applies to marginal increments to incomes of a given size, and the particular figures just cited also refer to joint returns only. For separate returns, which were not, of course, permitted to split their income, substantial relief would occur considerably lower down the income scale as would the transition from "over-" to "undertaxation."

[28] The rest of this chapter draws heavily on the author's book, *The Income-Tax Burden on Stockholders,* from which some materials have been selected for summary presentation here because they round out the discussion of the preceding section of this chapter. For a more thorough discussion, additional data, and more details on procedure than furnished here, the reader is referred to the book.

for their stockholder owners is differentially taxed. The overtaxation we found for distributed earnings could be exacerbated or moderated by the tax treatment accorded retained earnings. And this would be relevant to any discussion of dividend taxation since retention is the alternative to distribution. We shall find that the most salient conclusion about stockholders' taxation is not that distributed earnings bear an extra burden, but that when account is taken of their pro rata share of corporate earnings, whether distributed or not, stockholders are unequally taxed compared with other income taxpayers. And this inequality of taxation is not all in the direction of an extra burden.[29] On net balance, from this broader view, most stockholders are overtaxed, but some are undertaxed. Who they are and what this means will be spelled out as we go on.

The "Extra" Burden on Earnings for Retention

In our measure of the extent to which earnings for distribution (the pre-corporate-tax counterpart of dividends) were overtaxed, the burden of the corporate tax was moderated by taking account of the personal income tax that would have applied. Thus we imputed a marginal dollar of earnings for distribution (the pre-corporate-income-tax equivalent of dividends), determined the potential personal income tax on such an imputation, and compared with it the actual tax liability— viz., the corporate income tax on earnings for distribution and the personal income tax on dividends.

The degree to which the retained earnings component of stockholders' income is overtaxed is measured by a similar yardstick. In connection with that part of corporate earnings not distributed to the stockholder, in measuring what we again denote the extra burden, we consider a basic amount of corporate income, to be designated earnings for retention, which is the pre-corporate-tax equivalent of what is usually called retained earnings. Under our present tax structure, earnings for retention are subject to the corporate income tax. We, on the other hand, estimate the potential personal income tax which the earnings for retention would bear if they were fully distributed

---

[29] The reader is reminded that these conclusions are valid only on the assumption that the incidence of the corporation income tax is on profits. For only so far as the tax falls on stockholders is there validity in the charge of "double taxation" of dividends or in the finding of the overtaxation of distributed earnings.

(or imputed) to the stockholders,[30] and the difference between these two tax liabilities is the extra *burden* if the actual exceeds the hypothetical, the *benefit* if potential liability is bigger than the actual. The extra burden, taken as a percentage of earnings for retention, we call the differential against earnings for retention.

Add to the symbols used earlier in this chapter:

R = earnings for retention

C_r = effective rate of corporate income tax on earnings for retention (this is higher than C_e because earnings for retention are net of deficits reported by loss corporations)

N_r = absolute extra burden on earnings for retention

$\dfrac{N_r}{R}$ = differential against earnings for retention.

Then [31]

$$N_r = C_r R - PR$$
$$= R(C_r - P)$$
$$\frac{N_r}{R} = C_r - P.$$

It is apparent that the differential against earnings for retention can be positive, zero, or negative depending on the relative heights of C_r and P. With C_r invariant on stockholders' income and P a rising function thereof, the differential measured as a rate declines as stockholders' income rises, and if P is high enough at some point in the income scale, the differential will become negative. (Note that because the personal income tax rate schedule is progressive, the P that applies here is higher than the one in the differential against earnings for

[30] Use of this imputation procedure for retentions and distributions implies neither support for nor opposition to a change in the tax laws that would treat stockholders like partners. We adopted it as an analytical framework most relevant for assessing the equity that attaches to the income taxation of stockholders (given that the incidence of the tax is on profits).

[31] We could more properly write P_j, where $j \geqq i$ and, like i, runs from zero to the top marginal rate (see footnote 3 of this chapter). We felt this hypothecation of subscripts might, on net balance, hinder rather than help our expression of the basic relations involved here.

distribution formula. More precisely, since earnings for retention are taken to be incremental to earnings for distribution, they would be subject to marginal rates equal to or greater than those applying to earnings for distribution.)

As described, the actual tax load on earnings for retention consists simply of the corporation income tax, and the extra burden on this segment of corporate earnings is measured as the difference between the corporate tax and the hypothetical personal tax. This measure is designated variant 1 of our standard method. Values of the differential against earnings for retention (and of two additional measures described below—the differentials against net corporate earnings and stockholders' income—in the derivation of which this measure of the extra tax burden on retained earnings is employed) we call variant 1 values. Variant 1 is a clear-cut measure that tells us for a given year how much more (or less) income tax stockholders paid on their pro rata share of earnings for retention than would have been due if this income share had been subject promptly and in full to the personal income tax alone. But it leaves out something.

For it can be argued that some portion, at least, of retained earnings would show up as capital gains, and that some of these capital gains would be realized by stockholders in taxable form. Thus, because of current retentions, sometime in the future an additional tax liability would be incurred. Therefore variant 2 was developed. Under variant 2, in measuring the tax load on retained earnings (before corporation income tax), a term (explained below) was added to represent the present value of the future capital gains tax on the undistributed earnings of a given year. Unless otherwise specified it is the variant 2 values that are used throughout this section.

To make such an adjustment with precision is impossible, however. Too many factors about which little is known are involved. To what extent do retained earnings show up in share prices? What proportion of resulting capital gains is realized, and of this what fraction shows up in taxable form? Our adjustment, therefore, is arbitrary but reasonable in the sense that it is in the right direction, and that substantial changes in the assumptions used in its derivation would lead to only slight changes in the size of the estimated additional tax liability on earnings for retention.

Briefly, variant 2 incorporates an additional tax liability of stockholders—a capital gains tax—determined on the assumptions that for each dollar of retained earnings share prices rose by 72 cents, and that two-thirds of these increments in the value of stock were realized in taxable form at an even rate over a five-year period.[32] The adjustment for the future capital gains tax liability enters as an additive term in N_r/R.

But it might be argued that this adjustment does not go far enough. For one assumption used in the variant 2 estimate is that stock prices rose by only 72 per cent of reinvested earnings, or that 28 cents of every dollar of retained earnings failed to show up in enhanced stock values. Apparently, then, when earnings are reinvested rather than paid out, stockholders lose 28 cents per dollar of such earnings. Should not this be considered a deprivation and, while not a formal tax, should it not be taken into account in estimating the extra tax load on earnings for retention? Despite good grounds for answering this question in the negative (see the next paragraph), and because the matter is debatable, variant 3 was developed. Very simply, in addition to the corporate tax and the present value of the future capital gains tax due to reinvested earnings, variant 3 includes the present value of this 28 cents loss as though it were an additional tax on earnings for retention. This adjustment affects N_r/R, making it higher than the variant 2 values which, in turn, of course, exceed the variant 1 values of the differentials.

But variant 3 seems to cover too much. For there is a difference between a tax and the reduction in potentially disposable income caused by the failure of corporations to distribute fully. The latter lacks the strong element of compulsion that characterizes a federal tax levy. Stockholders are not forced to acquiesce in corporate distribution policies. They can press for fuller distribution by the companies whose shares they hold; or acquire shares in corporations whose policy it is to distribute more of their earnings; or make other kinds of investments. On this reasoning variant 2 was selected as superior. Variant 3 goes too far; variant 1 not far enough.

[32] The 72 cents comes from a finding for the period 1870–1937 "that every $2.50 of earnings retained by a corporation has, on the average, been associated with an increase of $1.80 in the value of its stock" (Alfred Cowles 3rd and Associates, *Common Stock, Indexes 1871–1937*, Principia, 1938, p. 42). The two-thirds and five years are arbitrary, but varying the fraction and the number of years would not change our measure much.

Measuring the Differential Taxation of Earnings for Stockholders

Combining the differentials against earnings for distribution and earnings for retention furnishes a net result—the differential against net corporate earnings, a weighted average of the differential against each component.

Add to the symbols used up to this point:

$$T = \text{net corporate earnings} = E + R$$

N_t = the absolute extra burden on net corporate earnings

$\dfrac{N_t}{T}$ = the differential against net corporate earnings.

Then

$$N_t = N_e + N_r$$
$$= C_e E(1 - P) + R(C_r - P).$$

Since

$$T = E + R,$$

$$\frac{N_t}{T} = \frac{N_t}{E + R}$$

$$= \frac{C_e E(1 - P) + R(C_r - P)}{E + R}$$

$$= C_e(1 - P)\left(\frac{E}{E + R}\right) + (C_r - P)\left(\frac{R}{E + R}\right).$$

NOTE: This is the formula based on variant 1 values of the differential against earnings for retention. With variants 2 and 3 the procedures are the same, but N_r/R and N_t/T are larger. Also note that we use the measure of the differential against earnings for distribution that applied in the period 1936–1953. The dividend credit and exclusion are not yet incorporated in our measure; they will be later.

The differential against net corporate earnings will, of course, have the same characteristics as its components. The higher the proportion of earnings for retention to total corporate earnings, the closer N_t/T

lies to N_r/R. Further, since both its components behave in the same way on this score, it will be a declining function of stockholders' income. Also, after a point N_r/R can (and in a number of years did) weigh so heavily that N_t will turn negative, i.e., an income tax differential in favor of net corporate earnings will exist at the higher income levels.

By now it is evident that an income as well as a tax liability adjustment is incorporated in these measures. That is to say, we conduct our comparisons on the basis of the size of stockholders' income after the imputation of their full pro rata share of net corporate earnings (defined as the sum of earnings for distribution and earnings for retention), or (the equivalent) the sum of dividends, corporate savings, and corporation income taxes (with corporate savings taken net of deficits). This distinguishes the results of this section from those presented earlier in this chapter. There for illustrative purposes we imputed small sums—marginal dollars. Now, however, in converting *adjusted gross income* which contains stockholders' dividends as the measure of their income from corporate activity to *imputed gross income* which includes their full pro rata share of net corporate earnings, we use a corporate earnings multiplier derived from the ratio of pre-tax earnings to dividends for the corporate system as a whole.[33]

Specifically this income adjustment was made each year as follows:

We used the data of *Statistics of Income,* primarily an array of dividend recipients (stockholders) cross-classified by size of adjusted gross income and dividend size class. The array consisted of over 200 cells—one, for example, containing the data on stockholders with adjusted gross income of $4,000 to $5,000 and dividend receipts of less than $100; another for those in the same income range, but with dividend receipts falling in the range $100 to $200, etc. To the average amount of dividends in each of these cells we applied the corporate earnings multiplier and obtained imputed gross income by adding this product to the average adjusted gross income in that cell. Then stockholders were rearrayed into imputed gross income classes; averages were struck and plotted, and from them we read off, for selected imputed gross incomes, the amount of corporate earnings and taxable income. With this information we proceeded in the manner already described to measure the degree of differential taxation of earnings

[33] Thus we measure the average experience and refer to our stockholders as typical or representative stockholders at particular imputed gross income levels.

for distribution, earnings for retention, and net corporate earnings. The data cover only individuals who were "double-taxed." They leave out fiduciaries (estates and trusts) and dividend recipients who were not subject to personal income tax.

The Net Extra Burden as a Percentage of Stockholders' Total Income

One more measure has been developed for this analysis. By relating the extra burden to the total income of stockholders, we obtain the differential against (or in favor of) stockholders. It enables us to ascertain how much more heavily, measured in terms of effective rates, stockholders were actually taxed on the whole of their income from all sources because of the combined (nonintegrated) corporate-personal income tax system than they would have been with the corporate tax abolished and their pro rata share of net corporate earnings subject fully and promptly to the personal income tax.

Add to the symbols listed above:

S = imputed gross income of stockholders

O = stockholders' income from sources other than net corporate earnings

$= S - T$

$\dfrac{N_t}{S}$ = differential against stockholders

$S = T + O$

N_t = the extra burden on net corporate earnings. This is also the extra burden on stockholders, since it is only on the corporate earnings component of their income that stockholders are differentially taxed.

Therefore:

$$\frac{N_t}{S} = \frac{N_t}{T + O}.$$

With O positive, the differential against stockholders lies below that against net corporate earnings. But, since the only difference is in the denominator, the smaller the value for O, i.e., the larger the proportion of T in S, the closer N_t/S to N_t/T. Thus, as we shall see, at the lower stockholder income levels, the two measures diverge considerably; near the top of the income scale, however, they lie very close together. This is a reflection of the fact that, except for the lowest portion of the income range, the proportion of T to S is a rising fraction reading up the array of stockholder incomes.

What we have given here is a brief description. For a more thorough explanation of these procedures, the reader is referred to *Income-Tax Burden on Stockholders,* Chapters 1 and 2 and Appendix B.

Differential Taxation of Stockholders in 1950

We turn now to the findings, and, to anchor the discussion, present them for a particular year 1950. Similar results, however, were obtained for all years 1944–1952. Modifications of the pattern because of the dividend tax relief provisions of the Internal Revenue Code of 1954 are considered later in this section.

Chart 9 and Table 44 summarize how heavy the differential taxation of net corporate earnings and of stockholder income was in terms of the four selected measures, for the 1950 data. The reader is reminded that the results are for "average" stockholders representing the aggregate experience in each stockholder income class, that the values plotted are those obtained from variant 2 of our standard measures, and that the income of stockholders includes their pro rata share of pre-tax corporate earnings. The marginal rate schedules for joint and separate returns showed substantial differences, except at the two extremes of the income range, because of the income splitting permitted married stockholders. Therefore, the differentials for each type of return were computed separately, and weighted averages were struck for plotting the chart.

Examination of line 1 in Chart 9—the differential against earnings for distribution—reveals that the double taxation of distributed earnings was substantial but became steadily less severe as stockholder income rose. At the bottom of the taxable stockholder income scale, earnings for distribution were subject to a tax more than 34 percentage points higher than would have been due under the personal income tax alone. At the $25,000 stockholder income level, the net extra burden averaged about 29 percentage points, and at the top of the stockholder income range plotted on the chart ($500,000) it was only 10 per cent.

177

CHART 9

Differentials, 1950

(variant 2)

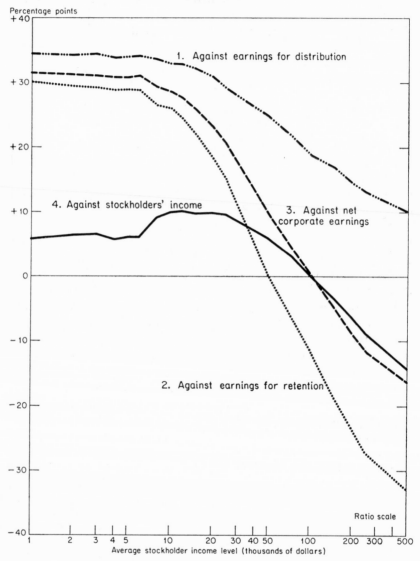

Percentage points

1. Against earnings for distribution

4. Against stockholders' income

3. Against net corporate earnings

2. Against earnings for retention

Ratio scale

Average stockholder income level (thousands of dollars)

TABLE 44

PERCENTAGE DIFFERENTIALS, 1950

Average Stockholder Imputed Gross Income ($000's)	Differential Against:									
	Earnings for Distribution Variants 1, 2, 3	Earnings for Retention Variant			Net Corporate Earnings Variant			Stockholder Imputed Gross Income Variant		
		1	2	3	1	2	3	1	2	3
1	34.3	27.3	30.0	43.6	30.0	31.7	40.0	5.4	5.7	7.2
2	34.2	26.9	29.3	43.0	29.7	31.2	39.6	6.0	6.3	8.0
3	34.3	26.8	29.1	42.6	29.7	31.1	39.4	6.2	6.5	8.2
4	33.9	26.1	28.7	42.3	29.1	30.7	39.1	5.5	5.8	7.4
5	33.8	26.3	28.8	42.3	29.1	30.7	39.0	5.7	6.0	7.6
6	34.0	26.2	28.7	42.3	29.2	30.8	39.1	5.7	6.0	7.6
8	33.7	24.0	26.5	40.0	27.7	29.3	37.6	8.6	9.0	11.6
10	32.9	23.1	26.0	39.5	26.8	28.6	36.9	9.3	9.9	12.8
12	32.7	21.7	24.6	38.2	25.9	27.7	36.0	9.4	10.0	13.0
15	32.1	19.2	22.0	35.5	24.0	25.9	34.2	9.1	9.7	12.8
20	30.8	15.2	18.5	32.0	21.2	23.3	31.6	9.0	9.8	13.4
25	29.2	11.3	15.2	28.7	18.2	20.6	28.9	8.4	9.5	13.4
50	24.9	−4.4	0.4	13.9	6.9	10.0	18.2	4.2	5.9	10.8
75	21.7	−12.4	−6.7	6.8	0.7	4.2	12.5	0.5	2.9	8.5
100	19.1	−17.3	−11.4	2.1	−3.3	0.4	8.7	−2.3	0.3	6.1
150	16.7	−24.6	−18.7	−5.1	−8.7	−5.0	3.3	−6.2	−3.6	2.3
200	14.6	−29.3	−23.4	−9.9	−12.4	−8.7	−0.4	−9.0	−6.3	−0.3
250	13.2	−32.8	−26.9	−13.5	−15.0	−11.4	−3.1	−11.5	−8.7	−2.4
500	10.0	−38.8	−32.9	−19.3	−19.9	−16.3	−8.0	−17.5	−14.3	−7.0

While the differential against earnings for retention (line 2 of Chart 9) follows the same general pattern, it is lower at all income levels, the difference becoming very marked over the upper portion of the stockholder income array. Starting at 30 per cent for the lowest income class, it falls rapidly to only 15 per cent at the $25,000 mark, above which the burden changes to a benefit increasing to a differential of −33 per cent at the top of the stockholder income scale. At this level ($500,000) the earnings for retention component of stockholders' income was subject to a tax liability 33 percentage points less than would have been the case had it been reached promptly and in full by the personal income tax alone. It appears, then, that on their share of earnings for retention some stockholders were overtaxed and others were undertaxed to significant degrees. The inversion from over- to undertaxation occurred, on average, at just over the $50,000 stockholder income.

The weighted average of these two measures, the differential against net corporate earnings (line 3), traces the same general path over the income range as the differentials that comprise it, and falls between

179

them. Reflecting the greater absolute magnitude of earnings for retention, it lies closer to line 2 than to line 1. Over most of the income scale the net corporate earnings component of stockholders' income was overtaxed, but for stockholders higher up the income pyramid, undertaxation occurred.[34] The heaviest extra burden falls on the lower stockholder income levels ($1,000 to $10,000)—between 32 and 29 percentage points. Above $10,000 the differential drops rapidly, reaching zero at about $100,000 and low point of −16 per cent at $500,000. Thus the substantial over- or undertaxation found on net corporate earnings depends on the stockholder's income level.

So far, we have measured the differential tax load on net corporate earnings and its components. Now we relate the over- and undertaxation to total stockholder income. How much heavier or lighter was the effective tax rate for stockholders than that applicable if their income (including their full pro rata share of net corporation earnings) had been reached by the personal income tax alone? [35] (The personal income tax is used as the benchmark throughout this analysis because it presumably measures the community's "consensus" as to the rates of income taxation appropriate at different income levels. I am not contending that this "consensus" has been deliberately arrived at; rather, the legislative structure of our community suggests that many considerations of varying degrees of merit and relevance, and numerous factors, some purposeful, others accidental, all are associated with the process by which this rate schedule was determined. Perhaps "consensus" is not the right word here. The community has never voted for a particular rate schedule per se, nor has it chosen from among candidates for legislative office on the basis of a particular rate schedule as the only issue differentiating them. Yet if we raise the question of what we have in fact established as our standard for personal income taxation, income being defined as regularly taxable income, it is to this schedule we must look for an answer.)

To put the choice of benchmark in a somewhat different focus, we might say we use the personal income tax rate schedule for this purpose because it is the rate schedule that applies to income (withdrawn

---

[34] In 1950, earnings for distribution totaled $11 billion, earnings for retention $19 billion. (These figures are the totals for taxable stockholders only.)

[35] Another way of putting the question is: How much heavier (or less onerous) was the combined corporate-personal income tax rate on stockholders at a given income level than the personal income tax on nonstockholders with a similar amount of income?

or retained in the business) generated by noncorporate business enterprises.

The answer is provided by the differential against stockholders' income, line 4 on Chart 9. It appears that the majority of stockholders,
having incomes ranging from $1,000 to $50,000, were liable to an ap-
preciable extra income tax of from 6 to 10 percentage points. Those
most severely affected were in the income range between $10,000 and
$25,000 with a maximum differential of 10 points. But near the top
of the income scale a different picture emerges, with the differential
declining very rapidly after the $50,000 point and reaching zero at a
little over $100,000. Stockholders with incomes above this point en-
joyed a tax benefit that became relatively more important as income
increased. Thus, at the $500,000 imputed gross income level we find
the combined corporate-personal income tax liability to be 14 percentage points lower than would have been the case without any
corporate tax but with stockholders' full pro rata share of net corporate
earnings subject only to the personal income tax.

Instead of falling constantly as income rises, the differential against
stockholders tends first to increase over a portion of the income range
and then, after reaching a maximum between the $10,000 to $20,000
level, to fall constantly thereafter. This difference in behavior compared with the other three differentials occurs because of uneven variations in the proportion of imputed gross income derived from corporate earnings. For the value of the differential against stockholders is
equal to that fraction of the differential against net corporate earnings
that net corporate earnings represent of imputed gross income. In general this fraction tends to rise with income. (This is why line 4 lies
closer to line 3 at the higher income levels.) Over the stockholder
income span from $6,000 to $20,000, the rise in the proportion of net
corporate earnings to imputed gross income more than compensates
for the fall in the differential against net corporate earnings, thereby
causing the product—the differential against stockholders—to rise over
this range.

The findings apply to average stockholders, and figures on how
many fell in the over- and undertaxed categories cannot be obtained
directly from these data. However, from a closely related set of procedures (detailed in Chapter 6 of *Income-Tax Burden on Stockholders*)
we can get some idea of the number of stockholders in each of these
categories. For 1950 the estimate is about 3.3 million double-taxed
stockholders. Slightly under 3.2 million paid a higher combined cor-

porate-personal income tax than would have been due under the personal income tax alone and were, in the sense adopted here, over-taxed. On the other hand, some 4 per cent, about 130,000, were under-taxed.[36] For the latter, a higher tax liability would have occurred if the corporate tax had been eliminated and their share of corporate earnings had been taxed in full as personal income. While small as a proportion of all stockholders, the undertaxed group assumes greater importance when its share of all double-taxed net corporate earnings is measured. Some 44 per cent of net corporate earnings was under-taxed.

The findings for 1950 are based on the tax treatment of corporate earnings then in effect. With the Internal Revenue Code of 1954, modifications of the procedure for taxing dividends were introduced —an exclusion of the first $50 of dividends ($100 for joint returns) and a personal income tax credit equal to 4 per cent of dividends over and above the amount excluded. How this dividend tax relief would have changed the results for 1950 is considered next.

But first we remind the reader that the findings just presented are for a given year and hence their specific magnitude depends on the particular levels of personal and corporate income tax, corporate earnings, dividends, and corporate saving that prevailed in that year. Values of the differentials annually from 1944 through 1952 can be found in *Income-Tax Burden on Stockholders,* Appendix A. We note in passing that for all these years the general pattern of results was similar, i.e., it shows differentials that decline with income, and, in the case of earnings for retention and net corporate earnings, decline sufficiently to lead to negative extra burdens. The income level at which this "crossover" from extra burden to benefit occurred varied, of course, from year to year. On a variant 2 basis, the lowest income level at which the differential against net corporate earnings "crossed over" was $30,000 in 1947; the highest, $138,000 in 1951.

Our findings are, of course, no more reliable than the assumptions used in their derivation. This is not the place to analyze all our assumptions or procedures, but two deserve specific mention. We

[36] These estimates, while germane, are not strictly comparable with the variant 2 values of the differentials that have been used in discussing the findings for 1950. For in deriving the number of over- and undertaxed stockholders, no account was taken of the future capital gains tax liability on reinvested earnings of 1950. An adjustment on this score would lead to somewhat larger overtaxed and smaller undertaxed totals than those given in the text. (See *Income-Tax Burden on Stock-holders,* p. 154.)

assumed, for reasons noted above, that the incidence of the corporation income tax is on stockholders via a commensurate decline in the income generated on their behalf. This is still a widely held opinion. But among students of public finance there is much disagreement about this whole matter. If the corporate tax is shifted to any degree, the findings given here overstate the extra tax burden and understate the tax benefit. The larger the fraction of the tax shifted, the greater this over- and understatement. We also accepted the tax law's definition of income which permits tax-free recoupment of the outlays on depreciable assets but only on a historical cost basis. And not all taxpayers have chosen the LIFO option for inventories. If corporate earnings were measured with regard to current costs of maintaining inventory and replacing depreciable assets, overtaxation would be found to be more severe than we have measured it, while undertaxation would be less pronounced. The effects of alternative definitions and assumptions on the measures of stockholder differential taxation are explored at some length in Chapter 4 of *Income-Tax Burden on Stockholders,* but we insert Table 45 here to show the effect of varying the two assumptions noted above.

TABLE 45

COMPARISON OF DIFFERENTIAL AGAINST NET CORPORATE EARNINGS UNDER
STANDARD ASSUMPTION AND TWO ALTERNATIVE ASSUMPTIONS, 1947

(per cent)

Average Stockholder Imputed Gross Income (*$000's*)	Differential Against Net Corporate Earnings		
	Standard Method	Assuming One-Half the Corporate Tax Is Shifted	Taking Account of Current Price Level for Depreciable Assets and Inventory
1	24.6	11.1	39.5
3	23.8	10.7	39.5
5	22.5	9.4	38.1
10	17.7	5.0	33.4
25	2.0	−10.0	18.3
50	−7.6	−18.1	10.1
100	−16.2	−26.3	1.7
250	−24.5	−33.9	−5.3
500	−25.7	−34.8	−6.1

NOTE: See pp. 81–103 of Holland, *Income-Tax Burden on Stockholders*, for an explanation of these adjustments.

Dividends Under the Income Tax

Effect of Relief Provisions on Differentials

The analysis in the first part of this chapter of the relief provisions of the Internal Revenue Code of 1954 ran in terms of marginal dollars. In order to determine how much relief on the average, rather than at the margin, tends to be provided by the Internal Revenue Code of 1954, its provisions have been applied to our average stockholder data for 1950. The results are shown in Table 46.

An examination of column 6 shows that the absolute reduction in the extra tax burden (measured in percentage points) is greatest at the lowest income and falls steadily as income rises. Apparently, this contradicts the point made earlier that the relief afforded by the dividend tax credit is the same at all income levels, while relief traceable to the exclusion of a flat amount of dividends rises with stockholder income. But this conclusion referred to marginal increments of earnings for distribution of the same amount at all income levels. Here, we are concerned with the total amount of earnings for distribution, and that, of course, varies with the stockholders' income. So the pattern

TABLE 46

EFFECT OF RELIEF PROVISIONS OF INTERNAL REVENUE CODE OF 1954 ON DIFFERENTIAL AGAINST EARNINGS FOR DISTRIBUTION

(estimated from 1950 data)
(weighted average of joint and separate returns)

Average Stockholder Imputed Gross Income ($000's) (1)	Earnings for Distribution		Differential Against Earnings for Distribution (4)	Internal Revenue Code of 1954 [a]		
	Amount (2)	Per Cent of Stockholder Income (Col. 2 ÷ Col. 1) (3)		Differential After Relief (5)	Absolute Reduction in Differential (Col. 4 − Col. 5) (6)	Relative Reduction in Differential (Col. 6 ÷ Col. 4) (7)
1	$ 70	7%	34.3%	24.3%	10.0%	29.2%
3	242	8	34.3	27.8	6.5	19.0
5	376	8	33.8	28.3	5.5	16.3
10	1,343	13	32.9	29.3	3.6	10.9
15	2,176	15	32.1	29.1	3.0	9.3
25	4,458	18	29.2	26.4	2.8	9.6
50	11,519	23	24.9	22.3	2.6	10.4
100	27,013	27	19.1	16.6	2.5	13.1
250	73,418	29	13.2	10.8	2.4	18.2
500	169,989	34	10.0	7.6	2.4	24.0

[a] Exclusion of $50 for separate and $100 for joint returns plus tax credit of 4 per cent of dividends in excess of excluded amount.

of relief we now get is a matter of weighting. At the lower stockholder incomes where the amount of earnings for distribution is small, the exclusion, which gives more relief per dollar, far outweighs the credit in importance; hence the large amount of relief (measured in percentage points of differential reduction). As we move up the income scale and the amount of earnings for distribution increases, the weight of the exclusion in the relief provided dwindles, while the credit grows in importance. For the highest incomes, the effect of the exclusion is negligible, and the absolute amount of relief (measured in percentage points of differential reduction) tends to approach the constant set by the credit alone.

Column 7 contains the data relevant to an appraisal of the degree of relief, i.e., the amount of relief relative to the severity of the inequity it is designed to ameliorate. Here the pattern is U-shaped. Proportionately the greatest relief is provided at the bottom and top of the income scale, with a lesser degree of easing of the extra burden in between. These results follow from two factors already noted—the relative weights of the exclusion and credit, and the fact that the differential moves inversely with income. At the lower income levels the exclusion has a substantial effect, accounting for the high degree of relief there. Moving up the income scale, the exclusion fades in importance, and the absolute amount of relief tails off toward the constant provided by the credit. With the differential declining as income rises, after a point (somewhere after $15,000 of imputed gross income on average), the higher the stockholder's income, the greater the degree of relief provided.

Since the differential against earnings for distribution is only one aspect of the unequal taxation of stockholders, it may be of interest to view the relief provisions against the net result of stockholders' differential taxation, i.e., with reference to the differentials against net corporate earnings and stockholders. This is done in Table 47. But our first conclusion is so obvious that no reference to the table is required. It is merely this: Relief is provided all dividend recipients, yet while some stockholders were overtaxed on their share of corporate earnings, others were undertaxed. Relief is granted to the latter as well as to the former. Specifically, the data of the table show that the differential against stockholders (taking account of both distributions and retentions on their behalf) is moderated but slightly, something on the order of 5 to 10 per cent (see column 5 or 9 of Table 47). On the other hand, existing undertaxation is made more pronounced.

TABLE 47

REDUCTION IN DIFFERENTIAL AGAINST NET CORPORATE EARNINGS AND STOCKHOLDER INCOMES DUE TO RELIEF PROVISIONS OF THE INTERNAL REVENUE CODE OF 1954 [a]

(estimated from 1950 data)
(weighted average of joint and separate returns)
(per cent)

Average Stockholder Imputed Gross Income ($000's) (1)	Differential Against Net Corporate Earnings				Differential Against Stockholder Income			
	Before Relief (2)	After Relief (3)	Absolute Reduction (Col. 2 − Col. 3) (4)	Relative Reduction (Col. 4 ÷ Col. 2) (5)	Before Relief (6)	After Relief (7)	Absolute Reduction (Col. 6 − Col. 7) (8)	Relative Reduction (Col. 8 ÷ Col. 6) (9)
1	31.7	27.8	3.9	12.3	5.7	5.0	0.7	12.3
3	31.1	28.6	2.5	8.0	6.5	6.0	0.5	7.7
5	30.7	28.6	2.1	6.8	6.0	5.6	0.4	6.7
10	28.6	27.2	1.4	4.9	9.9	9.5	0.4	4.0
15	25.9	24.7	1.2	4.6	9.7	9.3	0.4	4.1
25	20.1	19.5	1.1	5.3	9.5	9.0	0.5	5.6
50	10.0	8.8	1.2	12.0	5.9	5.3	0.6	10.2
100	0.4	−0.6	1.0	250.0	0.3	−0.4	0.7	233.3
250	−11.4	−12.3	0.9	7.9 [b]	−8.7	−9.4	0.7	8.0 [b]
500	−16.3	−17.2	0.9	5.5 [b]	−14.3	−15.1	0.8	5.6 [b]

[a] Exclusion of $50 for separate and $100 for joint returns plus tax credit of 4 per cent of dividends in excess of excluded amount.
[b] Denotes increase in differentials in favor of net corporate earnings and stockholders.

Of course this type of uneven result is frequently found for tax relief granted by the statutes; in the nature of the case, Congress will prefer measures which result in the application of fairly simple rules of computation of tax or tax credit; and inevitably the impact varies unevenly among taxpayers. This does not mean, however, that the dividend relief could not have been framed to fit the facts more closely without undue trouble for the taxpayer had the real nature of "double taxation" been used as a guide for the relief provisions. Moreover, some additional complexity, had that been necessary, might well have been worth the effort if providing greater relief at some future time were being seriously considered. For, as we have seen, the peculiarities of the method chosen become more pronounced as the rate of tax credit is increased.

Yet in pointing out the differential degree of relief the credit and exclusion provide among stockholders, we should not lose sight of the fact that some measure of relief has been provided them all.

INDEX

Index

Index